EMCEE
MONTY HALL

EMCEE MONTY HALL

Monty Hall
and Bill Libby

GROSSET & DUNLAP
A National General Company
Publishers   New York

Published simultaneously in Canada

Library of Congress Catalog Card Number: 72-79970
ISBN: 0-448-01551-X

First Printing
Printed in the United States of America

To those who cared, who helped, who encouraged, who had faith: my father, my friends, sometimes complete strangers, my children, and, especially, the two women of my life—my mother and my wife.

M.H.

Acknowledgments

The co-author wishes to thank, for their help in making this book as good and honest as he could make it, Monty and Marilyn Hall, his entire family, his *Let's Make a Deal* family, many other television executives and performers, many photographers, and the noted transcriber Mrs. Glenn Miller (Jacquelynn Kaysene).

B.L.

EMCEE
MONTY HALL

I

THEY HAVE WAITED *two or three years for tickets, these 350 people, and many of them have been standing in the street outside ABC's Hollywood studios for three hours. Ordinarily they are housewives, students, businessmen, doctors, teachers, but for this one incredible evening in their lives they are dressed as rabbits and hunters, as wine bottles and tubes of toothpaste, as ministers and policemen, as baseball players and baseballs. They have come with makeup and paint smeared on their faces and with hand-painted signs proclaiming they are prepared to make almost any kind of deal on earth.*

The show is Let's Make a Deal, *one of the most popular and longest running game shows in the history of television. Three nights a week during most of the year the shows are taped, two to an evening, some 271 shows every year. And 350 persons are sent tickets to each night's taping of two shows.*

Now they have come from all over the country to be contestants. They have watched the program, of course, and they know that by guessing the prices of items or by trading outright gifts of cash for what may be in a box or behind a curtain, they may win prizes of clothing, furniture, appliances, cars, boats, and all-expenses-paid trips around the world. Though they hope to win prizes, they know they may make the wrong trade and win nothing or, perhaps worse, win a "zonk," a gag prize, such as a couple of cows or sway-backed horses or a year's supply of spinach. But they are there, they say, really for the fun of it more than anything else.

Only a few admit to embarrassment at their outlandish costumes. They know that all of them cannot be on the show. Only thirty-one will be picked to go on the trading floor, and of those only ten or twelve will take part in the action on camera. The rest will be seated in the studio audience. They don't know how the contestants are selected, and they don't like to think about it. They admit they will be disappointed if they don't make it, but most agree that it will be fun just to be in the audience and watch the show's main attraction, emcee Monty Hall.

Ushers appear and walk up and down telling the people that the selections will soon be made and please don't wave their signs to call attention to themselves and hit the men who make the choices with them because they would not be apt to pick someone who has just poked out their eyes. Everyone thinks that is funny, but when the men come out to make their choices, the people, desperate to call attention to themselves, start to wave their signs and hit them anyway.

Two of the show's writers, Alan Gilbert and Bernie Gould, make the choices. They walk up and down the line looking at the people and their costumes, and the people jump up and down and smile broadly and shout that they want to be picked. Now and then a writer points at someone and he is picked, and he jumps with joy. An usher hands the lucky person a special ticket and hurries him out of line and into a special room where the contestants wait for further instructions.

The scene is incredible, like some sort of flesh market. Everyone yearns to be picked, and two men are walking up and down wielding an enormous power to choose and exercising it with swift jabs of a finger.

The writers say they don't care so much about the costumes or signs; everyone comes with costumes and signs. They are looking for lively, animated people, but they are also looking for a cross section of America— black and white, young and old, fat and thin, attractive and plain. What they do not want are those who are overenthusiastic, because someone who puts on a per- formance in the line may be just too obstreperous on the air; and already they know how ordinary people react in this arena of excitement and emotion. To place a wild extrovert onto that stage is to look for trouble.

There are no rules to guide them. They have been making the selections since the show began nearly ten years ago, and their record in picking people who work well on camera has been good enough for them to go on doing it in this way.

In less than half an hour the selections are made. The writers disappear. And those who have not been picked look stunned, as though it had never really occurred to them that they might not be chosen. A strange silence falls over them. A man in a Tarzan outfit puts his sign down and leans back against a wall and closes his eyes. They will have to sit and watch others go for the cars and the trips around the world. They say it was all right. They knew it would happen. They are disappointed, naturally, but it is just one of those things.

In a studio dressing room, Monty Hall lies on a couch, resting from a day at the office and preparing to resume his role as a performer. Hall is a major television per- sonality. In 1972 a respected poll rated him the public's favorite emcee by a wide margin over Ed McMahon,

Johnny Carson, Dick Cavett, Merv Griffin, Mike Douglas, and the others. He is tall, slender, dark-haired, and handsome. He is no longer a boy, but he still looks boyish and has a boyish charm. He has an easy smile and an easy way with people. Win or lose, the ladies kiss him on the show. He kids that when he comes home after a hard night at the studio with lipstick on his cheek and his collar, he looks as if he has had a head-on collision with an Avon lady. Women also kiss him in supermarkets and airports and restaurants and wherever else they encounter him. Men admire him, too. He is a television star, but he is approachable. He talks to his fans. He says he loves people and adds that if he didn't he wouldn't be nearly as successful as he is.

It is a tough show to do. It looks easy, but it is hard. And the people in the profession understand this. With some shows the show is the thing. With this show Monty Hall is the show.

Hall is up now, changing from casual clothes to the finery he will wear on camera, and Stefan Hatos, his partner, an intense, articulate, tough veteran from the heyday of radio and the early days of television, reviews the format of the night's shows with him.

A merchandising department has rounded up the prizes. More than $15 million in prizes were given away in the first nine years of the show. The prizes offered, however, amount to more, some $3 million a season on the daytime shows, and $1.5 million on the nighttime shows. This is approximately $10,000 a show daytime and $25,000 nighttime. The top prize daytime may top $4000, the top prize nighttime $14,000. More than half the prizes offered are won.

With the review finished, Hatos and Hall walk into the studio and run through limited rehearsals, because there are, as yet, no contestants reacting to the events of the show. Monty must know the sequence of stunts, the flow of the show, and what is in every box and be-

hind every curtain. Still, he rehearses only the nighttime show.

The show this night starts the way it has for more
than nine years and 2700 performances. Jay Stewart, a
pioneer announcer of radio and television, chats with the
audience to warm them up. The bright, hot television
lights go on, and the cameras swing into place. There
is a timpani roll. A studio monitor reveals the costumed audience on the trading floor. From backstage,
Stewart announces: "These people, dressed as they are,
come from all over the United States to make deals
here in the marketplace of America." The timpani roll
again. "And now . . . here is America's top trader . . .
TV's big dealer . . . MONTY HALL!"

Monty greets one and all with a bright smile and a
promise of fun and money, and the show is on. Between
spiels for the products and commercials, the contestants
make their pitches for prizes. Monty moves among them,
selecting those who will get their chances. A lady in a
football helmet opens a chest containing three $100
bills and after much hesitation takes a chance on trading them for what is in a bigger box, which turns out to
be a $1000 fur coat. She shouts with glee and hugs and
kisses Hall. A man in a clown costume works his way
up to $1700, then swaps it for whatever is behind a cur-
tain. It turns out to be a couple of cows. He shrugs and
smiles wistfully. Well, he came here with nothing. . . .
An elderly black lady trades for something behind a
curtain and wins an all-terrain vehicle—just what she
always wanted. Contestants cannot trade in their prizes
and must pay taxes on prizes worth $600 or more. They
cannot resell them to the manufacturer, though they
may sell them to friends. But whatever they win, it is
better than nothing, and it may be something special. A
fat couple costumed as farmers wins a set of furniture
and appliances simply by making the right selections of
boxes and curtains. They go wild and the audience

screams hysterically at their hysterics and Monty collects another kiss.

A man dressed as a devil picks a wallet packet containing $100 and is offered a trade for a large box. Before he can take the trade, Monty offers instead to pay him $200, then $400, $800, finally $1000. The poor devil is tempted, but the box is a greater temptation. He takes it and winds up with a thousand lollipops. The audience thinks it is funny. The man smiles thinly and shakes Hall's hand.

The show proceeds smoothly to the big deal, "worth $14,000!" The night's two biggest winners are pulled into the aisle to risk, if they wish, their winnings for whatever is behind three numbered curtains. Neither chooses to keep what he had. A bird in the hand. . . . Intensely nervous, they make their selections. Unselected is a curtain that, rolled back, reveals a houseful of furniture. Selected, a second curtain reveals an ox-cart. Oh, well.

As the tension grows, one competitor, her husband beside her, and one curtain remain. It rolls back. A picture of an airplane. No, she has not won a picture—she has won a trip around the world, complete with cash for expenses, which Monty peels from his pocket. She screams and throws her arms to the heavens, then embraces Hall and kisses him. Tears slide down her chubby cheeks. A large lady with a hefty husband who runs a filling station has won a trip around the world. Unable to contain their excitement, they scream, laugh, and cry. The audience applauds mightily. And Hall appears pleased, as if he himself had won.

As the show ends and the titles roll across the screen, Hall is paying a lady dressed as Cleopatra a dollar for every bobby-pin in her purse and a man costumed as a chicken $20 for every egg he has in his pockets.

Let's Make a Deal *is a target for the TV critics. For years everyone has taken a potshot at the program, but* the ratings stay up there, and in its tenth year are higher than at any time in history. With the new three-year contract that starts in January 1974, you would think that Hall was beyond the critics' barbs, but he is not.

"I have never maintained that we should get a Peabody Award for our show. We make no such pretensions. But we are in the entertainment business; and for what we do, we are the best. It is a costume show with people having a good time. They wait a long time for tickets. They come down to the show, and the excitement mounts. By the time the selections are made and the show starts, the air is filled with emotion and tension. When I point my finger at a contestant, she doesn't remember what her name is. Now they embark on a series of trades and gambles that may result in a very big score—or nothing. And at this point the most important refutation to the critics' claim of greed occurs. The woman looks at the five donkeys which she won instead of the car, turns and kisses me. We have had some fun. They have gambled and either lost or won, and for thirty minutes we have entertained them and the millions at home who play along with them. Doctors, lawyers, psychiatrists, as well as plumbers, policemen, and firemen, comprise our studio audience. And from my hundreds of personal appearances, I have discovered that they also comprise the viewing audience. Surely, we must be doing something right. As I said, we are in the entertainment business, and we entertain!"

The costumed crowd that convenes on those studio streets three times a week celebrates Monty Hall. The critics do not. He is a game-show emcee. But he is more than just that. And whatever he is now, he has had a long, hard time getting there.

1

I WILL TRY to tell it all, all the things that seem to me to
be of importance in my life, as openly as I can, without wanting to hurt anyone, but without wanting to
be dishonest about how it was, and how I saw it as I
remember it and feel it now. Being honest and open is
the most important thing, so that is the way I will go,
letting others have their say, and having my own.

It began for me in Winnipeg, Canada. My father's
parents and my mother's parents were among many
Russian emigrants who settled in Canada around the
turn of the century, driven from their homeland by
prejudiced, oppressive practices against Jews. They settled in Winnipeg, where there was not a large Jewish
population and where they and their children, who were
my parents, and their children, of whom I was one,
were often subjected to ridicule and discrimination.
When I was young, my family moved a lot and into
sections of the city where there probably were few
Jewish families. I was a sickly child and fair game for

the bullies. I lost many a fist fight until I could gain acceptance from my peers. These early memories serve vividly to remind me of my heritage. This, together with my mother's dedication, no doubt contributed to my own dedication today.

Winnipeg today is a city of around a half million persons, but it was only about half that when I was growing up. It was and is a tough town, a manufacturing and railroad center, strong on sports, with an increasing interest in the arts. Life there for me and my family was hard.

Oddly, there were nine children in both my father's family and my mother's. My father, the second oldest in his family, was born Maurice Halparin in 1899; my mother, the third oldest, was born Rose Rusen in 1900. My father's family had been in the cattle business for generations and they went into that in Canada, too. My mother's father, arriving penniless from Russia, turned to fruit peddling.

My paternal grandfather, Isaac Halparin, a hard man, strong and stern, was successful in business, and reared his three sons and six daughters in comfortable circumstances. Most of his daughters became schoolteachers. His two oldest sons, my father and his older brother, went to work for him early in their lives. He was a taskmaster. And my father's older brother was, too, in a way. As hard as nails and of very grim demeanor, he took a savage delight in beating the hell out of people—anybody—and he practiced on my father. It is claimed by many who knew him that in the proper surroundings, with the proper training, he might well have become a lightweight boxing champion. My dad tells stories of his youth that illustrate this toughness. When walking down a street, his brother would deliberately flirt with somebody else's girl or subtly elbow someone in passing, merely to provoke an incident. The incident would lead to words, and in a matter of moments, it was *smack, wallop*—and somebody was lying on the ground—but definitely not my uncle. In later years, proud as punch, tough and weather-beaten, he would lead parades on his palomino, ever the cowboy with his "I-can-lick-anybody-in-the-house" attitude. The two boys, with their father, ran cattle from fifty or more miles out of town into Winnipeg and they went on cattle-buying trips throughout Manitoba and Saskatchewan. It toughened my father, this male-dominated life.

My maternal grandfather, David Rusen, had five sons and four daughters. He became one of the major fruit wholesalers in western Canada. By contrast with my other grandfather he was a gentle man, who made a home of love and warmth for his children and did nothing to drive them out into the world, who stressed academic scholarship rather than studies in the school of hard knocks. Most of his children went to college, rather than right to work. Some of the sons became attorneys, doctors, dentists.

My mother became a teacher in the first part of her adult life. She and my father really began their romance when they were twelve. They were only friends then, but my father spent as much time in my mother's house as he could, preferring it to his own. He tried to stay out of the way of his father and older brother and away from their house of tension as much as he could. He partly grew up in my mother's house, where there was warmth, laughter, and singing.

My mother was the oldest girl and the third oldest child in the Rusen family. As a young girl, she was something of a tomboy, an athlete who played baseball with the boys. She had great talent as a singer and an actress and played the leads in all the student productions as she grew up. She was the president of every organization to which she belonged, from the time she was twelve until, who knows, until she died. Once when a group of youngsters were forming a new club in high

school, they came to her and asked her, "Rose, do you
want to join our club?" She answered, "Yes, if I am
president." And she was. There was some driving force
in her that compelled her to leadership. She was a dy-
namic person with a charming personality from her
pre-teen days. She was the heart of her family.

My mother was a schoolteacher by the time she and
my father became engaged to be married. She gave up
teaching with her marriage and the pregnancy that
soon followed. And she gave up much of her home life
when my father became sick and was unable to work
for a year and she had to go out to work to support us.
And later she joined him in his work at the butcher
shop, helping him without complaint. She still found
time to play a part in the social and charitable life of
Winnipeg, and she was a hearty humorist and superb
storyteller, a prominent club woman who presided over
organizations, starred in stage productions, and headed
fund-raising drives to benefit the needy. She was away
so much speaking for charities that I later joked I was an
organizational orphan. She was not a beautiful woman,
but a handsome one. She had a personality many remember as the most compelling they ever knew. She
had great strength, physically and psychologically. An
unusual woman, she influenced me enormously.

Mother had a remarkable equanimity no matter what
the situation. She covered for my father or anyone else.
She had a defense for the actions of all friends or family, her basic argument being, "We must love one another no matter what." Hence she was the mediator,
the placator, the negotiator. I recall that couples came
to her to try to solve marital disputes. Businessmen
called her into their plants or offices to settle employee
problems. When people were ill, they invariably called
for my mother as well as the doctor. And when a telegram came to a neighbor during World War II saying
that a son was missing in action, the first call came to

my mother. At a dinner honoring her in 1961 in Winnipeg, my brother referred to her as a lawyer who never attended law school, a doctor without a medical degree, a psychiatrist without a couch, a labor negotiator without a college background, a wife, a mother, an actress, a speaker, a playwright, an athlete—a woman for all seasons. She was this—and more.

We had our arguments. I wanted to follow in her footsteps, to be the storyteller, the actor, the singer she was. But this had brought her nothing. Later, when I went to college and started to study for a career in medicine, this pleased her; when I turned from medicine to the entertainment business, she regretted my decision but never offered one word of criticism. However, when I succeeded, she got great satisfaction from it. Still, she did not take me as seriously as I took myself. Once a reporter said, "Mrs. Halparin, I understand you are Monty Hall's mother." She replied, "Young man, where I come from, he's still known as Rose Halparin's son." Years later, when my parents came to New York to see me do a TV show called *Keep Talking*, they waited while I signed autographs under the theater marquee, which had my name in lights. I kept glancing at them to see if they were impressed. When I got to them, I said, "Well, Mother, what do you think of your star now?" And she said, "By me, when you replace Ed Sullivan you'll be a star."

Growing up, I always felt closer to my mother than my father. My personality was nearer hers, just as my son's now is closer to his mother's.

My father was a fine man who was frustrated by the fates. The roughness of his early life and the failures he experienced later stirred tensions and tempers that caused us to withdraw from him. Yet I remember respecting him, because no matter how hard he made me work in his store, he worked harder. He always found time to take me and my younger brother to hockey and baseball games or boxing bouts. It was a great treat when he came home and said, "How about taking in a hockey game?" And off we'd go, father and son, racing each other to the hockey rink.

My father left high school early and fled from his father and older brother and their harsh ways. At sixteen he caught a cattle train for Chicago and made it without any problem. There he wandered the streets looking for work. He soon ran out of money and resorted to sleeping under stoops and eating buns stolen from bakery windows. During one of the latter escapades a big Irish cop caught him and hauled him out of the bakery. Instead of rushing him off to the nearest juvenile judge, the big ruddy-faced policeman took him to a coffee shop, fed him, gave him some fatherly advice, doled out carfare to the outskirts of town, and my father hitchhiked back to Winnipeg. His arrival there was greeted with the kind of reception that warped him for years to come. His mother cried—and his father beat hell out of him for running away.

The next year my father used the family association with a cattle customer in Saskatchewan to change his life again. My grandfather had done business with the Doukhobors, a religious sect. Peter Verigan, the head of the sect, and known as king, remembered my father and gave him a job in the community, allowing my father to practice his own form of religion and ethics by living by himself in a hotel while working in the commune. However, a year of this, interrupted by occasional sojourns to Winnipeg to see my mother, was enough. He returned to Winnipeg where he was fortunate to find a job as a bookkeeper with a lumber firm, since he loved working with figures. He worked indoors in clean surroundings. He was able to dress well. At twenty, his life was going well, and he became engaged to my mother. A year later, they married and started their family. Then the reversals came.

He began to suffer from severe migraine headaches. A doctor told him he did not have the eyesight for bookkeeping and would have to give up such work or risk blindness. He accepted the advice and returned to the cattle business, the only other job he knew. But he worked with an uncle, not his father. Unfortunately, he did not make it with his uncle and was forced to return to his father and brother. He did not make it with them, either. Ridiculed by them for having dared try to make it without them, he was driven to go out on his own again. For a time he drifted from one job to another.

All of this has been passed on to me. My earliest memories of my father date from his middle twenties, when he had managed to acquire a little delivery truck and was running his own small meat wholesale business. This truck became the family car. We went everywhere jammed in the upright front seat of that little delivery truck. Its main use was in his business. He would go out, early in the morning, to the stockyards, buy meat from the slaughterhouse, and resell it to retail stores around the city.

When I was three or four years old, he often took me with him on his rounds. I kept him company. Although it is over forty years since I made those trips to the slaughterhouse in St. Boniface, a suburb where the stockyards were located, the stench has not left my nostrils to this day. There is a peculiar odor that is as foreign to our olfactory glands as any. It strikes you on your approach from miles away, and the closer you get, the worse it is. Inside, coupled with the squealing of the animals on their way to extinction, it is almost unbearable, a combination of sight and sound that never ingratiated itself upon my senses.

In his late twenties, my father was stricken with an awful attack of boils. For a year he was unable to work, and my mother had to support the family. It was dreadfully dispiriting for a man, and it almost broke him. He used to sit in our tiny living room listening to the radio and staring straight ahead. Sometimes he would lie in bed, staring at the ceiling, in intense pain, unable to stand or move around. He was deeply depressed because he had been invalided and his position as the head of the household had been curtailed.

When he was able to work again, he landed at a butcher counter, which he ran as a sort of concession in the corner of a delicatessen. He learned to cut meat. It was difficult for him, but he learned. It was the largest part of his life—or, at least, his profession, such as it was.

He was by nature something of a dandy. He was an extremely handsome young man, small physically, but powerful. He had been toughened by his upbringing, but he also had been bruised by it. He had no stomach for hurting anyone, for tackling trouble. And his year-long sickness seemed to sap his spirit. After that, he found something to do. He did not like it, but he did it.

He dressed more like a banker than a butcher. He wore suits and stiff-collared shirts to the shop as though he was going to an office. He did not shave himself, but went to a barber, though he could not afford it. He had his nails manicured. How many manicured butchers have you ever known? He insisted that his shop be spotless beyond reason. I know, because I had to clean it, scrubbing the block, washing the machines, and the rest. He kept his own books and prided himself on them, on the rows of neat, precise figures and the beautiful balances he struck. But he seldom cleared more than twenty-five to thirty dollars a week.

And he took this money and he went to the races or to his social club for long sessions at the poker table— always in quest of the killing, the big score that would buy him out of the butcher shop and give his family a better way of life. It was a killing that never came, a score he never made; and it frustrated him, as his life in the butcher shop frustrated him.

Many of the friends he had grown up with had gone on to become doctors, dentists, lawyers, successful merchants, and they were always aware of the gulf between him and them. They teased him, calling him "Butch," and that tormented him. He was unhappy, short-tempered, and given to excesses of emotion.

During one difficult period we lived with another family, relatives named the Spectors, who had two small children. The two families were forced to share one house to make ends meet. The two boys became like brothers to me. The younger, Joseph, was shot down in World War II. I still carry his picture in my wallet. And my Aunt Elizabeth is very special to me. Then my family moved in and out of a series of small apartments, always struggling to raise the rent. Before my brother Robert was born, six years after I was, we moved in with my mother's parents. They had what seemed like a large house. There were four bedrooms and another room which could be used a a bedroom. But living there were my mother's paternal grandfather and grandmother, her mother and father, my mother and father, six of her brothers and sisters, and myself. That was thirteen people living in that one house—and it had one bathroom. Somehow we managed to share it. Today we have five bathrooms, and when my three children are at home with my wife and myself they always seem to be in use at the same time. Our standards have changed. We no longer know what patience is.

We spent several years in my mother's home, and the experience made a deep impression on me. The family house was located on Hallett Street, which, when we lived there, was a lower-middle-class area; but a generation before it had been populated by rather comfortable citizens, including Premier Norquay of the Province of Manitoba. The street was about three hundred yards long, a sedate and genteel neighborhood which was going through a melting pot change. On this small street resided Jewish families, Ukrainian families, a Chinese family, old aristocrats, and new immigrants. Today, when I revisit Hallett Street, it is purely ethnic, mostly Ukrainian, still neat and orderly, but so miniaturized to my eye. And as I look at Number 107, I don't see how so many people could live in one house with grace.

My mother's brothers were not much older than I was, so they were and are more like brothers than uncles. I was like the tenth child and treated accordingly. Their family life was conducted in a hierarchy. I clearly remember my grandmother yelling to one of the boys, "Sonny, go to the corner store for some milk." And Sonny would turn and yell to the next youngest brother, "Charley, go to the store for milk for Mama." Charley would yell, "Sam. . . ." When they got to "Monty . . ." there was no one left for me to turn to and I would have to go. That is, I went until Robert was old enough.

That system is strong. And it seems to me somehow right and good. Growing up with grandparents had a profound effect on me. It is something my children have missed. It is respect. Not a pretense of respect. Real respect.

How can you explain to a child what it is like to live with great-grandparents in their eighties, to try to understand them and try to make yourself understood by them? Their hearing was failing. You had to work at talking to them. Their sight was failing. So the one who was nearly blind would feed the other who was blind. And you would help, learning to accept their infirmities. You had to help them upstairs. Youngsters today tend to turn from such tasks, but yesterday, when I was a youngster, I was warmed by it.

How can I describe to the kids today what it was like to take a ninety-year-old great-grandfather by the hand and walk him at a snail's pace to the synagogue on a Saturday morning. I talked very little to the old man; he talked less. My task was to deliver him; and if it took an hour to traverse the mile, then that's the way it was. In that mile walk I learned patience, tolerance, and respect. At the end of services, I was to bring him back to Hallett Street. Again, slowly, foot by foot, we made our way home, all the time a raging fire ready to explode inside me, because it was Saturday, a day when I could go to the movies—but something I couldn't do until the mission was completed. The old man would sense my anxiety. When we crossed Main Street, a very wide and busy thoroughfare with streetcars, there was only a half mile left to go. Then he would look down at me and, patting me on the shoulder, say, "Go now, go now." He could make the rest of the way on his own. I would run to my grandmother's house, have lunch, and with my three young uncles be on my way to the movies as the old man was still shuffling his last few steps home.

My grandfather, as the years progressed, brought out from Russia the members of his own family—sisters and brothers, nieces and nephews, and, eventually, countless other residents of Pavelitch, the small town whence he had come. Every year we children looked forward to the annual Pavelitcher picnic. Scores of friends and relatives all descended on Kildonan Park. The first order of business was to organize the soccer and softball games. Every member under the age of sixty was enthusiastically involved. After the games the participants moved to their own family picnic tables. Cloths were unfolded and spread on wooden benches. From huge baskets, epicurean delights miraculously appeared in an unending flow. Chicken and fish and salads and fruit. Pickles, dilled to perfection, and an assortment of Jewish delicacies, blintzes and knishes, were majestically arrayed before the expectant diners. Some tables exchanged goodies. The excitement was contagious. What a feast! And for dessert, we children were given nickels to run to the pavilion where we bought ice cream cones. Overfed and overtired, we boarded the family cars or trucks and wended our way homeward to revel in what was the most glorious of days. There were other times when just the four of us went on a picnic—Mother, Dad, Bob, and myself. We played ball and ate and laughed. It was the best of times. To this day, mention a picnic to me and my eyes get misty.

Eventually we had to leave my grandfather's house, and we moved first to an apartment, then to a small house. We still had little money and it was a terrible struggle to pay the rent, to meet the bills, to have enough left over for food. There were times when the lights and gas were turned off in our home because we weren't able to pay the bills. Every Friday night we went to dinner at my maternal grandparents' house. Every Sunday we spent the day and had lunch and dinner there. These were our best meals of the week. And before, during, and after the meals was the family comedy hour. Laughter sustained us. At home, we often made a meal of porridge. We sometimes did not have enough wood for the furnace. Our warm clothing was old and well-worn. When the rent was due, there was terrible tension between my parents.

Aside from the meals, my grandparents rarely helped us. In later years I asked my family why, and no one seemed to know. Apparently, my parents were too proud to ask, and my grandparents were too busy with their own problems to think to offer. In those days it was accepted that people made their own way.

I was a bright child. My mother had been a teacher and I was brought up among people who were interested in education and willing to work with me. In my first year of school, I skipped from grade one to grade two. When we moved from my grandfather's house, I entered a new school and was put back to grade one. This lasted one day. They put me in grade two. This lasted one day. Then they put me in grade three. At the end of the year they put me in the fourth grade. I still was only six. When I was seven, I missed half a year of school because of two serious ailments. At first they tried to put me back, but finally they advanced me to grade five at the age of eight. I ended up finishing high school at fourteen.

The studies came easy, but other things came hard. Because I was ahead of others my age in school, I was always the smallest or one of the smallest boys in my class. I was put down a lot. Brightness seldom is admired by other young boys. Toughness is preferred. I, too, wanted to be tough, but I wasn't. I was always being moved to a new area and a new school and always had to make new friends the hard way, in the crucible of hard knocks.

The first of my two misfortunes as a seven-year-old came when I was playing in the kitchen with a cousin. We stacked up some furniture and placed a rocking chair atop it all. There always seemed to be a pot of soup boiling on our stove, and somehow the rocking chair hit the handle of the pot and flipped the boiling soup over my head. I screamed. I can still hear the scream. I was severely scalded and in terrible pain. My mother ripped my clothes off and smeared butter all over my body.

My face was wrapped in bandages, and I was fed through straws for four or five weeks. At the end of that time, the doctor came to my house to remove the bandages. There was great apprehension that I might be scarred and my skin discolored for life, and my parents concealed this fear from me. But when the doctor unwrapped one arm and my parents saw that it was horribly, violently, red, they recoiled.

My mother rushed the doctor from the room. Years

later she said she simply was stalling because she was afraid of what my face would be like. Many are not as fortunate as I was, however. My mother returned with the doctor, who resumed the ordeal of removing the bandages. As he finished, there were gasps and tears of joy. I was rushed to a mirror. My face was fine. The skin came out smooth as a baby's.

One sidelight is significant to me: My father used to nag my mother about keeping the boiling soup on the stove and letting me play nearby. But after the accident he never said anything to her or in any way blamed her for the mishap. To me this is remarkable.

At the time, I weighed forty pounds. Sipping meals through a straw did not build me up, and I probably started to go out on the streets with the kids sooner than I should have. One night I got up feeling sick and, going to the head of the stairs and seeing what I thought was my uncle Sonny, called for help. "Uncle Sonny, Uncle Sonny," I yelled desperately. But it was not Uncle Sonny, only a coat hanging on a stand at the foot of the stairs.

They found me in the morning, huddled up at the bottom of the stairs with a raging fever. An ambulance was called to take me to the hospital. In the ambulance, the doctor told my mother, "I don't think he's going to survive." I had double pneumonia. I was in an oxygen tent for seven days, delirious the whole time. I recognized my mother, but not my father or anyone else. It was touch and go for a while, but I pulled through. I returned home thin and weak, lucky to be alive.

The rest of the year, I was kept home from school. From the time I was burned until my recovery from pneumonia I spent most of four or five months in bed. As it turned out, this was a productive and not unpleasant period for me. My mother, the former teacher, tutored me. My father, the former bookkeeper, challenged me at arithmetic. We put a large blackboard by my bed. My mother would write a long list of figures on the board and my father and I would race to see who could add them up faster in his head. I went on to multiplying, dividing, and subtracting in my head. I became a very fast reader and a whiz at math. Once, in my freshman year at college, a professor asked me why I was not writing down a trigonometry problem as the rest were. He didn't believe me when I said I already had worked out the problem in my mind, and he was startled when I gave him the correct answer.

About the only practical use I've ever found for this ability has been on *Let's Make a Deal* whenever contestants must guess the price of various products and the amount they are off must be subtracted from the money they started with. I am always able to throw the dollar-forty-nines and the twenty-seven cents and the four-ninety-eights around in my head and provide accurate accountings while announcer Jay Stewart is writing things down and figuring them out. I have never yet been found wrong. The fellows in the control room try to catch me, but they haven't yet.

Lying alone in bed while I recuperated, I invented football, baseball, and hockey games that could be played with a deck of cards, a piece of paper, and a pencil. Later, I created "playing fields" on which "players" might be moved with everything from Mah-Jongg pieces to tea service. Unfortunately, I never patented them—they were similar to games devised and sold successfully in later years. They were a satisfying diversion, however, and when I started to play outside again and couldn't keep up with the other kids, I used these games to lure them back to my house.

My father was intrigued by my ability to read the racing form and select winners. He would play this game with me each night and challenge me to dope the races. The boy genius did just that, juggling the speed ratings and past performances and class of competition

and jockey's abilities and coming out with a remarkable record of winners. At home, that is. When I was
taken to the track, I lost the skill, and was wiped out.
No one beats the races—not even a smart-aleck kid.

We moved to the Elmwood section of Winnipeg and I
started at Lord Selkirk School. The kids in that area
were rougher and tougher than any I had experienced,
and they took turns beating the hell out of me. My
classmates were older and bigger, and I was overwhelmed outside the schoolroom. I had nothing. Every
year I looked forward to the annual show put on in an
arena by the Native Sons of Canada. They staged ama-
teur boxing bouts and gave free hot dogs and soft
drinks to the kids. That was the highlight of my life
then.

When my father was sidelined with boils, my mother
went to work selling life insurance and advertising for
a local newspaper. After he recovered and became a
butcher, she helped out in the store. And so did I. The
conditions were dreadful. The money I earned was for
the family, not for myself. Sometimes I worked as the
delivery boy so my father would not have to pay another
helper. I never had the ice skates I wanted, or the
bicycle, or the new leather jacket. My folks gave me
what they could, but they could not give me much.

Actually, I started helping my father when he began
as a butcher and was running the concession counter
at the delicatessen. Soon I spent my lunchtime there,
then my time after school and my weekends. Using a
wagon in the summer and a sled in the winter, I made
deliveries to nearby customers, while he took the truck
to make more distant deliveries. After he got his own
shop, he no longer had his truck—it had broken down, I
suppose—and he had to borrow a car from relatives.

Soon he got me a bicycle so I could make deliveries
all over town. I was eleven or twelve years old and
considered strong enough. I weighed less than a hun-

• dred pounds and used to pile more than a hundred pounds of meat into a large carrier on the front of my bike and start off. I could make the north end deliveries in a series of short runs, but the south end deliveries had to be made in one long trip, which included twenty to thirty stops and took several hours.

It always seemed to me I covered a hundred miles a trip. In recent years I returned to my old route, went over it in a car, and found that it ran somewhere between sixteen and twenty miles. I remember sweating in the summer heat, and, much worse, freezing in winter temperatures that sometimes dropped to forty below zero. I wore moccasins and heavy breeches and a winter jacket of some sort, and what we used to call an aviation helmet, like those worn by pilots in World War I. It came right down over my ears and buckled under my chin. But it couldn't keep the cold out. My nose ran, my eyes watered, my feet and fingers grew numb.

I would sneak into stores to warm up along the way. A few customers were kind enough to invite me in and give me something hot to drink. Others could care less. They would leave me standing outside while they closed the door and took their time getting the money together. I remember all of them, the ones who were kind and the ones who were not, and some of them come up to me now and are surprised that I remember them, their names, even their addresses. One thing I never will forget is making those deliveries on my bike in the bitter cold. I still feel that cold. I remember those years all too well, and it is not a pleasant memory. I hated those days.

When I was about thirteen and in the tenth grade, my father bought a 1929 Whippit, a little four-cylinder car that had to be cranked up when it wouldn't start. The car cost $150, and my father swung it by borrowing $50 apiece from three friends. Our business had grown some, and customers complained I was not getting their deliveries to them fast enough with my bicycle. My father figured I would do better with an auto, although I was not legally old enough and so small I could hardly see over the steering wheel. My father took one day to teach me how to drive. He put me in the car and he said here's the gas pedal and here's the brake and here's the clutch. Here's how you shift into first, second, third, and reverse. "Now you get behind the wheel and you do it." I did it terribly, and he yelled at me a lot. But soon he decided I was set.

That very day he drove me back to the butcher shop and he gave me an order for a customer about two blocks away. "Here, take the car and deliver this," he ordered. I was scared to death. My mother was scared to death. She screamed, "He can't drive. He could get killed. Or he'll kill someone." But my father said, "He'll manage. By the time he gets back, one way or another, he'll be driving the car." So I got in that car and I went. Somehow I started it and I bucked and heaved my way down the street. I practically ripped up the gear box. I was terrified, but somehow I made it. I got back to the butcher shop in one piece without having killed myself or anyone else.

By the time I was fourteen, I had been driving for two months. Strangely, no one ever stopped me. The longer I drove, the better I got, and it made my life much easier. There was a heater in the car so I froze only when I had to get out to make a delivery. Physically, I was not as exhausted.

When I graduated high school at fourteen, I began working full-time in the butcher shop. The boy who had been working part-time was let go so my father could save the $6 a week he had been paying him. Most of my friends were sixteen or seventeen years old and ready to start college or go to work. I had been able to spend little time with them, and now they began to drift away from me. They joined fraternities and made new friends. For a while I was invited to their parties on Saturday nights, but I usually could not make it because I had to work late at the shop. Soon I was left alone.

I found new friends among others who could not afford to go to college or had not found steady jobs. This was during the depression, and many young men were without much to do. It was like the old song, "Standing on the Corner Watching All the Girls Go By." That's what we did. I was beginning to be interested in girls, but few were interested in me. I could not afford them. The girls in my high school group were older than I and by then were dating college boys. So my drifting friends and I patrolled the streets of our neighborhood in the evening and, with ten or fifteen cents in our pockets, ended up at Oscar's delicatessen, where we occupied a booth or two at the back.

We spent half our free time in these booths. Oscar was a kind man. For five cents he gave us a plate full of small slices and crusted ends of rye bread that he otherwise would have thrown away and a thick slice of salami and, for another nickel, a Coke. For ten cents we had a feast with all the free mustard we could use. We talked, we ate, and we sat. And then we went home. Sometimes we went to a movie. But that cost ten or fifteen cents, and when we got older it cost twenty-five cents. We just couldn't afford it very often. That was my life and I didn't like it.

My life revolved around the butcher shop. There I worked hard—without pay—yet I was treated as just another worker. My father was a difficult man to work for. He never hit me, but his temper was like a whip. His voice used to cut me to shreds. He'd buy a small side of beef for as little as possible and have to sell every part of it to come out ahead. But most customers obviously wanted the best parts for the least money. My mother took phone orders and tried to talk customers into taking common cuts. If she failed, my father would be furious and take out on her the wrath he felt for the customer. He was always insulting customers, and my mother was always trying to soothe their ruffled feelings. Customers were important to us.

My mother was the buffer between my father and his customers, between her husband and his sons. She suffered those days in the butcher shop, this brilliant, gifted woman, so she could spend nights with her clubs, with her charities, with the shows she often wrote and produced. This was her social life, because my father refused to share friends.

He suffered those days in the butcher shop, and he lived for those nights at his club. And when he came home late and my mother reproached him, they would argue bitterly. I would hide my head under the pillow so as not to hear them.

Still, she was a diplomat by nature. I remember one Saturday morning when I was about fourteen years old. My father had been out all Friday night and had not yet come home. My mother was waiting at the window, weeping. Seeing me, she wiped her eyes and called me to her. She said, "Monty, I want you to do something for me. Your father will be coming home any minute now. He's been out all night playing cards. He does it because he is desperately trying to make some money for his family. And he always fails. We have to show him that he doesn't have to be a big financial success to be a big man to his family.

"When he comes in, I'm going to get into an argument with him because there is no way that I can just let him stay out all night without a word and worry me to death without complaining about it. But after we have been arguing for about ten minutes, I want you to come into the room. I will draw you into the argument. I will say something about how terrible it is to stay out all night, and I'll ask you to tell him how terrible you think his actions are. But, instead, I want you to tell him you think he's right, that he has a right to stay out if he wishes, that he is the man of the house and is just trying to help his family, and that I am wrong for arguing with him and complaining about it. I want you to take his side."

I was too young to understand what she was up to, but I trusted her and she talked me into doing as she asked and also into never telling him about it. When he came home, my mother drew him into the inevitable argument. After a while I walked into the room and she turned to me and said, "Ask the child, ask him how he feels." Feeling full well that my mother was right and he was wrong, I said what I had been told to say about the rights of the man of the house. I said, "Daddy's right. I'm on his side." My father at first seemed stunned, but then swiftly accepted the unexpected and turned triumphantly to my mother and said, "You see, you are wrong. Even the boy says I'm right. So it shows what you know." And he stormed from the house.

I was almost in tears, but my mother gathered me in her arms and said, "Don't worry. You did your job well. Wait and you will see what happens now." Ten minutes later my father returned with a quart of ice cream and a big smile on his face. My mother started to smile, and then they both started to cry. Soon we were seated at the table eating our ice cream happily amid laughter and tears. Slyly, my mother winked at me, warning me. I realized then that somehow she had handled it just right. I saw how she saved a man's pride and shown him that he was loved. I will never forget it.

II

ON A TRIP to *Hawaii, Monty and Marilyn Hall visited the Variety Club's school for retarded children. Surrounded by students, they stood talking to the school's director, Mrs. Rose Lee. Suddenly from one corner of the room came a young boy's voice. "Mon-ty Hall . . . Mon-ty Hall . . . Mon-ty Hall," the boy said, slowly, over and over again. He had been standing facing into a corner with his back to them when they entered, but then he had turned around to sneak a peek at the visitors. His eyes widened when he saw Monty and he kept repeating, "Mon-ty Hall . . . Mon-ty Hall."*

A hush settled over the room. "This is an autistic child," Mrs. Lee explained. "He has not communicated with anybody. His mother brings him here every morning and leaves him in the hope that we can help him, but we have not been able to break through to him. He seems removed from all reality. He stands in the corner by himself. At lunch he even takes his tray of food into the corner. He doesn't play with any of the children. We haven't been able to get him to say one word to anyone. Until now." As she speaks, she starts to cry.

At this point, the boy's excitement rose. "Mon-ty Hall . . . Mon-ty Hall . . . Mon-ty Hall," he said faster and faster. Monty bent down, embraced the boy, and began to cry. The other youngsters seemed touched, too, and tears filled their eyes.

Later, Mrs. Lee thanked the Halls and asked them if they knew how much their visit meant. Monty, embarrassed, smiled and said, "It's my privilege," and he and his wife left, deeply moved by the experience.

One is inclined to contrast the contestants on Monty Hall's show with the people who benefit from his charities. The contestants reach out eagerly, laughing, not really needing, but wanting. The others reach out regretfully, sometimes weeping, often not wanting charity, but needing help.

They are the people of Monty Hall's two worlds. He is a man who has given much of himself to others. It has had its rewards, he says, though it has not come without sacrifice and disappointment and even, he admits, some regret.

I am a star. Others can judge for themselves how much of a star I am, but I know I am enough of a star in the entertainment industry to be a celebrity and instantly recognizable to many people.

One of the privileges stardom produces is the opportunity to help others. I am a salable commodity. My presence as toastmaster at a dinner, emcee of a variety show, or host of a telethon builds up the audience and increases the returns. There are other personalities whose name and presence could mean as much, but many of them do not do as much charitable work as I believe they should. Some lend their names, but do not serve on committees or donate money. My participation means a lot. I am in demand a great deal, and I respond—so much so that I am stamped as a soft touch and sought out constantly.

Some performers, such as Danny Thomas with St. Jude's Hospital and Jerry Lewis with the Muscular Dystrophy Fund, concentrate on one worthy cause. I give a great deal of time to as many as I can manage to help. I average fifty major charity performances a year, all around the country and in Canada. I receive invitations to approximately 350 of these affairs every year. I cannot begin to guess how much money I have raised for charity, but it runs into the many millions of dollars.

I have stated that a concomitant of success is responsibility and obligation. Those of us who have made it have the responsibility to make sure we put something back into society, and we have the obligation not only of giving of our time and talents, but of our money as well. The caring for the sick and handicapped, the building of hospitals and communities, are not to be left only to the doctors and lawyers, builders and oil tycoons, but entertainers as well. We are also citizens. Taking this position, I am often at odds with my fellow performers. I have told them that doing one benefit is not a commitment. I urge them to sit on committees, give money, help build, whatever it is. For this and my other speeches, I am sometimes labeled with derision a "do-gooder." I am surprised that a do-gooder in our society today is a dirty word. Maybe it shows the extent to which cynicism has taken over.

I am not ashamed of what I do, and I don't want any medals or honors, although I have accepted some. From the Variety Club, I have run the gamut of winning the Heart Award in Toronto in 1953 to a similar award in Los Angeles in 1971. I have been honored by countless numbers of organizations whose plaques adorn my walls. But I turn down ten for every one I accept, especially those labeled "Man of the Year." The "Man of the

Year" award is a running gag among those of us in show business. What usually happens is that an organization decides to have a dinner, gets a plaque, fills in the legend on the plaque for the recipient who is being honored, but leaves the recipient's name off until they get somebody to accept. It is more a build-up for the gate than it is the respect paid the recipient. I myself have been the toastmaster at a score of these Man of the Year dinners where the presentation of this honor almost made me retch, especially when I knew that the recipient was somebody who hadn't done a damn thing to earn it.

Then there are those performers who receive huge fees for doing so-called charity events, whether they be fund-raising dinners, speeches, or telethons. I do not accept a penny other than expenses. I did so on only one occasion, years ago, at the insistence of the host because everyone else was being paid; and I immediately donated mine back to charity. I have two fees—one is very expensive, for television and commercial appearances; and the other is gratis, for charitable and worthwhile causes. But by having such standards, one can run into some terribly frustrating experiences. I was called to a charity event in Canada. When I said I would be pleased and would waive the $3500 fee, the woman caller was delighted. Since I had five days free, I requested round-trip fare and hotel for my wife and myself for five days. The woman wrote me, saying that they would pay for the plane but only two days at the hotel because that was the length of their bazaar. I was furious. If I had accepted the $3500 fee, it would have cost them thousands more than my request. Since my mother belonged to this organization, I grabbed the phone, called her long distance, and before she had time to say hello, screamed all my frustration and anger at her. And what do you think she replied: "Good for them! You can afford it more than they can!" Never underestimate the power of a woman, especially a club woman, especially my mother. Naturally, I went. (P.S. We stayed four days, and the organization paid for all four nights at the hotel.)

Working for charities can be lonely and thankless. Often I have traveled thousands of miles to do a show, to be met at the airport not by the chairman, but by a flunky; booked into a hotel room without air conditioning; and left to my own devices for twenty-four hours until my appearance. Sometimes the audience is nowhere near as large as promised when you accepted the invitation, and you realize that you have been had. Little surprises are always in store for you. You arrange for one performance, and you find that you have been booked for three, and so on. Still, I continue to make these appearances because, in the final analysis, the result is more important than one's ego and comfort.

I also admit that my motivation is not altogether purely philanthropic. These appearances enable me to exercise talents I do not get to use as emcee of *Let's Make a Deal.* I might write a satirical piece or a mature monologue. I pride myself on being able to go into a town, read the local newspapers, familiarize myself with the names of important people, and deliver a highly personalized monologue that evening. This pleases me, and it pleases me further when I gain a measure of respect from my show-business confreres.

However, I have reached the point where I think I am doing too much, giving too much. I can't easily say no and it's gotten out of hand. I know I am being taken advantage of, but I don't know how to get out of it. I have neglected my wife, my children, and my work. I'm going to cut down, but I'm not sure how or where, because I'm caught up in it.

My charitable activities expanded with my membership in The Variety Club, the international show business organization that aids underprivileged and handicapped children around the world. I joined the organization in Toronto in 1948. Our aim was to raise funds to set up a vocational guidance school for handicapped kids. Land was donated by the province of Ontario, and we were left to finance construction and operation of the school. We needed more than $200,000 to get going, and we launched many money-making projects.

I organized a series of Sunday night movie shows all around the area. In those days, movie theaters were closed on Sundays in compliance with Canadian blue laws, but we got permission to stage our shows. The films were first-run and were given to us free. We put together a vaudeville show to play with the movies, and we worked all the small towns around Toronto. Everyone from ushers to performers donated their time and effort. I emceed the show and performed in it. At the intermissions we asked for additional contributions. Often a show made $600, $800, even $1000, and we did them for years.

Most of the money came from an annual baseball game. Jack Kent Cooke, now the owner of the Los Angeles Lakers and Kings, then the owner of the Toronto Maple Leafs, donated the use of the park for the night, and we did raise a considerable amount of money. This, plus our out-of-town appearances and other donations, finally resulted in the construction of one of the greatest vocational guidance and residence schools for handicapped children in the world, Variety Village. I will never forget the dedication of this school and the pride that we all felt on that day.

In East Los Angeles, where many Mexican-Americans are struggling, the Variety Boys Club has three thousand members who swim and play and learn arts and crafts. In a wealthier section of Los Angeles we support a children's heart clinic at UCLA. We support pediatric research at Cedars-Sinai Hospital. We have bought dozens of "Sunshine Coaches," vans with special seating and ramps that are donated to organizations to transport handicapped youngsters to hospitals, to places where they receive treatments, to parks, to ball games, and so forth.

I've worked with many other organizations that do wonderful work. I once visited the Southern California Adolescent Psychiatric Center at Los Angeles County Hospital. Noting how excited these troubled teenagers seemed to be by my appearance, Dr. Ruth Sinay asked me to stay for lunch. We had sandwiches and lemonade. Then each child took me to his room and proudly showed me his furnishings and belongings. For hours I talked to them, kidded with them, teased them, hugged them. They seemed like normal, joyous youngsters.

One struck me especially because she was as beautiful as any teen-aged girl I've ever seen. She looked as if she could step out of this institution and into a studio and play "Gidget." I mentioned this to Dr. Sinay. She sighed and said, "Yes, but she is one of our worst patients. She has tried to commit suicide on more than one occasion. Her body has been slashed with knife and razor wounds."

As I was leaving, Dr. Sinay said: "You've done more with these kids in two hours than I've managed to do with them in the last two months." I was ripped right through with two contrasting emotions. On the one hand, my heart ached for these youngsters. On the other hand, we had just shared two hours of sheer delight. Driving back to my office, my car never touched the ground. It was a warming experience. We *do* have the power to do so much, and there is so much more we can do.

I have had a hundred such experiences, over hundreds of visits to the children's wards of hospitals, where I have tried to cheer up and make contact with the emotionally disturbed, mentally retarded, and seriously or incurably sick or crippled youngsters. Their faces etch themselves on your brain forever. You do not have to be an especially sensitive person to be moved by these visits.

Celebrities have a curious power, and I don't believe we should turn our backs on it. One time the city of Wichita declared *Let's Make a Deal* day. I appeared at luncheons, did radio, television, and newspaper interviews, and was hosted by the city's mayor and the governor of Kansas. Shortly before we were to meet with the mayor, my host was chauffeuring me around. He mentioned that my biggest fan in town was a man with incurable cancer. I said, "Let's go visit him." My host said, "That's what I was hoping you'd say." We went to the hospital.

This man clearly knew his days were numbered. But he played his role to the hilt. He talked about his family, about how he was going to get well, how he was going to go out to California to be on my show and wear one of those crazy costumes. We laughed and talked and pretended life for him was not what it was. But when we parted we shook hands, and in his eyes, and I'm sure in mine, there was an honest admission of the realities. It is difficult to describe the feelings that sweep over me at times like this. I feel good and I feel bad. I know I am doing no more than the Bob Hopes and Martha Rayes and countless other performers. Because of our interest these unfortunate people know they have value, that others care. It is not much to do, but if we give them one more laugh, or even a smile, it is something.

My secretary, Jerita Ingle, has been with me for twelve years. She screens my mail: the requests for tickets, pictures, or money—and there are many of those —or the crank correspondence. She tries to protect me from people who would pester me, but she knows I want to see the personal mail. So she brings it all to me, sometimes with a tear in her eyes and the comment, "I didn't want to show you this one." Maybe the letter is from a mother whose daughter is dying of leukemia. As the child lies in bed she watches *Let's Make a Deal* every day and loves Monty Hall. Could I possibly send the child an autographed photo with perhaps a short note? I send a letter, using whatever information the mother has given me—the name of her dog, the school she went to, her favored friend, and so forth—to make it as personal as possible. I say that when the child gets better I want her to come out to see the show as my guest and visit me. But these children seldom get better.

Perhaps they answer my letters. I reply, sending a souvenir, something, anything. And one day I'll get a letter from the mother telling me that the child read and reread my letters and propped my picture up beside her bed and talked to it and watched our show until the day she died. The mother will thank me on behalf of the family for the happiness I provided this child. Then Jerita and I can only look at each other and try to restrain our emotions. The mother has lost a child and is thanking *me*.

I am Jewish and have worked hard to raise funds for Israel and for the United Jewish Appeal, but I have also represented almost every religion and many nationalities the world over. One week I emceed a Communion Breakfast for Cardinal McIntyre, was honored by the Armenian Society of Southern California, and received the Mitzvah Award from the Sisterhoods of America. Another week I made appearances in Los Angeles, New York, Miami, Chicago, and Montreal. I have worked so many charity affairs at the Beverly Hilton, the Century Plaza, and a few other hotels that the staffs and I are on a first-name basis.

One interesting comment I can make about the variety of groups I perform for and a generalization I can easily make, whether they are Italian, Armenian, Irish or Jewish: the women all embrace you the same way, they kiss you the same way, and they look at you with the same love. The men have a warm smile and a hearty handshake that doesn't differ from black to white, senator to sanitation worker. And conversely, no one group has a monopoly on driving you crazy.

I have also found that if you find time to talk to one group in one community, ten other groups from ten other communities are immediately writing or telephoning to demand that you honor them with an appearance, too, and are insulted if you do not. They also are disappointed if you do not make a contribution to their cause or at least shower the group with color television sets, washing machines, and other paraphernalia.

On *Let's Make a Deal* we pay for the expensive prizes. The rest of it is given to us only to be handed out on the show with plugs for the products. I do not get cut-rate prices or outright gifts from any company. I buy my cars at dealers and my TV sets at discount stores. The public doesn't seem to understand this, however. Heads of charitable organizations seem to think all we have to do is pick up the phone and order a few hundred free cars or cameras and have them delivered immediately.

I once spoke at a memorial luncheon for my mother in Palm Springs. Afterward the president asked if I could get them a color television set wholesale for their bazaar. I said I was sorry but I could not; I had no such connections; I had nothing to do with the prizes we gave away on our show. The president would not take no for an answer. A few days later she wrote to ask if I had found a color TV for them. I wrote back politely saying I was sorry I couldn't help. A few days after that she called to ask me if I had located the set for them. I was losing patience fast, but again I said I couldn't help. She called again. I exclaimed in exasperation that I had a color television set in my office. I said, "Look, if you can have someone over within an hour to pick it up, you can have it." She thanked me triumphantly. Sure enough, within an hour someone showed up at my door to haul away the set. A few days later, the president of a Desert Hot Springs group called to say she'd heard of my gift to the Palm Springs group and asked if I could get a color TV for them!

I spend most of my time on the other side of television sets, anyway. Often it is spent hosting telethons, a very special sort of charitable endeavor. I'm usually on the air twelve to eighteen hours at a stretch. Most telethons originate in New York or Los Angeles and are broadcast on as many stations across the country as will carry them. Most of the pledges are telephoned in and the organizers must follow up with letters and telephone calls to those who are slow in mailing the amounts pledged. The results are inconsistent. As a rule, if you receive more than 70 per cent of the sums pledged, you are satisfied. It is a fact, however, that some telethons have netted more than pledged. Some who can't or don't try to get through on the telephone still contribute.

Among the most successful telethons is Jerry Lewis's annual pitch for muscular dystrophy funds, which has raised millions. Others don't do nearly as well. A telethon is not like any other television show, and putting one together properly is tricky. It must be broadcast from a single center with a single emcee front and center. The audience must be given a sense of structure and continuity. People do not watch telethons for five or ten minutes and then send in money. They watch for a long time, often for many hours. They become almost mesmerized and after a while they begin to identify with your cause. Their reserve and resistance is slowly, carefully rubbed away until they are moved to contribute. It is important to attain some success from the start. As the figures on the tote board mount, others are inspired to jump on the bandwagon. Pleas based on building up low totals seldom work. No one wants to go with a loser. The success of the Lewis telethon starts with the success of his past telethons. They have been winners. There is always a healthy total from the previous year to be topped. The early returns usually are large and bring more in turn as the telethon progresses.

In the summer of 1972 I appeared on a telethon for the Democratic National Committee. It was broadcast from different centers with a variety of emcees and got looser and looser until it fell apart. As the show shifted between Miami and Los Angeles, people were cut off in mid-speech, mid-song, and mid-dance. There were too many entertainers, and viewers were more aware of the multitude of talent than the money that was needed. I emceed the first two-and-a-half hours and was pleased when critic Cecil Smith of the Los Angeles *Times* commented that I projected an image of class. A lot of other classy citizens were available to follow me, but the producers turned instead to members of the younger set, and it is doubtful if their long hair, tie-dyed shirts, and blue jeans were right for the more mature, moneyed audience they were trying to reach.

I was disappointed, though not surprised, by the results. The Democratic Party was more than $9 million in debt. The telethon raised less than $5 million, a poor total for a show with an unusually large and strong national network of 175 stations and a product that generally attracts large donations from wealthy men. The show cost approximately $1,500,000 to put on, so $3.5 million was all that was left—provided that much was sent in—to lower the debt.

Although I am not affiliated with any political party because of my Canadian citizenship, I still feel that I

want to make a contribution to the political process in
the United States; and helping to preserve a viable two-
party system through the telethon was my contribution.

In the spring of 1972 I did an Easter Seals telethon in
Las Vegas. It must have had the classiest cast in telethon history: Jack Benny, Bob Newhart, Alan King,
Robert Goulet, Debbie Reynolds, Bobby Darin, and
many others. Sergio Franchi, who had been out on the
desert camping with his son, drove 500 miles in a jeep
to appear. Then he gave $500 himself.

The show was telecast from the enormous convention hall in the Sahara Hotel. It was beset with problems. The local Las Vegas station we were using had
burned down and could provide only rudimentary
equipment. Our mikes often were not working. We were
seen in New Orleans, but not Los Angeles, where no
station would give us time. Still, we raised nearly a
million dollars.

I worked terribly hard, as I do on all telethons. After
a week of taping my own shows, I flew to Vegas from
Los Angeles late the night before the show, checked
into the suite provided me by the organizers, and early
the next morning, went to rehearsals. Most of the stars
do not rehearse in advance for such shows, but the or-
chestra must practice its music, the cameramen must
know what to shoot, and a schedule has to be plotted.
In mid-afternoon, I took a nap. I had dinner, shaved,
and was dressed by seven P.M. The show started at
eight. I was on from then until four in the morning. I
returned to the show at ten A.M. and stayed on it until
it ended at four in the afternoon.

You don't feel tired while you are working on a telethon. Performing carries you along and keeps you going.
You hit a peak and maintain it. In a place like Las
Vegas, there is a large live audience out front stimu-
lating you. You eventually become dazed, however, and
must rely on instinct and experience to hold things to-

gether. When you are finally through, it seems as though you have been working for a week and an enormous sense of exhaustion settles over you. But if the show has been successful, you feel an enormous sense of satisfaction, too—that is, if it isn't taken away from you. At this telethon, Mr. Easter Seals, the gentleman from the Midwest who was national chairman for the cause, flew in to make an appearance during the last hour of the telecast, shook my hand, then flew away again.

It happens too often. As with other charity shows, the front men take the credit, while the emcee and the others who work as hard as people in this business can work to make a success of a show are fast forgotten at the finish without even a private expression of gratitude, an offer of dinner, or a ride to the airport to ease our weariness. Men like Dennis James are called upon to work many telethons because they do them beautifully and succeed with them. There are only a few such experts, yet Dennis had many a lean period between telethons, his expertise suddenly forgotten.

I worked a local telethon in Nashville, Tennessee, once. The chairwoman was a Mrs. Hoity-Toity. The show was on for about twenty hours, and I was on for about sixteen. I never saw Mrs. Hoity-Toity until that last hour when all the Big Wheels arrive on camera to accept credit for the cause. I never saw her again.

This show raised $270,000—a lot for a local show, and the best this one had ever done. When it ended at six o'clock, with a great, spirited rush of music, I was exhausted, though exhilarated. The show was broadcast from a sports arena, and a trailer backstage served as a sort of dressing room. I went to the trailer to stretch out for a minute, leaving word of where I had gone. I fell asleep. When I woke up, it was silent and dark. Everyone seemed to be gone. I had worked sixteen hours for their cause, and not a single one of the spon-

sors had hung around long enough to thank me or
see if there was anything they could do for me. The
stillness was broken by a solitary figure who poked his
head into my trailer. "Are you still there?" he asked.
"Where the heck do you think I'd be!" I replied, "and
where is everybody?" Sheepishly, he explained, "I think
they've all gone to the country club for a celebration
dinner. They must have figured you had gone back to
Hollywood." "By the way," he continued, "what are
you doing for dinner?" I looked at him pleadingly. "I'm
having it with you if you're free." And we did.

A few years ago when the Wichita State University
football team was wiped out in a charter-airplane crash,
I organized a special national telecast to raise funds for
the families of the victims. I put together a plan for
an all-star show to be broadcast from campus with all
of the proceeds coming from the sale of seats and from
contributions we would seek from the TV audience.

I called my manager, Ray Katz, and told him what
I wanted to do. He wanted to help. We placed a call
to Martin Umansky at KAKE, our ABC affiliate. He
told us that, by coincidence, they were in the process of
placing a call to me because they felt I would be willing to help. Swiftly, we agreed on a plan. I would emcee
the show in the school's fieldhouse and set it up with the
help of Ray Katz, who would line up the talent. Stars
and even technicians would be flown into Wichita. No
one would be paid anything. A date was set.

A committee was formed in Wichita to help organize
things there. One of its members, a former writer long
removed from the Hollywood scene, apparently said,
"The show idea is okay, but who the hell is Monty
Hall? I can get you Jerry Lewis." And someone or another apparently said, "Oh, wow, Jerry Lewis—well,
wouldn't that be something!" The next thing I knew
I received a call from someone at Wichita State asking
me if I would share the spotlight with Jerry Lewis. I

asked how Jerry Lewis had got into the act. I was told that someone there could get Jerry Lewis, and, of course, he was such a big name that it would probably boost the show's impact considerably. I suggested that what he really wanted was for me to step aside. He admitted this was so. I said that was fine with me. I wished him well and hung up.

A few days later I got another call from the same official. He said the deal to get Lewis had fallen through. They were in trouble and would appreciate it if I took over again. I suppose I should have told him where to go. But the cause was worthy, and I agreed to resume. Maybe I should have displayed some ego. In any event, I put off my own work in order to work on this special show.

Then the plane carrying the Marshall University football team went down. This second tragedy was so close to the first that we felt we had to include them in any fund-raising project. The Wichita State officials agreed, but the Marshall people were not so sure at first. It was right after their youngsters and coaches had been lost and they felt a show might be in bad taste. They did not seem to trust Hollywood people in general. But we were concerned that it would seem strange to the public if the show was done for the families of the ill-fated players of one school and not the other. Eventually, Marshall agreed.

We rounded up stars such as Bill Cosby, Lou Rawls, George Gobel, Leif Erickson, Marilyn Maye, Phil Ford and Mimi Hines, The Young Americans, and Kate Smith. Lear Jet put planes at our disposal, and we flew in Hollywood musicians and engineers. Conditions in the fieldhouse were not up to professional standards. Final rehearsals were chaotic. Late in the afternoon we lost all electricity and had to resume by candlelight. As show-time neared that night, the power had not been restored and it began to appear that there would be

no telecast. All was madness. At ten minutes to eight,
forty minutes before showtime, power was restored.
The Wichita Power Company had erected giant poles
and brought power in from miles away. Just like the
popular song, the "Wichita Lineman" had come through.
The show, lasting two and a half hours, was a smash.
Bill Carruthers, who directed, kept his cool through
all the problems and did an amazing job. Mind you, he
did all of this without benefit of a camera rehearsal.
As we say in the business, "He winged it," and he didn't
miss a shot.

The fieldhouse was packed. At $10 a ticket, those
10,000 or so seats raised $100,000. The show was carried
on an astonishing 202 stations. Most carried it live, but
some carried a cut version later. These stations produced hundreds of thousands of dollars. Carroll Rosen-
bloom, then owner of the Baltimore Colts and now the
owner of the Los Angeles Rams, contributed $100,000.
It all came to more than $700,000, which went into a
scholarship fund for the children of the players and
coaches of the two teams.

Sadly, there were some unfortunate postscripts to this
story. Ohio State football coach Woody Hayes telephoned a personal letter from President Nixon, con-
gratulating us on what we had done. Later, I thought
it might be nice to have a copy of the letter, and I wrote
to the White House for one. Sometime later, while playing golf at the Hillcrest Country Club, I was paged to
take a telephone call from the White House. When I got
on the phone, a lady who described herself as an assistant to the President said, "In answer to your letter,
Mr. Nixon does not believe in signing the same letter
twice." I asked, "What does that mean?" She said, "It
means we'll send you a copy of the letter he sent to
Mr. Hayes, but it will not be signed."

I was stunned. It seemed sort of silly to me, but she
did not agree. Nor, apparently, was the situation worth

a new signed letter. I was sent the unsigned letter. It is not my proudest possession.

Reflecting on the episode, I thought it strange that the President, who will call to congratulate winners of golf matches and football games, will not write a note of congratulations to one who does what I did. It seems strange that the White House would even go to the expense of a long-distance call simply to tell me the President would not sign a letter I was being sent.

I never received even an unsigned letter from anyone at Marshall. As far as I know, the money had not been distributed because the two schools were squabbling over which was to get what share. The whole thing is incredible, but there you are. It is experiences like these that sometimes take the edge off, but still I continue them. I would like more time to live a normal life with my family and to work creatively at my profession. But it is not easy to turn from endeavors that have produced so many satisfactions. And I remember. It is not as if I were not given help when I needed it.

2

THE TWO years between high school and college were unpleasant. While my friends all went on to college, I worked full time for my father in the butcher shop without pay, unable to participate in a teenager's social activities. On Saturday nights I frequently had to deliver meat to homes where my friends were giving parties. Frequently, too, the kids would sing the old classic, "The butcher boy, the butcher boy, I'm going to marry the butcher boy. . . . Oh, Mama, oh, Mama, how happy I will be. . . . Oh, Mama, oh, Mama, the butcher boy for me."

Too young to handle this embarrassment, I'd hang my head and leave as fast as I could. I was a lonely boy who desperately wanted to go to college. I knew my parents could not afford it, but I was determined to raise the money. My mother was all for it and argued with my father, who was more realistic about our finances and who long since had given up on dreams.

Finally my parents decided to start me off at the University of Manitoba and see how long it could be sustained. Tuition was $150 a year at that time, and the cost of books and student activities was $25. My mother had put aside a lot of twenty-five cent pieces over the years, and these small savings and some money my father raised saw me through the first year of college.

My clothes were a big problem. All my life I had worn hand-me-downs from my mother's younger brothers. I had not had a new suit since I was thirteen, and now that I was seventeen my mother felt I needed one. My father did not. A new suit at that time cost about $18. A hand-me-down from one of my uncles could be altered to fit me fairly well for $2 or less. In the end my parents compromised and bought me a heavy sports coat and a new pair of slacks. I think I wore that same outfit for three years.

Going to the university was an emancipation. I was freed from the butcher shop. I was back with my peers, and college excitement loomed ahead. I arose between six and seven in the morning, took a streetcar across town to the university, and did not get home until after six in the evening. My father began to use my younger brother more and more in the store and took on more and more of the side duties himself.

I still made deliveries on Saturdays and collections on Sundays, but the butcher shop no longer was my prison. The first year of the university, the equivalent of our last year of high school today, was considered a period of adjustment. The studies were easy, and I had plenty of time to go out for athletic teams and drama programs.

After a summer back in the butcher shop, I was at first relieved to return for the second year of college, then depressed to find it much tougher than the first year had been, simply because I had rushed headlong into extracurricular activities. I wasn't prepared and I began to do poorly. By this time World War II was in its

early stages. I was nearing draft age and was serving in
the Canadian Officers Training School, a sort of ROTC
program. I got the idea it would be glamorous to become
a young officer, and I volunteered. When I was turned
down, I was deeply disappointed. The war was just
starting, and officer selection was still being handled
on an elitist basis.

Reluctantly, I returned to my studies. I dropped out
before the final examinations, and anyway I had run
out of money. It seemed to me that there was no point
to going on with college. I had to go to work, but I
did not want to go back to the butcher shop. I took a
job in a wholesale clothing house, making $9 a week.
Lunches cost twenty-five to thirty-five cents a day, and
the job was close enough that I could walk to work.
Since I lived at home, other expenses weren't high. So
I figured I could save $5 a week and put my kid
brother through college some day.

If I had been humbled by working for my father at
the butcher shop, I was humbled more by working for
a stranger. The boss was a hard man who spoke broken
English. Receiving an order on the telephone, he would
shout out to the help: "Do we got there sufficient
sizes?" He had trouble remembering names, but that
didn't bother him. He referred to Mr. McCorkindale, the
manager of Eaton's, the finest store in town, as "Mr.
McCockendoodle." He didn't even try to remember my
name. He asked the accountant what I was called. When
the accountant said "Monty," the boss sneered, "What
kind of a name is Monty?" From then on I was called
either "Say" or "Boy." If he wanted me, he'd merely
raise his voice and shout, "Say, go get me two boxes
of underwear." Or if I was not in sight, he'd yell to
someone, "Call me the boy."

My job was to do all the small things others were too
big to do. I arrived in the morning before anyone else
and swept the floors with a long broom. When I finished,

I went upstairs, uncrated clothing, and stacked it onto shelves. Then I made deliveries to department stores. At six, after sweeping all the floors again, I was finished. At night I went out with my young friends and tried to play the man about town on my small wages.

I worked there for a year. Then came the first of two turning points of my life in Winnipeg. One day another clothing man called me and said, "I have a buyer in town I want to do business with, but he has his son with him and I don't know how to get the boy out of the way. I'm sure he'd like to go out, and he's about your age. Get a date for yourself and somebody for him, and take him out. I'll lend you my car and give you enough money to cover your expenses. It'll be a free night out for you and a life-saver for me."

This was a bonanza for me, and I readily agreed. The boy turned out to be a fine young man. I found us a couple of dates, and we had a great time, and laughed the night through. I played the big sport and insisted on picking up all the tabs. He had no idea someone else had paid the bills and thought I was quite a high liver. He called the businessman the next day to tell him how pleased he was to have been entertained by such a splendid lad.

That afternoon my boss decided that the front steps needed washing. "Get the boy and tell him to wash the steps," he ordered. Soon the boy was on his hands and knees with a bucket scrubbing the steps. As I was working away, a visitor almost stepped on my fingers. "I'm sorry," he said. It was the young man. Our eyes met when I looked up, and in a second we realized the truth about each other. We were both embarrassed, and in another second he was gone. I never saw him again. But I never forgot him.

This was one of the most humiliating moments of my life. I had pretended to be something I was not, and what

I really was, was brought home forcibly to me. A cruel embarrassment. That night, in tears, I told my mother what had happened. She gave me a lecture in pride that I have never forgotten. She pointed out the indignities she had suffered throughout her life and how she had endured them. I realized that this magnificent woman who had achieved much more than I had and who had been subjected to so much more abuse, had learned to handle herself with regal dignity. Now, it may seem corny now, but I will never forget my mother looking into my eyes and saying: "Do you know the Rudyard Kipling poem 'If'? And let me quote the first few lines to you: 'If you can keep your head when all about are losing theirs, . . .'" Such was her way of restoring my confidence and picking me up.

The episode in the clothing store was a turning point of consequence. All the years of working in the butcher shop, all the hours of wire-brushing blood-stained cutting blocks and delivering heavy loads of meat in below-freezing weather, all the uncrating of clothing, of sweeping floors, of scrubbing steps, of being treated as if I were less than nothing, all the embarrassments I had suffered with my friends—all of it suddenly stiffened by desire to succeed in life. I determined somehow to make something of myself, to rise in the world and bring my mother, father, and brother up with me. I resolved to return to college and study to be a doctor. But how could I make it? A second turning point provided the answer.

Across the road from the wholesale house in which I worked was another run by a man named Max Freed, who was about ten years older than I was. His father had established the operation and made his son president at twenty-one, and now, at thirty, he was running the business by himself. He ran it well, and it was an enormous success. All of which others overlooked when they criticized him. People said his father had provided him everything, and now he was wasting it. He was a handsome young man and a bachelor, and he was quite a young man about town.

Freed noticed me making deliveries to his plant. One night, when he encountered my father playing poker at a club, he asked him what I was doing. Why, he wondered, was such a fine young man working at such a poor place? My father said, "It's very simple. He has no money. We have no money. What alternative is there?" When Freed suggested that I should go to college, my father replied honestly, "I imagine he would like that very much, but what about money?" Freed said, "Have him come to see me tomorrow."

When my father came home, he told me of the conversation, but I didn't get my hopes up too high. Nevertheless, I went to see Freed the next day. He asked me if I wanted to return to college. I did. What did I wish to study? I mentioned medicine. "Well, I'm going to arrange it," he said. "You will go back for as many years as you need, taking whatever courses you need. I want you to write down how much money it will take for tuition and books and clothing and your weekly expenses. In a few days, when you have figured it out, show it to me and I will give you the money."

I was stunned. I couldn't believe it was this easy. Why would he do this for me? I went away and made up my list of expenses and kept it modest to make sure it was not too much. I left out the clothing and limited the lunches, streetcar fares, and so forth to $2.50 a week. Nervously, I took the list to him. He looked it over and said, "You haven't included anything for clothing." When I replied that I didn't need any, he said, "I want you to have a couple of nice suits. We'll add that on. And you can't possibly handle your other expenses on $2.50. We'll double that so you can go like a gentleman." It came to about $300 a year.

Then he explained why he was doing this. He said,

"I have had everything in life given to me and I want to help people who have nothing. I have already tried it with a couple of others, but they have disappointed me. One showed signs of being a brilliant scholar, but both dropped out. I don't want you to disappoint me. So there are several strings to my proposition. One, you must report to me monthly and show me you are maintaining a high grade average—or the deal will be dropped. Two, you must promise to eventually pay me back every penny. Three, if you can, you must help others in the same way some day. And, four, you must never tell anyone about this except your parents."

I agreed, and though I never became a doctor, I kept every promise except the last one. I reported regularly and formed a firm friendship with this amazing man. I got high grades. I paid back in full the $900 he advanced me. When I could afford it, I began to help others and have sent several through college. But I could not keep his secret forever. When others criticized him, and put him down as a playboy, I could not resist straightening them out. The so-called playboy had moved into my life where the town's aristocrats had failed me.

I had a new outlook because I had a new obligation. Before, my parents had been behind me, but they had not pushed me. Now, this friend was behind me, too, and he was pushing me hard. I pushed myself. I could attend classes without worrying about how to pay for them. I could live well while pursuing life as a student. I had decent clothes on my back, my hair was cut, and I had a few bucks in my pocket.

Although Freed wanted me to restrict myself to my schooling, I insisted on working at his wholesale house one day a week and at my father's shop on Saturday nights. I picked up other jobs after school and on weekends from time to time and worked every summer to help out as much as I could.

I plunged into university life. I lettered in athletics, wrote for school publications, performed in school shows, headed school organizations. I became, in fact, a "big man on campus." I was spirited. Although I could not be compared to the rebellious youngsters today, I was always an outspoken activist for various campus causes and was frequently in hot water with university officials and my professors.

When I finished my final pre-med semester of studies, I stood in the top ten of those who were applying to medical school, some three hundred in all. But although seventy were accepted, I was not. The explanation: there was a quota system at the time, though no one would talk about it. Winnipeg had a large ethnic population, and many Jewish students applied to med school. The school accepted three or four students from each minority, including women, and gave the rest of the places to Anglo-Saxon Protestants.

When I told Max Freed, who had been so proud of my progress and so sure that admission would be granted me, he was furious. But he encouraged me to remain in school and seek admission again.

Disappointed, but intent on making med school the next year, I remained at the university and took another year of science—the recommended procedure for promising rejects. Again I got good grades, and was elected president of the Science Student Body. The latter was considered the highest honor a student in science could attain. I was called "Senior Stick" and my benefactor and my parents were tremendously proud of me. I was also the president of the University Booster Club and active in athletics. Again I applied to med school, and again I was not accepted.

The next year I did well a third time, and at the end I was elected president of the entire student body of the university. But I still failed to make med school. Then I decided to remain in school for a fifth and final year—and to fight the med school's prejudiced admissions practices. I joined with several prominent attorneys and businessmen who started to investigate the situation and apply pressure to have it altered.

Meanwhile, as president of the student body, I tried to right other wrongs. At this time there was considerable public criticism of the university as a hideout for "slackers" from the war effort. Despite the fears of officials, I organized an "open house" at the university campuses. The public was invited to see the university at work. Thousands went through laboratories and classrooms, listened to lectures, watched their young at study, and came away convinced that there was purpose to such endeavor. The press stressed that much of the research being done would benefit the war effort. The open house was a smashing success. But college officials never forgave me for going against their wishes, and this probably resulted in my loss of the alumni medal.

Every year the alumni presented its medal to the outstanding student on campus. At the end of my fourth year, the alumni met and decided that I would be the recipient; but because I elected to go on for a fifth year, they decided not to make the award but save it for my graduation the next spring. As a result, no award was made that year to anyone. When the alumni met with student representatives in my fifth year, I was expected to receive the medal. But the alumni and the professors sitting on the committee had other ideas. They voted the medal to another student. Whatever their reasons for literally stealing my medal away, they remain theirs to this day. When David Robertson, my close friend and my successor as president of the student body, came directly to me to tell me the news, he broke down. "There was no discussion," he said. "It was a fait accompli when I arrived at the meeting." I was crushed. I had had a great college career, probably one of the greatest any student had ever had at that university;

and I was left with the taste of bitter ashes. It is a generation since then, but I have never forgotten.

In my final year I had begun to work for the local radio station. I had a disc jockey show seven nights a week. Before that there were other jobs, and some of them were less than grand.

I got a summer job building airfields with the Department of Transport. The fields were strung throughout Canada, and I was assigned to Portage La Prairie. I became a chain man, which is the lowest job on a survey team. Although the temperature was ninety or more, we wore dungarees, heavy shirts, hats, and boots because the air was thick with mosquitos and flies and we usually worked on swampy farm land. The surveyors staked out the land and the airstrip area and used hand signals to instruct us where to string our chain. It was backbreaking work, lasting ten to twelve hours a day and paying forty cents an hour six days a week. I averaged about sixty-five hours and $25 or $26 a week—out of which I paid $8 or $9 for breakfast and lunch as well as the room I shared with another worker. I had to pay for my suppers. If I wanted to go out on a date or buy a bus or train ticket for a trip home, the rest of my salary was wiped out. I was not saving a dime.

The foreman was tough. One scorching afternoon a truck stopped to dispense lemonade and drinks to the field workers, and the survey gang asked him if we could have some. He laughed and told us to forget it. I could have murdered him on the spot.

When the crew moved to Souris, there were no reasonably priced rooming houses, and we had to stay at the hotel. Room and board was $15 a week, which really left little for other expenses. One weekend I went home, and on Sunday night I caught a train from Winnipeg to Brandon, where I expected to make a connection to Souris, thirty miles away. When I got to Bran-

don, however, I found there was no train to Souris, and
no bus until the next morning. It was eleven P.M., and I
was due on the job at seven A.M. or I would be fired. I
had only enough money for the ticket on a nonexistent
train, not enough for a room for the night or any other
kind of transportation. So I started to walk.

I hoped to hitch a ride, but with gas rationing in
effect there were few cars on the highway. So I walked
on through the dark, deserted, lonely night. For a
while I whistled. Then I stopped whistling and began
to tire. Fortunately, I had no luggage. By six in the
morning I had covered eighteen miles, and it was light.
A bus bound for Souris came along, and I had enough
for a ticket. I arrived at my hotel at seven, just as my
roomie was leaving for work. He said, "Hurry up or
you'll be late." I was too weary to care. "To hell with
work," I said, and fell down on the bed. And I added,
"To hell with the Department of Transport and to
hell with the foreman." In the late afternoon I woke
up and walked over to the office where they were wind-
ing up work for the day. The foreman said I was fired.
I said I quit. A traveling salesman was parked outside
the hotel, and I hitched a ride home to Winnipeg with
him.

The summer was far from over, and I needed another
job. So I went to work for the Canadian Wheat Board.
At that time there was a surplus of wheat and farmers
were being paid by the government to keep their fields
unseeded. Inspectors checked out the size of the farm
so each farmer could be paid properly. A fellow sitting
at one desk read these reports aloud. I sat at the next
desk and entered the details in large ledgers. There
were rows and rows of us at desks doing the same thing.
It may have been the most boring work anyone ever
did.

The only break in the monotony came when it was
discovered that I had some small theatrical background.

Asked to put on the board's annual show for employees, I became the producer and director, and I also took part in it. It was a great success. A few days later, however, I was caught conversing on the job. Other than the reading of official reports, no one was allowed to talk while working. I always talked and I had been warned. This time the straw boss fired me. So that was all for that summer. As a producer-performer, I was accepted; as a talker, I was fired.

During the winters I began to work for a troupe that traveled around entertaining at service installations. The war was in full swing, and people put together shows privately and visited bases and hospitals. Harry Zimmerman, an old Chattaqua circuit vaudevillian, came out of semi-retirement to start a troupe with his wife, Elizabeth, and I got a spot with them. Our shows were called "Priorities of 1941" and so on.

After my last class in the afternoon I hurried to catch a bus that rushed us 50 or 100 or 150 miles to an army post or airfield or hospital. We did two shows for the enlisted men and a third for the officers. Then we climbed back on the bus and returned to town. Often I arrived about seven in the morning and had to go straight to class. It was wearying but exciting. I emceed the show and did comedy routines. I also sang alone and with a girl singer. It was the best training I ever got in show business, and I loved it. Among the local kids in that show were Morley Meredith, now with the Metropolitan Opera, Iva Withers, who headlined on Broadway, and many others who toured in Canada and the States.

Coached and encouraged by my mother, I had been performing in school and club shows since I was a child. In college I played the lead in an original musical comedy *You Can't Beat Fun.* David Yeddeau, who directed the show for us, went on to direct radio shows and asked me if I wanted to work for him. I said I did, and whenever I could get away from classes I worked at Station CKRC, whose studios were in the Royal Alexandra Hotel in Winnipeg.

My first show was a disaster. I had a small dramatic part. After our dress rehearsal we had a half hour until air time. Someone said Lily Pons was in the lobby of the hotel. I had grown up listening to opera records and I idolized the great performers. I rushed to the lobby in hopes of getting a glimpse of Miss Pons. I never found her. Suddenly I remembered the show. Dashing back, I found Yeddeau reading my lines on the air. He froze me with a chilling glance, thrust the script into my hands, and went into the control room while I went on with the rest of the script. Later, other members of the cast took me aside and explained how bad it was to miss a cue, much less a show, without good reason and sufficient warning for a replacement to be found. The director must have assumed I learned a lesson from this mishap because he never said a single word to me about it. I was not fired, as well I might have been, which probably would have nipped my show business career just as it was budding.

I began to do a great deal of radio work. I pinch-hit as an announcer and did small acting parts. In my last year of college Esse Ljungh, a prominent producer and director of drama for the Canadian Broadcasting Corporation in Winnipeg, auditioned me and hired me to play the parts of many young men in his shows.

I was young and indoctrinated early into the hard-talking, hard-drinking, free-living life of the broadcasting people of those days. They played a lot of practical jokes on each other, and I took part in them. Our sportscaster, Arthur Morrison, was about seventy years old and fair game. Once, when he sat broadcasting into a mike, we filled a wastebasket with news clips and set them afire at his feet. Our newscaster, Ron Alderson, always had his four o'clock newscast prepared by two o'clock. No matter what happened in the world during the intervening two hours, he was set. Once we inserted a recipe for frying fish into the middle of his copy, and he read most of it before he realized what he was reading.

Another newscaster, Cy Cairns, always was able to make me laugh with a line or a look. It got to the point where he could simply stand in front of me while I was broadcasting and he would break me up. The sponsors started to complain, and I determined to get revenge. Cy did the twelve o'clock news in one of our glass-walled studios. Sitting at his table, he faced directly into a corridor. I put a pile of chairs and junk atop a desk and shoved it all in front of the window while he was broadcasting. I then stood on the desk, stripped off all my clothes, and sat stark naked atop the mountain of rubble. Cy didn't crack a smile. He had anticipated something of the sort, and he had lettered a sign, which he held up as he continued speaking into the mike. I was so surprised by the funny obscenity that I fell to the floor—and limped the rest of the semester.

My work at the station on the six to midnight shift covered lots of different shows—a singing program, a quiz program, and a disc jockey program, along with various acting and announcing roles and the job of directing an ethnic musical show. How I got the singing show is a strange story. I sing, but I'm no Sinatra. The station had a musical program, *Concert at the Console*, which needed a soloist. I had a friend I felt could fill the role and I arranged an audition for him. I went along, and after he had finished, I was asked to sing, too. I did—and I was hired. My friend was not. And that is how I beat out Morley Meredith of the New York Metropolitan Opera for a singing job. It is possible that the people at the station were not the best judges of talent.

I was now making $50 to $60 a week working part-time on radio in Winnipeg while my father was making

$25 to $30 a week working full-time in his butcher shop. I had paid my own way through my fifth and last year at the university and wanted to begin repaying Max Freed. I had stirred an investigation into the quota system at the medical school, but after my fifth year I did not bother to apply again. By then I was fed up and finished with that and excited by thoughts of a career in show business.

That year, of 78 or 80 who were accepted for Medical School at the University of Manitoba, I believe 26 were Jewish, and many others were members of other minority groups. My closest friend was among these. But I was not. I was satisfied that I had played a part in righting a situation that was dreadfully wrong.

As so often happens in life, a bad experience had good consequences. I might have been a good doctor. Who knows? I do know that I have been successful in show business and that I am happy with my profession. But at the time I started up the path into show business, I had not the slightest idea how tough the way would be.

3

ORIGINALLY IT APPEARED that the world of entertainment would somehow have to wait until I had done a hitch in the service and the war had ended. I had been serving in the university's reserve officer training corps and therefore was protected from having to serve in the regular Army. I did not feel guilty about it, because I'd volunteered at the start of the war and been rejected; and I had later volunteered for the army's entertainment corps and been rejected for that, too. But now, with my college career concluded, it appeared I would be going into the army.

The colonel in charge of our college officer training program was not one of my biggest boosters. In Canada, we had a service review board that was supposed to classify college graduates according to their fields. But as is the case with most such classification systems, the graduates' backgrounds were ignored and they simply were inducted into the infantry. I wrote an editorial in the student newspaper pointing this out and suggesting the board was a waste. The colonel did not like it and threatened to court martial me and strip me of my reserve officer's status.

I then enlisted to serve in the European theater where the Canadian Army and all of the British Empire forces were primarily involved. I was to go to camp as usual for two weeks, after which I would be transferred from the reserves to the regulars.

While we were in camp, V-E Day came. The colonel wanted a solemn ceremony staged at the camp and suggested I put it on. In short order I rounded up some talent, rehearsed a choir, and presented an essentially religious program. Backed by a large chorus, I sang "The Lord's Prayer." Near the end, the colonel was introduced to offer official comments. He gave a speech. It was a great moment in his life and he wept. The show was well received and later he came to me to tell me all was forgiven.

Then it was discovered that because our enlistment papers had covered only service in the European theater, we had fulfilled our contract and were free of commitment. We were asked to volunteer for the Asian theater, but I declined. The colonel came to me and said, "Do you realize that as the president of the student body of the college you are a leader and an example for the others? If you don't sign many of them won't either." "I don't care what the others do," I replied. "I just want out." Suddenly, I was back on the outs with him and he was as angry as it is possible to be. But he was also helpless. I was a free man. In his frustration he followed me into civilian life, went to CKRC, spoke to the station manager, Gerry Goetz, and demanded I be dismissed as a slacker. Goetz threw him out of his office—for which I have always loved him.

The colonel's only revenge came when he refused to permit me time off from camp to attend my graduation ceremonies. I received my Bachelor of Science degree anyway and went to work for Goetz and CKRC, beginning my real career in June 1945. My immediate supervisor was program manager Jack Kemp. He was a marvelous man who believed in me. His inspiration carried me through many a frustrating period that year.

I remained on the six-to-midnight stint, but I worked every other shift, too. When I wasn't working, I was at the station helping or trying things out. I did music shows, sports shows, quiz shows, dramatic shows, interview shows, man-on-the-street shows, every single sort of show. On V-J Day, for instance, I reported on the celebration in downtown Winnipeg. I stood on top of a recording truck and described the incredible scene of celebration. I jumped on a streetcar to interview people. It was a great, wild, exciting day, the most memorable of my life for years. I also learned a lot about how to produce and direct, and I spent a lot of time creating new shows in the hopes they would get on the air some day. I learned some of the engineer's duties. I did everything they threw at me, and loved it all. It was hard to tear me away from the station. I was only making $60 a week or so, but I was satisfied.

I seemed to be making it. At least, I was off to a swift start. I sent Max Freed a $100 check at the end of the first year. I was to send him another $100 check at the end of the second year, and a $700 check the third year, wiping out the debt. Much later when I was in New York and he wanted World Series tickets for four business friends, I promised to get them for him. I refused to accept any money and willingly paid a scalper $200 for four fine seats, never letting Max know how I got them.

That first year out of college my best friend, who was to start medical school, came to me and asked for help. He said, "I have enough money for my tuition and just about enough to get through the year, but I haven't enough money for my books or microscopes or other supplies. Now that you're working, could you lend me some money?" I had $225 in the bank. I withdrew it all and gave it to him. He took it gratefully and returned to school and later repaid the loan. Today he is a successful doctor, and we remain close friends. This was the first interest payment on my promise to Max Freed.

People in my position are constantly asked for cash to cover rent or operations or some need for some desperate circumstance, but obviously we cannot respond to the many problems of strangers. But from the time I had money to give, I have given it to those who seemed deserving. Often I have been paid back, often I have not.

I was paid little in my early years in radio, and after the first flush of enthusiasm for my new field wore off, I began to feel frustrated. At CKRC the veterans were content to coast and laughed at the hustle of an ambitious youngster like myself. Yet they got the choice jobs and the top money. I was used only as a fill-in. If the sportscaster tied one on and didn't show up, I was rushed in to pinch hit. If the newscaster played sick, I served in his place. Yet they kept their positions, while I couldn't seem to improve mine. One night the Dominion Network blacked out and we had to improvise several hours of programing. I went to my desk and pulled out a quiz show, a sports show, and two musical shows I had worked up and put them on. From 7:30 to 10:30 that night, I was the producer, the director, and the star of all our shows. I was our station. I was proud but received little recognition.

This situation was especially depressing because I had been burying myself in work deliberately. Since the summer of '44, I had been going with the daughter of a Los Angeles couple who returned to Winnipeg each year. After my first date with her, a blind date, I began to see her every day or night, and we swiftly grew serious about each other. So much so that her father checked with friends to find out why I had not been accepted into medical school. He liked me. But his wife did not like the idea of a broadcaster, a son of a butcher, with about $18 in the bank as a prospect for her daughter. She tried to discourage us.

Nevertheless, at summer's end, when she returned to Los Angeles, we had an understanding that we were at least unofficially engaged. If I did not make med school in my last year, I would go to California to work in broadcasting. There I could be near her, and we could pursue our romance. All my final year in college I corresponded with her. But near the end of the school year, she wrote me a "Dear John" letter. She had met someone else; she had fallen in love; she had just become engaged. Shortly thereafter, I heard they were married. I was young, and a romantic, and I was crushed and resentful. So I plunged deep into my radio work after graduation. And when I swiftly felt frustrated, I acted.

Early in 1946, I went to see Gerry Goetz and told him I thought I rated better than I was getting. He agreed, but he did not offer me more. Instead, to my surprise, he spread a map out on his desk. He said that it was a map of Toronto. I pointed out that my plea had nothing to do with a map of Toronto. He disagreed. "This is where you have to go. Toronto is the big time for broadcasting in Canada. I've been watching you ever since you began with us and I believe you can make it in the big time. I could give you a few dollars raise or a new show. I don't want to do that because I don't want you to stay here. If you do, you'll become like the other regulars—fat and lazy, and going nowhere. You're young and you're going somewhere. And my advice to you is to go. Go now." I thought about it. There was nothing to keep me in Winnipeg. Toronto, indeed, was tops in Canadian broadcasting. So why not try there? Why not try Montreal, too—and even New York? I had saved another $250. On the night of my parents' twenty-fifth wedding anniversary, I announced I was on my way. I remember friends and family were there. I was explaining, "First I go to Toronto and make several calls at stations there for five or six days. Then I go on to Montreal and spend four or five days visiting stations there. And then I'm going to take a week in New York and try the big city." And someone asked, "And then what?" My grandfather interrupted, "And then Monty comes back home to Winnipeg." And everybody laughed because they all believed that would happen. But I was determined that it would not happen—and it did not. I left Winnipeg and returned thereafter only to visit.

In mid-February 1946, I got on a train with all my belongings easily squeezed into a single valise and went off to Toronto. I moved in with a friend and began to make the rounds. Selling myself was not easy. I had budding talent but couldn't prove it in a brief interview. I had a good personality, but not the beautiful baritone voice of Orson Welles, Lorne Greene, Joseph Cotton, or Howard Duff, some of whom began as announcers and went on to become actors.

I went to see Andrew Allen, head of CBC Drama in Toronto, and others at the Canadian Broadcasting Corporation. I went to CFRB but received no offers. Then Don Insley offered me a job with CKEY for $175 a month. I thanked him and asked for some time to decide. I went on to see Jack Part at CHUM and he seemed impressed but not enough to make me an offer. I ran out of Toronto stations. Before I went on to Montreal, though, Jack Part changed his mind and offered me $225 a month to join CHUM. I told him I would let him know. In Montreal, I was asked to work on overseas broadcasts for the CBC's International Division, but that didn't appeal to me. I went to New

York and got exactly one interview, which was arranged by a cousin who was working as a writer there.
The man told me, "You're an emcee, are you? Listen,
son, when I want emcees I call Danny Kaye or Bing
Crosby or Bob Hope, not a kid from Canada." It scared
me half to death. I couldn't even get in to see anyone
else. I stood on the sidewalk watching the St. Patrick's
Day parade, then went to a telegraph office and wired
Jack Part in Toronto, accepting his offer and saying I
would report for work at CHUM as soon as possible.

In a few days, I was there. Jack Part was short and
stocky with wavy gray hair and the dancing eyes of a
pitchman. He owned a patent medicine business, and
he recorded programs for his elixirs and placed them
on stations throughout Canada. His remedies were doing well, but his station was not. CHUM was a daylight station, operating from sunrise to sunset, and it
was not making any money. Part, however, was a joy to
work for, and we took to each other right away.

One thing Part didn't like was my name. I was
Monte Halparin then and he thought I needed something short and sweet. We tried a lot of combinations
without hitting on one we liked. Then I suggested,
"How about just cutting my second name in half?" He
said, "Monty Hall, that's fine." I did not know that he
did not know how to spell my first name. I woke up
one morning to find billboards all over Toronto announcing a new show with "Monty" Hall. I shrugged and accepted it. Later I had my name legally changed. (My
brother, Robert, also changed his name to Hall, not
knowing that Robert Hall was a familiar name in clothes
in the U.S.)

Jack Part asked me what sort of show I'd like to do.
I had done a musical morning show in Winnipeg with
that lovable old pianist-newscaster Cy Cairns, and I said
I'd like to do such a show in Toronto. I said I needed
a partner who could not only play the piano but sing

Monty at eighteen months

*With mother and father at
twelve months, and again,
at age eighteen,
with parents and brother Robert*

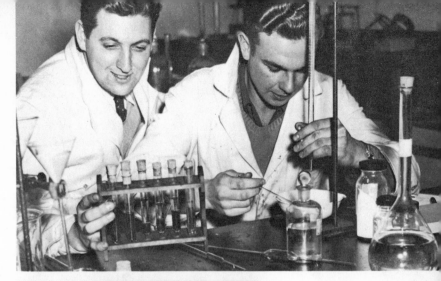

The pre-med student,
the Senior Stick, and the surveyor

*The wedding of
Marilyn and Monty,
with Monty's parents (above),
and the young performer—
with Mildred Morey
in a Crippled Children's
Charity Show at Maple Leaf
Gardens (right), with
partner on early morning
radio show,
Wake Up and Smile (middle),
and interviewing
Danny Kaye on
radio (bottom)*

*Monty with a contestant
on his first game show,*
What's Cookin'? *(top),
and with others
on the set of*
Video Village *(bottom)*

so we could harmonize some. Part said he had someone who would be almost perfect, a pianist who both sang and wrote his own songs. The problem was that he drank heavily and might not appear every now and then.

I gave him a try anyway, and he turned out to be almost perfect. He didn't mind taking orders from a kid eleven years younger than he, and he did everything beautifully. We called the program *Wake Up and Smile,* and it was on seven to nine every morning dispensing songs and snappy patter. Only on the fourth morning he failed to show up, and I had to resort to records. He promised it would never happen again. A week later it happened again. I devised a solution. Every day a taxi picked me up and took me to his apartment house, where, hungover or sober, he was roused, showered, rushed to the studio, and shoved behind the piano. This worked for many months.

However, he had another problem. He adored his estranged wife and spent almost all his money phoning her in New York and pleading with her to take him back. One morning I found his apartment empty. There was no word from him for three days. Then he called from New York to say he had gone there to make his pleas in person, but had been refused and was returning. Later he announced that he had accepted an offer to do a show in Winnipeg for more money. So that was that.

I found another partner, a talented man but not an outstanding pianist and it didn't work out well. I tried others, but the chemistry wasn't there. Finally, the program was dropped. Most shows have short lives, and this experience taught me that there are many and varied factors behind their troubles—not all of which are apparent on the air.

Again, there was a silver lining to the cloud. The death of my show probably helped the birth of my marriage. I had begun to go with a lovely young lady named Marilyn and was head over heels in love with her. I suddenly found myself becoming a romantic of ridiculous proportions. I decided I would serenade her every morning on the show, dedicating one or another love song to her. I always asked her later how she'd liked it. She realized it was important to me and tried to be enthusiastic. The problem was she was going to school, working as a radio actress on the side, and going out with me nights. I could get by on four or five hours sleep a night, but she could not. Getting up at seven in the morning to hear me sing "Embraceable You" when her first class didn't start for three hours was beyond love or duty. Fortunately, the show went under before our romance did.

There was no shortage of shows for me. I did radio sports shows and play-by-play. Since my early days back in bed with burns and pneumonia, I had studied sports record books, especially Frank Menke's *Encyclopedia of Sports*, and I was full of trivial facts about sports history. At CHUM, I had a sports quiz show on which people asked me such things as Rogers Hornsby's lifetime batting average and who held the flyweight boxing title in 1907. I could answer almost all the questions then, though I can't now.

I loved doing play-by-play hockey and football games. But I loved even more doing live on-the-spot broadcasts, something that sadly has almost disappeared from radio. With an "actuality" broadcast, you never know what might happen. On a show broadcast from the steps of City Hall called *What Do You Think?*, I interviewed passers-by on topics of the day. Larry Mann was my assistant. Larry now is a prominent character actor in Hollywood and remains a close friend. Larry's job was to select interesting-looking persons and talk them into going on mike with me. He was my "grabber." I trusted his judgment. One day he shoved someone in

front of me and I asked: "What do you think about the
Hamilton steel strike?" The man replied with a startling
string of obscenities. The show was live and his words
were going out over the air. In panic, I turned and
started to run from him. He started to chase me, and
only Larry's flying tackle saved what was left of the
day.

Another time Joe Louis, then still the heavyweight
boxing champion of the world, came to Toronto to play
a golf exhibition. He said he didn't want to do any
interviews, which disappointed the radio men of the
area. I figured if I could get to talk with the champ it
would be quite a coup. I was young and brash. I raced
over to his hotel, went to his room, and announced I
had a parcel. In a big, booming voice, he said, "Come in."
So I went in, portable recorder in hand instead of a
parcel. I said, "I'm sorry for the deception, champ, but
I was desperate to see you for an interview." He
growled, "I said, 'NO interviews.' " I said, "I know you
did, but I'm a young guy working hard to get ahead and
an interview with you would be a big help to me." He
looked at me a moment and then said, "All right," and
waved me to a seat. It was one of my first "scoops."
Today Joe is a "greeter" at Caesar's Palace in Las Vegas,
and I see him from time to time. He recognizes me, but
it must be from television. I'm sure he has no memory of
that morning I crashed his room. I call him "champ."
Life has turned difficult for him, but he will always be
"champ" to me.

I also covered the arrival of Alexander of Tunis, who
had become the new Governor-General of Canada. The
government gave him a parade, which was to wind up at
the 48th Highlanders Building. I found a perch on a
wide ledge just above the first story of this building and
broadcast from there. To our disappointment there were
no speeches. As the parade ended, Alexander was hurried into the Highlanders Building. As I was climbing

down, I happened to look into the room below me and there was Alexander and an aide. On impulse I jumped into the room through an open window and went up to Alexander with live microphone in hand. "Sir, would you be so kind as to say a few words to the people of Toronto?" I asked.

Even as I spoke I knew something was very wrong. The aide looked terrified. Then I saw that he was holding Alexander upright. I took a closer look at the Governor-General and realized that he was three sheets to the wind. Suddenly, I was terrified. Thanks to my rash act Alexander's reputation was at stake. And I couldn't back out. I had to leave the microphone in front of his face. With the majestic bearing and resourcefulness that had preserved the British Empire for centuries, Alexander somehow rose to the occasion. Drawing himself erect, he gave a glorious, articulate address to the people. All the while his eyes were rolling in his head. Swiftly, I thanked him and announced we were returning to the studio. And Alexander collapsed on a couch.

I also broadcast our city's welcome to Field Marshal Montgomery, the Empire's greatest World War II warrior. He was paraded to the City Hall, but the caravan was extremely late, and I had to fill in a lot of empty time. I had done my homework and had much material on Montgomery to pass on to the public. My eyes swept over the waiting crowd and saw mothers with babies in their arms, decorated veterans, and other interesting types, and I described the scene as colorfully as I could. There were other stations there, too. They had teams of three or four while I was alone with an engineer. But they weren't as dedicated as I was. Floundering to fill time, one had inched closer to me and was beginning to repeat almost exactly what I said. It was as though I had an echo. Soon, I noticed another moving near him and repeating his words. I was getting angrier and angrier.

Finally, Montgomery arrived and was ushered without a word into the mayor's office. Through a friend in the office, I knew he would be there only briefly. Guessing that the others might not know this, I made a swift decision. As the cheers of the crowd were dying out, I announced, "And that covers the arrival of Bernard Montgomery of El Alemain to Toronto. I thank you for being with us. We now return you to our station." The others said some of the same, signed off, and began to pack up. As my engineer prepared to pack up, too, I whispered to him to fake it, and I said quietly into the mike, "However, it is possible the general may return shortly, so we will play some music and we hope you will wait."

The others had packed their gear and were leaving when Montgomery suddenly emerged with the mayor. I was the only one with a live mike and I moved up to them and asked the general, "Sir, would you say a few words to the people of Toronto." He did just that, then departed. I had an exclusive interview. The others stood there in surprise—and how they cursed me! I could have cared less.

Jack Part liked me well enough to make me CHUM's program manager at $500 a month. I felt pretty important. But Part also made a fellow named Roly Ford sales manager, and we didn't get along at all. Ford said he couldn't sell the programs I programed. I said he couldn't sell anything. In radio and television, the sales manager always wins. I'd had my new job for only a few months when Jack Part made Roly Ford the station manager and told me I was to report to him. Roly Ford told me I was no longer the program manager, but I could remain as a performer at $500 a month. Having no alternatives, and no loss of income, I accepted the demotion and continued to work my shows.

There is also a moral here. I have often preached that no matter what jobs you may lose or what con-

flicts you have with your superiors, "Always leave the
door open when you leave." The fact that I accepted
Roly Ford as my new superior without a scene resulted in my continuing on without loss of salary.

Esse Ljungh arrived from Winnipeg to take up a new
position as a producer for the CBC in Toronto. I applied to him for acting work but was turned down. He
told me he didn't want to be accused of using his pets
from back home. He didn't have to use me, of course,
now that he had the cream of the crop to pick from. At
one point, I was asked by John Crosby of Dancer, Fitz-
gerald and Sample advertising agency in Toronto to emcee the Canadian version of *Truth or Consequences*
which Ralph Edwards was emceeing in the U.S. I was
excited by the opportunity to do my first national network show, but nothing happened. I checked into it and
found that the advertising agency and the CBC were at
odds over the format. The CBC had shows that gave
away money, and they also accepted advertising on
shows, but they objected to a program that gave away
merchandise in exchange for free plugs from companies,
which then did not have to buy commercials. This has
always been a sore point in the business, and in this
case CBC finally rejected the program.

Disappointed, I went to the CBC to protest to Ernie
Bushnell, who was the head of programing and an
important man there. I pointed out that I was being
deprived of my big break because a show that was considered good enough for the U.S. was not considered
good enough for Canada. Bushnell said he was sorry,
but that was exactly the case because the CBC had
certain standards it felt necessary to uphold.

But he then opened up a folder and pulled out a dos-
sier, and he said, "I've been doing some research on
you. Frankly, I feel you have shown enormous ambition,
imagination, and talent. I can't imagine why you are
worried about losing a job as emcee of a quiz show. You

have much greater potential than that. I'm so sure of it I'll bring you into the CBC right now as a producer."

I was stunned. Many men had worked for the CBC for years without attaining that height. As sure of my ability as I was, I would not have even thought of seeking such a position at that point in my career. I was flattered. The CBC was the cultural network in Canada and had a country-wide audience. As a producer I would have the opportunity to do important shows. Unfortunately, my first reaction was to ask him how much the job would pay. And when he said $4500, I was disappointed. I had made $4800 my first year in Toronto and was making $6000 my second year. At the CBC everybody started at a set salary his particular job called for and got small raises periodically—a typical government operation.

I said, "Mr. Bushnell, you're asking me to go back to making less money than I made in my first year in Toronto broadcasting." And he said, "Yes, but look at all the prestige you will get working for the Corporation. This is as high as one can go in broadcasting in Canada, and you can become a truly creative artist." And I said, "I am aware of all that, but I have been a poor boy all my life. I hope to become creative in broadcasting, but I must do it on a level in which I can be well paid for my efforts, and I don't think the CBC answers that need. I am truly grateful for your offer, but I have to decline it." He seemed astonished. It was the first time but not the last that I looked at a situation and took the road toward greater earning potential rather than creative opportunity.

I must add I never have regretted turning down the CBC offer. Ego didn't enter into it because I would have had much more prestige as a CBC artist than as anything I've been since. I would have liked that, but at that time in my life $6000 was a lot more money than $4500 and a lot closer to the $10,000 I was shooting for.

If I had taken the job, who knows, I might still be in Canada earning $15,000 to $18,000 a year and being terribly frustrated because there was insufficient moneys to produce something the way I wanted. I might be rated a creative talent, perhaps even an artist, but I would not be nearly as happy as I am at present. Today I am making big money and have had the opportunity to do things for family and friends. But I must admit that if an equally lucrative chance came along, I'd try to escape the game shows and establish myself as an artist in another area of show business.

III

"The truth is, I'm not prepared," he admitted. "And I want so much for this to work." It was around noon and he sat backstage in his little dressing room waiting for the final rehearsals before his opening show that night. He was worried about what he had to do because he had not done it for many years, and in a way it was more than he had ever done in his life. He looked tired and somehow he seemed frightened.

It was the spring of 1971. Monty Hall's Let's Make a Deal was in its eighth year on television. It had made him a star with a tremendously loyal following. But though it was the most successful game show in broadcasting history, it was still a game show and he was still a game show emcee, and he had reached the point in his life and career where he hungered for more.

Some entertainers, friends and colleagues, needled him at times about being a "game show emcee" who could always buy his way out of a tricky situation by giving away a refrigerator. Many openly admired his skill, such

85

as *Red Skelton and Jack Benny, and Jimmy Durante
and Don Rickles. They said they couldn't do what he did
nearly as well as he did it, and said they watched his
show and loved it and admired his work and were fans
of his. Hall was grateful, but he wanted to do the things
they did, too. He was an entertainer and he wanted
recognition as an all-around performer who could succeed singing, dancing, talking, or telling stories.*

*Now he was about to open in the Congo Room of the
Sahara Hotel in Las Vegas. Since the nightclub business has almost disappeared, these big hotel showrooms
in this gambling town have become the biggest of the
big time for singers and dancers and comics. If you can't
make it here, you are not truly a star. And for the first
time Hall was trying to make it where his most gifted
friends had made it.*

He didn't want any part of Let's Make a Deal *in his
act, but his manager, his agent, the writers, and the
hotel executives told him he had to have some of it anyway. Reluctantly he agreed to end his Sahara show
with some routines from his television program, but he
insisted that he do a monologue at the beginning and
then sing and dance. To help him he hired a group
called The Kids Next Door, a comic named Carl Ballantine, and his* Let's Make a Deal *aide and announcer,
Jay Stewart. A month before the show was to begin, he
started to learn his songs and routines.*

*The Sahara contracted him for $80,000 for two weeks,
which is a large salary, not as large as a Sammy
Davis commands, but larger than the amount received
by many who play Vegas regularly. Out of this he had
to pay for his supporting acts. The hotel offered additional money and gambling "scrip" for prizes. In return
he felt an obligation to repay the house with a hit and
a series of sellouts or near sellouts for the fourteen
nights and twenty-eight shows he would work.*

The Sahara management told him not to worry. Every-

one was excited by his appearance, and he was certain
to be a smash. He was thrilled to see his name and face
up in lights outside the Sahara, on billboards throughout the city, and in newspaper ads. He kept telling himself he was making the right move. He was gambling,
but this was a town for gamblers. "It might be a pass-
port to a new career or an interesting experience," he
said. "At worst, it can't hurt me. I have my television
show. I'm not dependent on being a hit in a saloon. But
I have to admit I'd like it. And I keep thinking it could
lead to great things."

He shook his head as if to shake away his worries. He
studied his cue cards intensely. He was up against it
now. Time was running out. Tonight he had to go on.
"I can do all these things, but I haven't been doing them
for a long time. I have to remember the words to my
songs. I have to synchronize my dance steps with the
other dancers. I have to get the timing down. I have to
get it all down."

Outside, Carl Ballantine, who had taken ten years off
from the saloons to act on television in McHale's Navy
and other shows had just finished rehearsing his old
act—magic tricks that don't work. The Kids Next Door
were onstage working on their routines. Most of them
started their careers with The Young Americans. They
were young, enormously attractive, and apparently talented. They worked hard on their numbers, starting,
stopping, starting all over again as their director drove
them toward perfection.

They ran through the opening routine in which they
introduced the star of the show by coming on carrying
Let's Make a Deal *signs,* wearing Let's Make a Deal
costumes, and singing a Let's Make a Deal *song:* "Just
got in from New Orleans . . . With money jingling in
our jeans . . . Just arrived from North Dakota, and we
aim to win our quota. . . ."

They rehearsed and rehearsed while others set up the

lighting and microphones in the near-deserted supper club. Outside it was another world, with a hot sun pouring over the people by the pool and bright lights illuminating intent players at the slot machines and crap tables. But there in the casino where there were no windows and no clocks, and it was never night and never day, Monty Hall came out to rehearse his routines with the group. He smiled and made small talk with several of them. "He's a very nice man," a girl said. "He makes us feel like we're friends. It's not like a star and the supporting cast. How good is he? At this? I don't know. He has a nice personality. He's good looking. He can sing some and dance some. It might work for him. I hope so."

And they went back to work, sweating away the long afternoon on stage in this shadowed place. Hall strutted through a straw-hat-and-cane number with the kids, trying to get his steps right, trying to reach his turn at the right point in the song, trying to get it straight and come out even.

One doesn't realize how hard they work to prepare what must appear to come easily that night. Finally, the kids were released and sent away to rest up for a few hours. You look closely at some of them, and you see their watering eyes are winking, and they are breathing hard. Watching a pretty girl in a skimpy outfit depart, you notice the muscles twitching under the skin of her back, and you see that her eyes have gone hard and cold.

Monty rehearsed on, perfecting his routine with Ballantine. He placed himself in a box and let the "magician" shove swords through it. "This is a trick, isn't it?" Hall asked. "I've been doing it for years," Ballantine replied. "Never with a live person, however." No one laughed. Finally, it was time to knock off. Show time was only a few hours away. Walking slowly, Hall returned to his dressing room.

On the door it said "Johnny Carson." He was the last

headliner here, and the management hadn't removed his name. The room was small. The wall were paneled in brown wood. There was a gold rug, a sofa, a few chairs. A bouquet of roses sent by the hotel sat on a table. Before the night was over, Hall had received 131 telegrams of good wishes. The wires said, "Good luck . . . All the success in the world . . . The best of luck . . . Go for broke . . . Knock 'em dead . . . Be a smash . . . Be a hit . . . Be a smash hit . . . Wishing you a hit . . . Wishing you a success . . . Wishing you another success." Some of them say, "Congratulations," although the show had not yet started. One said, "Imagine ham from a kosher butcher shop."

Monty smiled at some of the messages and shook his head wistfully at others. He handed them to his wife Marilyn and looked at the gold carpet. They brought in a tray of food and he tried to eat, but he couldn't. He picked at it, then pushed it away. Someone came in to say, "Richard Nixon called." It turned out he had— only it was another Richard Nixon. Monty got up and went into another room to lie down. He lay there in the dark with his eyes open for an hour.

After a while he began to talk. "I don't see why I can't do this," he said. "I know I have the talent. It's just a little rusty. And the audience is accustomed to something else from me. What I do, I do damn well."

He sighed and was silent for a moment. The only sound was the hum of the air conditioning. He started to talk again: "It's tough when you've been away from something for so long. I used to do variety shows in Canada. I haven't had much chance in this country. I'm just rusty. I'll be okay. I'm not nervous, just tired. There's no place I'd rather be. Really. It's very exciting. For someone in show business, headlining a showroom in this town is really something. Only the best play here. Some good ones never make it here. I don't need it," he said, "but I want it."

He grew silent again and did not speak until later

*when he got up. He went into the outer room where his
wife and his manager and his agent and his writer and
his choreographer and the producer and the director
and others were wedged in and waiting.*

*He got help dressing and with his makeup. His pants
didn't fall quite right, and he kept smoothing his hair
and looking at his cue cards. He started to speak the
lyrics to one of his songs: "There's no place I'd rather
be . . ." Then he began to sing the song. After a few
words, he stopped. "I know it," he said. "Of course, you
do," his wife replied. His manager said, "Don't worry,
you've got it cold." There was a lot of commotion in the
room, and finally it was decided Monty should be left
alone for the last half hour so he could compose himself.
Only the writer stayed, sitting in a corner, watching,
listening, not saying anything.*

*Monty sat before his make-up mirror and touched up
his face. Several of the bulbs were out. "I wish I wasn't
doing any* Let's Make a Deal *out there," he said. "It's
my show. It's a great show. It's brought me everything.
I love it. But I wanted to get away from it when I
worked here. I wanted acceptance on a totally different
level. I wanted to do the other things, not this thing.*

*"The hotel backed out on some of the extra money
they were going to give us for the gambling scrip. We'll
have to take money out of pocket. Our budget is tight.
We have our big prize, a little car, behind one of the
curtains tonight. It should last several shows before
someone picks it. Then we'll turn to a color television
set for a big prize. That should get us halfway through
the first week. . . ."*

*He shook his head. "What the hell, this isn't my real
racket. Show business isn't my best thing. My real business is benefits." He picked up his cue cards and started
to study them again, then flipped them away. "I don't
know why, but this has awakened so many memories. I
keep thinking back to my boyhood. The butcher shop.*

*Delivering meat on a bike in twenty-below cold. I almost
became a doctor, did you know that? I went into radio.
Then television. It's been a long haul from Winnipeg to
Toronto to New York to Los Angeles. And now Las
Vegas. Everyone wishes me luck, but they all think I'll
need a lot of it. They say, 'My God, what the hell is he
going to do on a stage in Vegas?' Not many think I
should be doing this. They figure I'll make a fool of
myself."*

His head hung down, and his hands were clasped as
though in prayer. "Well, what the hell," he said. He got
up and snapped off the loud speaker and lights and sat
back down in the dark and was silent, lost in thought. A
hotel official came in, snapped on the lights again, and
said, "Twelve minutes. Good luck." Monty thanked him.
The man said, "We've got a full house outside. The dinner show is sold out. Seven hundred and fifty people to
see you." When Monty asked whether all opening nights
were not sold out, he was told that not all were. "There
must be a convention in the hotel," Monty said. The man
smiled. "There is. But no one forced them to come see
you. Don't worry. Just be yourself. That's why they
wanted you here." Monty said, "Well, there's no place
I'd rather be."

When his wife came in to kiss him good luck, he put
his arms around her and held her close to him for a
minute, then let her go. She returned to her seat at one
of the long tables near the stage. The room was full.
The people had polished off their meals and were drink-
ing their coffee and chattering away waiting for the
show to begin. Marilyn smiled and said, "Last night
Monty said, 'This is coming fifteen years too late.' I said
it wasn't. I said, 'Maybe five years. . . .' "

The lights in the room went down and the stagelights
came up. A voice boomed out, "The Sahara is proud to
present the Monty Hall show, starring Monty Hall, the
amazing Mr. Ballantine, and The Kids Next Door." The

Kids, costumed now and seeming fresh came on: "Just got in from New Orleans. . . ." Monty entered, smiling and at ease. "A lot of people wonder what the hell is he gonna do," he began. There was laughter. "I've been performing since I was five years old," he continued as he went into his monologue.

Some of the stories worked, some didn't. Some got laughter, some only smiles. He began to work a little faster. Still, the routine ran long. Then the Kids came back on and did their stuff. The audience kept breaking into spontaneous applause during each bit and then rewarded them with cheers at the finish. They beamed through their make-up, their eyes gleaming. Then Monty joined them in "Mame," working hard and well.

Marilyn's eyes were riveted on the stage and on her husband. She was almost expressionless. A thin smile tugged at the corners of her lips. Hard lights sparkled in her eyes. She was very intense, worried, reserving judgment. Ballantine did his stuff and the people out front laughed a lot.

Next Monty and Jay Stewart moved among the audience. He sang "The Anniversary Song" to a couple and got a tremendous response. He offered $5 for every lipstick she had. She had two. He gave a man $5 for something else. It was time to offer the big deal located behind one of three curtains at the rear of the stage. A lady guessed the right curtain and won the car. The crowd reacted with applause but no great excitement.

Monty moved into his closing medley, singing songs like "Everything Is Beautiful." He sang attractively and was well received. As the show closed, the crowd applauded. There was no standing ovation, but everyone seemed pleased. Someone said, "We need more shows like that."

It wasn't a bad show. It didn't lay 'em in the aisles, but it wasn't bad. The monologue needed punching up.

The singing and dancing were successful. The show did need a faster pace.

After a quick round of opening night parties full of false smiles and pretense at celebration, the people around Monty began to tear the act apart. The managers and agents and directors and producers and executives crowded around Monty telling him that it hadn't worked as it should have worked and that they had to make some changes fast. He seemed surprised. He kept saying he thought most of the things came out pretty well. But the others insisted that this thing hadn't worked and that thing hadn't worked.

Each one had a different idea, and no one had a final say. Somebody picked up a grease pencil and began slashing stories from the routine. And another picked up the cue card for the songs and began to cut material there. Monty sat back and closed his eyes, and his wife sat off to one side looking down at her hands.

When he went on for the second show, he was doing less of the other things and more of Let's Make a Deal. *The house was half empty. He worked hard but the show faltered. "The Anniversary Song" had been slashed and was missed. He and Ballantine had trouble with their routine, and a lady picked the curtain that concealed the color television set. When it was finished, the people applauded and left, returning to the roulette and blackjack tables. Monty and his wife received friends in the dressing room and tried to retain a "high." They smiled and accepted congratulations and chatted with visitors, but conversation was forced and uneasy.*

Finally, at three in the morning, he and Marilyn walked out through the crowded casino and got into their car and drove quietly to the handsome house that the hotel furnishes to its stars. As he drove down the sparkling strip and turned out into the dark night, his wife huddled close to him. Outside the house, he parked the car and stood under the stars. "It wasn't too bad, I guess," he said. "But it wasn't what I hoped it would be." Suddenly, he seemed exhausted.

The review in the *Los Angeles* Times by John L. Scott referred to the act as something new in Las Vegas shows, pointing out with surprise that a car had been given away at one show, a color television set at another. He wrote: "It's difficult to appraise Monty Hall's work except on the basis of his host activities. He's a genial master of ceremonies, glib and personable, but I hesitate to predict a great future for him as a singer and dancer. (As if he cared.)"

The review ran eleven paragraphs. The ninth and tenth paragraphs described Ballantine as a real pro who had the crowd in stitches. The eleventh and last paragraph said: "The Kids Next Door, a lively group of singers and dancers, provided the youthful accent on the Sahara's bill." It was the only mention they got. Some reviews did not mention them at all.

Most of the reviews said it was a nice show, but not a knockout. Variety, the bible of show business, said Hall was personable and sang well and was supported by good acts, but suggested that the people who patronized his shows were not apt to be the high rollers favored by Vegas hotels. Some of the reviews said it was a bad show for Vegas. Ralph Pearl in the Las Vegas Sun said Hall was "a personable, charming rascal," but his show was bad and boring and there was nothing more boring to café-goers than to watch other café-goers win goodies.

The best of the goodies were gone the first night, and the Hall team had to dig deep to produce new superprizes and wound up giving away fives and tens to visitors who were throwing away tens and twenties on a single roll of the dice in this place where money soon means nothing even to a miser. The best of the reviews were forgotten and the worst remembered, and more *slashes were made in the show—until Monty Hall wound up doing more of the thing he least wanted to do,* Let's Make a Deal, *and less of what he most wanted to do, singing, dancing, telling stories.*

He never had a chance. He wasn't so bad. He was good. If they had let him polish his performance, it would have worked, but he didn't get to try it out at Tahoe or Reno. He got one show in Vegas, at the top, and when it wasn't perfect, they panicked and started to slash away at his act, not one man paring prudently, but several men each hacking out what he didn't like, shoving the headliner back to where they believed he belonged. And Monty Hall let them.

They made him a game-show emcee again. Attendance at the shows dipped. It was the off-season, anyway, and he soon was struggling before houses that were less than half full, embarrassed and dejected, just waiting for his run to end. He waited through lonely days, waited for his wife's visits, waited for the nights when he could put two more shows to rest. He was thrown into a jungle and torn to pieces. He came close to what he wanted most in life, but this time he never had a chance.

Over the years I received offers from time to time to take *Let's Make a Deal* to Vegas. I never was interested. I knew I could take the show on the road and succeed with it everywhere—people are people. But why leave home to go on tour? I couldn't see playing it in the showrooms because I couldn't see people paying $10 to $20 to see our show there when they could get it for free on television six times a week.

Johnny Romero, the Sahara publicity chief, had insisted that with my following I could do a stand-up comedy routine and be a success. But I didn't want to play the lounge. Then he began to talk about doing a show in the main room. Other hotels sent out feelers to see if I'd be interested in trying a show in their main rooms. I began to become interested. I wanted to prove to everyone, including myself, I was an all-around performer.

Raymond Katz became my manager because he felt he could develop me into such a performer. We agreed that we would try it for a while, and if it didn't work we would part company. Raymond knew I wanted to break away from the game show emcee rut and move into the variety field, and he felt I could and wanted the opportunity to set it up for me.

Others warned me against it, but I knew they were worried about my making a break from projects in which they were involved and putting a hole in their personal worlds. If they felt I would fail, they weren't so bold as to say it to me. They just said, "Monty, who needs it?" Well, I felt Monty needed it.

Katz signed me for the Sahara. Since it had been a long time since I sang or danced extensively, I knew I needed practice. I worked on my dancing and took singing lessons from a variety of teachers. That was a wild experience in itself. I went to three singing teachers, and I was fortunate to survive. I found there were as many charlatans in voice coaching as in anything else. The first one I went to started me out with long-winded recitations on his philosophy of singing. He likened me to a tree in which the sound started out in the roots, rumbled up through the trunk, spread through the branches, and poured out the top. I couldn't follow him at all. So he switched to a metaphor in which I was a gun and the bullet was my voice and I pulled the trigger and sent the bullet through the barrel blasting out my mouth. I couldn't follow this either. He kept saying, "Don't you see it? Don't you feel it? Shoot it! Let it go!" I let him go.

I turned to a teacher recommended by Sandy Gallin, Raymond Katz's partner. Gallin explained that the man used unusual methods but had worked wonders with others. I went to his office where the teacher pounced on me and began to pummel me and apply half nelsons and headlocks. He twisted my neck until I screamed. His philosophy was that we don't use most of our vocal capacity because our vocal cords are too involved with our physical movements and bodily tensions, and that to use them to capacity we must somehow separate them from the rest of us. It seemed to me he was trying to tear my head off.

As I left after my first lesson with him, he smiled and said, "I'll probably never see you again." He was right.

The third teacher was less a modernist and more an old-fashioned sort who had me singing scales and learning to project properly. I spent several sessions with him and he was a help. However, he was always expressing delight and amazement at how good I was and what a great potential I had. I felt he was spreading it a bit thick. I can carry a tune, I have a pleasant voice, I can sing as well as most nonsinging performers—but I am not Andy Williams. My last teacher helped me, but he didn't fool me. At least, he didn't kill me.

I taped my numbers and listened to them everywhere I went. I began to rehearse more with an accompanist, Jack Elton, and The Kids Next Door. I began to get better.

I was having trouble with my monologue. I had met with comedy writer Martin Ragaway and spun some amusing true stories, which he enjoyed and incorporated into the first draft of my routine. But the routine was a combination of stories and jokes. The jokes leaned heavily on *Let's Make a Deal*. I had to temper them because I have made it a rule not to demean the participants on the show. I have had a lot of fun with them, but I have never deprived them of dignity. As a result, the jokes were lukewarm and did not blend well with the long stories. Ragaway tried hard, but neither of us could find the right combination.

Ragaway kept saying, "Don't worry. You just take what you want from this draft, and I'll keep bringing you more stuff." But the more he brought me, the more I worried. He was a skilled specialist, but he was used to working with comedians like Bob Hope, and the rapid-fire joke just did not work for me. I tried some of the material out on benefit audiences, and I got more smiles than laughs. We did part of the show at a temple's annual meeting and received a lukewarm response. But everyone kept saying, "Don't worry. We're working out the wrinkles. It will work in Vegas."

One of the problems was that I simply did not know what *would* work for me in Vegas. I should have studied other nonsingers and dancers who have done well there. I should have been sent to the minors to master my act. I rushed into the hottest spotlight in the industry without proper preparation. As experienced as I was in show business, I was a babe in the woods on the saloon circuit. I paid people who didn't protect me properly. And I didn't insist on doing the right things when it began to go wrong. I wasn't strong enough.

We left for Vegas on the Sunday before the Tuesday we were to open. We spent all day Monday and Tuesday rehearsing the entire show with the entire cast on stage. It wasn't nearly enough. We gave it everything. We worked and sweated almost in a panic. We just didn't have time. I had only one workout with Ballantine. Our routine didn't work at all, but he insisted he was an old pro and would pull it off when the time came.

I had a lot of workouts with the Kids and they were great. In this, they were the veterans, and I was the beginner, but they were marvelous to me.

Meanwhile, all was bedlam around us. In Vegas one show closes and the new show opens the next night. In very short order the technicians throw a new setup together, and for a while all seems madness. Then the Sahara backed out on its contribution of scrip to the prize fund. We screamed bloody murder to no avail. With fourteen shows a week, we were reduced to $400 a show in prizes.

Again we made a tactical error. We should have refused to go on without the big prize budget. How could the biggest giveaway show on television go into the biggest gambling colony in America and offer pennyante rewards to high-rollers. My gut instinct was that it just could not play that way. Later, my fears were proved right.

By opening night I was straining to keep myself together. I could see that we had only the skeleton of the show I wanted to do, and that it was a fragile package that could come apart as we unwrapped it in public. I knew we faced the toughest audience a performer can face. The critics would not consider the circumstances of my situation and would review it as a finished act instead of a debut.

I was worried, but I kept telling myself I probably was just suffering opening night jitters, especially since I was doing something different, and I should respect the optimistic views of those around me that we had something that would work. I figured they knew better than I. I was wrong. Whatever we do, we know better what is right for us than others do.

My wife's spirit sustained me. Without her it would have been tough to get through that first night. Marilyn is a lot of my strength and I leaned on her a lot as that first show neared. The fears began to build up and a strange sort of loneliness assailed me in which I was driven by memories of all the steps I had taken that had got me to Vegas. I was lucky that I didn't need success there. But I would be lying if I said I didn't want it badly. I felt as though the eyes of all my family and friends and fellow performers were on me.

I went to work before a full house. But there was a Variety Club meeting in town and a convention in the hotel, and an opening night always attracts an audience. So I didn't kid myself that it meant much. Still, it stimulated me. I thought a lot of things worked well, but I saw that some things did not. I felt strangely let down. I suppose while I had not expected it, I had hoped for more.

After I got through the between-shows parties and the false smiles and the expected congratulations and the routine glad hands and backslaps and returned to the dressing room, I was startled to find all the people who had thought our format was perfect now were prepared to pull it apart. Instead of using a surgeon's scalpel, they began to wield axes. No one person was in charge. I should have been, but I wasn't. They grabbed the cue cards and everyone began to cut something. If something wasn't perfect, they didn't try to figure out how to improve it, they just cut it out completely. They chopped some of the best or most promising items. They panicked. I let them pull my show apart. I figured they knew best.

The second show was very different from the first. I led off cold with the monologue, which was cut to five minutes. From start to finish the show was chaos. The house was only about half full and far from fascinated. It was depressing, and I left in a trance.

The reviews were better than I expected, but the bad reviews were the ones we reacted to. My writers axed out more stuff and rearranged further. The monologue was removed completely. Ragaway felt terribly guilty. He had been paid well, and after the first night his material was not used again. After he went back to Los Angeles he kept calling me to offer lines that I could use in the audience or on stage or anywhere, anything that could be considered a contribution. He was a faithful friend.

My *Let's Make a Deal* section, which I hadn't wanted to do in the first place, and which I really hadn't wanted to do under the restrictions of money and prize availability, didn't work out as a giveaway show. So we resorted to the only thing we could do: we made it into a comedy segment. I knew I was in big trouble when I went up to a corpulent lady in the audience and offered her $50 for any kind of pill; and when she didn't have one, I chided, "You just blew fifty bucks!" She looked at me and said, "Honey, I just blew $3000 at the crap tables. What the hell is another fifty bucks! Just give me a kiss and forget about the money!" I had to do a lot of kissing during that two-week engagement.

We had some sellouts or near sellouts, but mostly we drew crowds of, say, 250 for the supper show and 200 for the late show. The high-rollers weren't interested, and the Las Vegas townspeople, our natural audience, couldn't afford it. The visitors support the Vegas shows, not the locals. I'd peek around the curtain, see the tiers of empty tables, and grow more and more depressed. The Sahara people pointed out that it was the off-season and the hotel was only half full. I was drawing as well as could be expected. Only Tom Jones at Caesar's Palace was pulling big crowds. This was true, but it came as scant consolation.

I'd stand in the wings and Jay Stewart would smile and say, "Well, this tests you as a performer." I tried to meet the test. I gave the smallest crowds the best I had and the receptions got better and better. The people came to be wonderfully responsive, but there just weren't enough of them.

Later, some of my fellow performers seemed to regard me in a different light simply because I had played there, no matter how successfully or unsuccessfully. It was as though I had become one of them, and I was greeted with new respect. Just playing Vegas was almost enough. Almost.

It was not enough for me, however. I know now that you do not go into a main showroom in Vegas without a polished show. I do not blame the people for staying away from the show I gave them. If I were them, and I wanted to see a comic, I'd go to see a Buddy Hackett; if I wanted to hear a singer, I'd go to see a Tom Jones; and if I wanted to see a variety show, I'd go to see the Follies or the Lido de Paris. I'd go to see a Monty Hall only if I read or heard that he had put together something special and appealing. And Monty Hall hadn't done that. He had an idea that might have worked, but he let others pull it apart.

After the first few nights, the shows became an ordeal. Unlike other stars who only work the last half of their shows, which perhaps I should have done, I was on stage much of the time from start to finish, and it was exhausting.

I would go out to dinner at two in the morning with Ray Katz, my wife, or friends who were playing Las Vegas, like Danny Thomas and Abbe Lane. There is a strange camaraderie among Vegas performers. When they meet each other backstage or in restaurants, they cling and embrace with surprising intimacy—like survivors of a holocaust. It is a lonely world, and it seems as though they are together in strange, hostile territory while all around them is alien, and they show a desperate need for one another. The same effusive embrace in Las Vegas is just a casual hello in Los Angeles.

Danny Thomas softened my hurt with a pretty good lecture at four in the morning. He asked, "Why are you so low?" And when I responded that I had only 175 customers at the supper show, he raised an eyebrow and hurled back: "I only had 150. Look, kid, this is my business, and I love it, and there are some times when you are going to have an empty house, and then at others you'll be turning them away. It's all part of the business, and you can't take it personally. For crying out loud, Juliet Prowse had a dozen people the other night, and you wouldn't suggest she give up the business would you? Stop suffering. Do your best and enjoy it."

All this was good advice from a veteran star; but he had earned his spurs in the nightclub business, and I had just been thrown off my first horse and found it tough to climb back on. During the days I loafed around the house, conserving my energy, waiting for the nights, dreading them and, like a prisoner, scratching the dates off the calendar.

Strangely, in light of my feelings about the experience in Vegas, other hotels want me back. I still feel I can succeed there, but I won't go until I can present something properly prepared and foolproof. Recently, Joe Delaney, Las Vegas television host and critic, asked me whether I was coming back. When I said no, he responded, "Nonsense, you will be back. The people love you."

4

I MET MY wife through a mutual cousin named Norman
Shnier. I was a cousin on his father's side, and she was a
cousin on his mother's side. Norman had been a prisoner
of war in Germany. Released early in 1946, he decided
to resume life in Toronto and arrived there when I did.
He told me about his other cousin. He said, "You just
have to meet her. She is adorable." I asked, "How old
is she?" And he said, "She is eighteen, and a senior in
high school." I smirked. "Oh, she's too young for me.
I'm a college graduate." "But she's a radio actress," he
added. "You have something in common." And I said,
"My God, if there is any one person I don't want to
meet it's some precocious eighteen-year-old radio
actress."

Norman wangled a dinner invitation to her family's
home. While we were standing outside talking, this girl
came walking toward the house. It was Marilyn. She had
a trench coat draped over her shoulders and a model's
even walk, and as she approached I saw that she had a

lovely face. Something inside of me seemed to say, "Look out." She gave me a soft smile and said hello in a gentle, pleasant voice.

We went in. Her parents were separated, I learned. She and a younger sister, Peggy, and a maiden aunt lived with her mother in this small, modest six-room house on Eastbourne Avenue. Marilyn was working as an actress and helped to support the family. She had read about me in an interview printed in *Radio World Magazine*. In the interview I had spoken about being president of the student body at the university, and about all the broadcasting I had done at an early age, and about how I hoped to reach the top in Toronto when I got there. For a guy with a buck and a half in his pocket I exuded confidence to the point of cockiness, and that's the way Marilyn read it. All during dinner she baited me. I didn't expect that from an eighteen-year-old, and some of her needles had sharp points.

She let it be known that while I had been doing bit parts for Esse Ljungh in Winnipeg, she already had acted coast-to-coast as Alice in *Alice in Wonderland* and *Alice Through the Looking Glass*. She still was getting top ingenue parts around Toronto, while I was just breaking in with an early-morning show. She was making as much as $90 a week at eighteen while I was making $60 at twenty-three.

Marilyn had the upper hand on me. She wasn't obnoxious about it, but she did make me feel less mature than I was. Her mother was very nice until she realized I was serious about Marilyn. She wanted more than me for her daughter. Not that her daughter was throwing herself at me. In fact, she refused my first requests for dates and did it like an adult turning down a child. Once at dinner I sent her a little note asking, "How about going out with me this weekend?" She passed me back a note saying, "No, I can't." Then when she saw my expression, she passed me another note that said, "There, there, don't be too upset." I was being patronized, but I persisted and I finally got a date with her.

By the oddest of coincidences I had already met Marilyn's father. He had been the Toronto manager of Warner Brothers motion picture company and had been slated to become the Canadian general manager. His separation from his wife disrupted his life, however, and he was passed over in favor of an underling, who promptly fired him. He found a new position as Canadian General Manager of Monogram Pictures, and every morning he had breakfast in the same place I did before doing my show. After I found out that Marilyn was his daughter, he and I began to eat together every morning. As so often happens in such separations, the mother had given Marilyn and her sister a one-sided version of their marital difficulties, and it had turned them against him. He seldom heard from them and was eager to hear what news I could pass on. Whatever the marital troubles, whoever was to blame, he was a nice man who missed his wife and daughters very much.

There still were little things to be settled between him and the family, and Marilyn agreed to go out to dinner with me one night to discuss them. Another night we went to a dance. Later she went away to a camp, where she was a counsellor, but when she came back she wanted to have dinner with me again because I could be the go-between between her family and her father. We went to an Italian restaurant. She looked beautiful to me and I realized how much I had missed her and how much I wanted her. Then she told me she was going to marry someone else.

She said that a fellow she had been dating on and off for a couple of years wanted to announce their engagement when he returned from a business trip. I said, "Does he know that when he gets home he will have lost his girl friend?" Marilyn laughed a little and asked,

"What do you mean by that?" I smiled. "I mean you are going to belong to me." "Oh, really?" she replied. "Really," I said. She just laughed again.

We went together all through the rest of that month, getting closer and feeling the love developing between us. We hated to part at night. When we had night broadcasts, we'd often walk back to her home. On one such walk my break-through came. Her boyfriend had been away for six weeks and was due back the next day. I said, "I think it's time you told him about us." She looked at me a long time, then smiled and said, "All right." The next day she broke the news to him.

Immediately her friends started dropping by her house to tell her she was making a mistake. If I was there, they'd ask her to go outside for a minute so they could talk to her. Some of them, I suppose, were sent by her boyfriend. I laughed it off, figuring that they would not get very far in trying to divert Marilyn from her course. I was right.

Marilyn's mother applied considerably more pressure, however. Other young men were interested in Marilyn. One was heir to a real estate fortune, and another was in medical school. Here was Marilyn committing herself to a radio announcer without any certain future. Through the next winter Marilyn and I fought all efforts to break up the romance. On May 17, Marilyn's twentieth birthday, I gave her the gold ring that I had received as president of the university student body and we announced our engagement.

Marilyn was at the University of Toronto and was acting on radio on the side. Her mother kept trying to get her to change her mind about me. She enlisted other relatives, who would call up to counsel Marilyn not to act rashly. Marilyn was a strong girl, but that summer she was down to ninety-four pounds and I was worried about her.

We decided on a date to get married and so informed both sets of parents. But Marilyn's mother had one last shot to fire. She called Marilyn's father, buried her pride, and asked him to try to talk his daughter out of it. He wanted us to marry, but I suspect he was willing to do almost anything to win back his wife's favor. So he telephoned Marilyn and started to talk against the marriage. Luckily, I happened to be there and I took the telephone from Marilyn and said, "Joe, the wedding is going to take place on September 28 in Winnipeg. We invite you to give the bride away. If you don't come, someone else will. But the wedding will take place, with or without you." In a sad voice he said he was sorry for having interfered and he wished us well. Marilyn's mother was out of ammunition.

I felt sorry for him. He kept up a bold front while his life was falling to pieces around him.

Marilyn and I were married on September 28 in Winnipeg, as I had announced. We restricted the guest list to close family and friends, so we had only three hundred or so in attendance, and upset several hundred we didn't invite. My family had lived in Winnipeg since the turn of the century and had spread out in great numbers in that area. Marilyn had family there, too. Her mother and father and sister came. Her father gave the bride away. Marilyn had saved $2000, and she paid the railway fare from Toronto for herself, her sister, and mother. She also bought her own trousseau and new dresses for her sister and mother. I had about $1500 saved up and I blew most of it on a second-hand 1941 Ford we called Crasty, short for procrastination, so named because I procrastinated a long time before buying it.

My family gave us $500. I'm sure they didn't have a thousand dollars in the bank, and it was a tremendous gift from two people who were barely getting by. Of course, my father always was a sport, and when it came to the marriage of his first son, he was going to dig deep. It was a grand gesture.

It rained the day of the wedding, and Marilyn, leaving where she was staying to go to the hotel, spilled a suitcase full of everything she had. It looked like a bad day all around. But a friend from my army shows, Harold Green, provided his quintet as a present, and when we walked down the aisle at three on a Sunday afternoon, the sun came out and shone through the windows on us.

We were to have honeymooned in the lake area of Minnesota, but I had just been offered a new radio show which was to start a week after our marriage, and we felt it was wise to cut the trip to a short holiday in the Toronto area.

On our wedding night, we boarded a train for the trip back to Toronto. An uncle was supposed to have booked us a private bedroom compartment, but all he could arrange were upper and lower berths. Boldly, I broke the news to my bride that we were not going to be split up on our wedding night and would share a single berth, no matter how narrow.

It may sound old-fashioned and unlikely, but the truth is Marilyn and I had resisted the terrible temptation of sex throughout our courtship. But now the time had come. Maybe it was not the perfect place, but it was time. I stood outside in the aisle while Marilyn struggled out of her clothes and into a nightgown and robe in the cramped lower berth, and then she waited outside while I struggled out of my clothes and into my pajamas. I called my lovely bride to me and she climbed inside the berth. That was when I saw the face staring at us.

It was a teen-aged girl and she was peering at us from through the curtains of the adjoining berth. I was sure she had seen us come on board with Marilyn wearing a corsage and had guessed we had just gotten married. She had observed us changing into our night clothes and knew the honeymoon was about to start. She was curious and fascinated. I whispered to Marilyn that I was not about to make love to her as long as that girl was watching and listening. Nor were efforts to out-stare the girl successful. She just kept staring back. I can still see that face.

So we lay side by side in our little berth and stared out the windows at the rolling prairies of Canada and hoped the girl would go to sleep, but she seemed determined to stick it out to the finish. Every time I opened the curtains, there was the face! Eventually we drifted off to sleep. In the morning, I called the porter aside and asked if our berth could remain a bed for a while and he smiled patiently as if to say even a newlywed must realize there is a limit. He was sorry but he had to fold them up into their daytime seats. It was a one-day, two-night trip from Winnipeg to Toronto. As we entered the dining car for breakfast that morning, I spotted the teenager sitting with her mother. The kid had blood-shot eyes and looked as if she had been up all night, which indeed she had. We sat up all day and talked, and that night when my bride and I got back into our berth, there was that teen-aged face. We didn't even attempt to wait her out this time.

Arriving in Toronto, my bride and I sped off to the Guild Inn in Scarborough, on the outskirts of Toronto. It was the opening day of the World Series. I was a big baseball fan, and I wanted to hear the game. I sat down and pulled a pencil and a paper out of the desk drawer and started to draw lines. Marilyn, who was unpacking, asked me what I was doing. I said, "I am making up a box score." I will never forget the expression on her face. She knew nothing about the World Series, and thinking that this was the day her sex life was to begin, she was stunned.

I reassured her, but insisted on listening to the game.

I believe it was the Yankees and the Dodgers. If I remember right, the Yankees won. In any event, after the game we finally won.

We moved into our first home—a bedroom. That was the only room we had. We rented from a couple with a three-bedroom house in the Rosedale section in Toronto. The family had been comfortably fixed until the husband suffered a stroke and the wife had to let out the two smaller bedrooms to make ends meet. She built a tiny bathroom for us on top of the garage. The bathroom was unheated, and we endured some chilling cold that winter. And the night we moved in, part of the bed collapsed under us. We didn't bother to fix it, not that night. Youth can put up with a lot of things.

We made do with a small hot plate and a toaster, which we kept in our room. Every morning Marilyn went down to the kitchen and got our milk and maybe some bacon and eggs from the common refrigerator and made us a hot breakfast. Then we'd go off to our places —me to the radio station, Marilyn to her second year at college.

One morning we went off without remembering to turn off the hot plate. We returned that night to screams of outrage from our landlady. We had decided to hard-boil some eggs and left in a hurry with the element still on, and they had exploded all over, staining the ceiling. The pot had burned and the room reeked of sulfur. It took days to get rid of the terrible smell and we never did get rid of all the stains. They may be there yet.

After work I picked Marilyn up at the college library and took her out to dinner, though we couldn't afford anything fancy. Afterward we went home to .our one-room home, and Marilyn studied and I read or listened to the radio unless I had radio work to do. It was a confined way of life, but we were young and didn't mind. We paid $87 a month for that one room, and I had to pay $10 more a month to rent a garage for our humpty-dumpty car. We didn't have a lot left.

After a few months we managed to find an apartment in the center of town. Apartments were hard to get, but I managed to find someone who would be an intermediary in the pay-off of $300 key money, divided among the intermediary, the superintendent, and the house mistress. It was torture to pay the $300, but we desperately needed a place to live that at least had a heated bathroom, to say nothing of a kitchen.

The new apartment was across the road from a Catholic boys school, De la Salle College, and I have three distinct memories of that school. The first is that a rich benefactor died and left the school $5000 to purchase new brass instruments for its marching band. Every Saturday morning at the crack of dawn the trumpets and cornets started to sound, disrupting my sleep. How I cursed the benefactor! The second is that Marilyn and I used to take a football over to the grounds and play tackle football, rolling over and over in the snow, until we were so fatigued we couldn't move. And the third recollection is that on Sunday afternoons I used to take my ice skates and hockey stick and join the boys in a hockey game. The kids thought I was a member of the faculty and called me "Brother." I hope that when they read this now, they will forgive me. I needed the workout. Come to think of it, they certainly treated their Brother with little respect. More than once they gave me an elbow in the chops and the butt end of a stick in the ribs.

Our apartment was so small that I swear even the mice were hunchbacked. We had one who visited us regularly. We called him "H.B." (short for "hunchback"), and he terrorized Marilyn. Coming home from a hockey game one night, I found Marilyn semi-hysterical. With tears streaming down her face she announced,

"H.B. was here." I waited for him that night, got him, and gave him a respectful funeral.

We lived there for two years while Marilyn continued her classes and part-time acting. I had left CHUM to free-lance, and I often had free time. Frequently, I made our breakfast, made the beds, and cleaned up around the place. Often I could meet her for lunch. She studied a lot in the library, and I passed a lot of time in the local pool hall. A friend and I played what must have been the longest-running billiards series in history. It lasted through two semesters while the girls studied. The loser and his wife were to take the winner and his wife out to dinner at the best restaurant in town. Believe it or not, after six months it came down to the final ball in the final game. I lost, and Marilyn and I had to pop for a fancy meal.

One year a friend told us he could get us a hamburger stand at the Canadian National Exhibition Fair. It may not sound like much, but it presented possibilities. I had worked as a performer for $5 a show almost around the clock during fair week. It was one of the largest fairs in the world, and 250,000 to 350,000 visitors a day had to be fed. Concession locations were hard to land and could be converted into fat profits if you knew what you were doing—which we did not.

We invested in the stand, and my brother Bob joined us to help out. Wes Cox, who had worked for me in radio production, offered to work for me in hamburger production. We decided we needed something different and special to lure customers and Wes came up with an idea in which he sliced a warm hamburger bun in half and ladled cream of mushroom soup over it. Imaginatively, we called it "cream of mushroom on a bun." Later we added "cream of chicken on a bun." We broadcast pitches for our concoctions over a loudspeaker all day long. After the first day, however, we had to make a new tape pitching our hamburgers because so many customers had asked for their money back that we had to discontinue our special snacks.

Marilyn, Wes's wife, Alva, and other relatives helped out at the stand. It turned out to be a tough trick. As we pulled the soft drinks out of the cooler and popped the caps off, water and spray splattered onto the floor, and by evening we were standing ankle deep in slop as we served our customers. Unfortunately, there were not enough of them.

Our biggest days came over the Labor Day weekend. Len Starmer, who now is an executive with the CBC, and his wife and sister came by elegantly dressed and, seeing us swamped, moved right in to help. Len took off his suit coat, rolled up his shirt-sleeves and started to sell. His wife and sister took off their white gloves and wide-brimmed hats, sat down on crates behind the shack, and began to peel onions. I will always remember them in their Sunday best, perched on those crates, peeling onions, tears streaming down their faces and messing up their makeup. But what friends!

At the end of each day we would take the cash receipts and compare them with the goods we had used up. They never balanced, not once, not one single day. It was simple to estimate the number of buns and hamburgers sold, but the money always came out short and we never figured out where it had gone. We took whatever money we managed to hang on to, usually a few hundred dollars, home with us at night and hid it. We'd take ice cubes out of the trays and stuff the money in and keep it in the refrigerator. We called it our "cold cash."

There was a sad footnote to this period. Marilyn had become pregnant for the first time that fall, but miscarried. That was a deep disappointment to both of us. She suffered another psychological setback when her father died in Vancouver, a broken man. But tough times matured her a great deal. She buckled down and did exceptionally well during her final year in college. And I bore down, too, and formed my own production company in 1949.

Our first child, Joanne, was born in June 1950. My folks had come from Winnipeg to be with us and joined me in a thirty-two-hour vigil. Poor Marilyn was a wreck, and the three of us pacing the waiting room were no better. Finally Marilyn was taken up to the delivery room, and shortly thereafter a nurse walked down the hall and called out: "Father Hall!" My dad screamed out "Yes!" and ran down the hall toward the nurse. My mother was second, and I placed third. The three of us stood like children at a candy store with their noses pressed up against the window, just gawking. We had a daughter.

Our son Richard was born two years later in June 1952. I was in New York on a three-day conference when I received a call from Marilyn saying she was in labor and my brother was rushing her to the hospital. I forgot about the conference. There was a bus and taxi strike in New York, but some of us at the hotel wanted to get to the airport and hired a limousine for an awesome amount of money. By the time I got to Toronto and the hospital it was evening. But our baby had not yet come. I waited with my mother-in-law until eleven that night, when Ricky arrived. He was born jaundiced. Marilyn has Rh negative blood, and it was touch and go for a while, but he made it and all went well after he survived the early crisis.

We had never definitely picked out a name for the second child because he came three weeks prematurely; but when I rushed to be beside Marilyn when she came down from the delivery room, she looked up at me, semi-conscious, and said: "We have got our little Richard David." Thus it was decided.

At the time my father's business was not going well

in Winnipeg. I helped where I could. My brother, who was now married himself, was still in law school. I flew back to help Dad move his shop to a different part of town but after a couple of good years, business began to fall off again. He was in his fifties and beginning to feel frightened about the future. I started a small monthly retirement fund for him, and my brother agreed to contribute as soon as his law practice began to pay off. We hoped to see him through his difficulties and wind up with savings of perhaps $25,000.

Eventually, we got him into another business, then retired him and my mother to Palm Springs. But in the early fifties we were all struggling financially and unsure of how well off any of us would be in the future. I was hustling to make my way in radio and by now television. It was an exciting time but an exasperating one.

IV

Maurice Halparin

I REMEMBER THE *day Monty was born. It was the proudest day of my life. To become a father with a son was something to me. I didn't want to give my son a hard time, but those were bad times for us. We needed his help, and he resented some having to give it. I don't blame him, but I couldn't admit it at the time, which frustrated me and made my temper short and words often sharp.*

My own father originally was going to be a rabbi. He got a Hebrew education, but wound up going into business. He was a Russian who went to Winnipeg at forty with a family of nine. He supported his family, but he had no warmth left over in him for them. He was from a stern, old-fashioned sort of background and demanded discipline and respect and did not know how to love. He disciplined with a strap. He used to beat us badly. It made my older brother tough. It hurt me. He was a cattle buyer who dealt in wholesale meat. It was rugged outdoor work, and he took me and my brother with

*him. I was not cut out for it, but I could not get out of it.
I met Monty's mother when we both were in third
grade. We were to go through life together. I found
warmth and love in her house. She had a warm, loving
family. Rose was a remarkable woman. Everyone knew
that right from the time she was a young girl. She was
outstanding in every way, bright and talented, a leader.
Why she bothered with me, I'll never know. Love, of
course. We loved each other.*

*I never liked being a butcher. For some men, it is
fine, but it was not for me. Still, I labored at it. I was
lucky to bring home $25 a week. I could not afford a
delivery boy, so I had to use my son. He must have
known I did not want to. But how else could we eat and
pay the rent and buy clothing if we did not scrimp
every penny? He worked hard, I know that. I pushed
him. I had no choice. My temper was short.*

*I am not proud of it. I could not give my son the
material things other sons get from their fathers. I
hated this. I ran from my life as much as I could, trying
to be something even when I had nothing. I had my
pride. I always tried to dress nice, to be neat, to leave
the stain of the bloody shop behind me, to wash it away.
I gambled some. I enjoyed the companionship of other
men. I never ran around on my wife. She had her clubs,
her charities, her friends, too.*

*I wish I could have done more, but a man cannot be
ashamed of doing as much as he can. I know my son
realizes I did all I could do. I was never as close to him
as his mother was. They had a very unusual relationship. I never saw so much love between a mother and
a son as they had. My son was much like his mother.
He is talented and outgoing and confident, as she was.*

*Monty is one child in a million. It has been a struggle
for him in show business, but he never quit. He always
had ham in him, always was in every school play, al-*

ways was headed in this direction. I was afraid that it would be too tough, but he was tough, too, and never quit. I am proud of my son who struggled to become such a success.

Robert Hall

Monty can remember harder times than I can—he helped our family out of them. Monty can remember the rent collector coming and our dad hiding out back because we could not pay him. Monty can remember when dad had to drive him at the butcher shop because he needed his help. Monty retains resentments of those early days I never formed. I think he is wrong, and I have told him so. But then I was six years younger and never took the full brunt.

My dad suffered in comparison to my mother. He did not have her personality, her popularity. But my dad was a good family man and father. He suffered frustrations which made him temperamental. But he worked a lifetime at work he loathed, endured the intolerance of others, and gave us everything he could.

Monty favored our mother. He was incredibly close to her. She has been his inspiration above and beyond all others, even his wonderful wife. He became closer to our father in recent years, but he did not give him his due most of his life. I have argued with Monty about this. It is about the only argument we have had.

Monty has been magnificent to me. There was a fantastic relationship between us despite the difference in our ages as we were growing up. He was my mentor, wanting me to be all the things he had not been able to be. He coached me as a boxer and baseball player. He counseled me. He encouraged me to go to the University of Manitoba, to make as much of myself as

*possible. He urged me to go back to law school and
financed me in the early years.*

*Whatever I wanted to do, Monty was for it. He
represented strength to me. Financially, he was always
behind me. I never had to worry about losing out. I
remember once he bought an extra car just so there
would be one for me to borrow, because he knew I
needed one and would not have accepted it as an outright gift. He has always done for others. He did for me,
our mother and father, other family and friends, his own
family, of course, and countless strangers through countless charities.*

*When no one could help him, he helped himself. In
the early days in Toronto and later in New York when
he was not getting anywhere and he had to survive
layoffs, he was sure enough of himself, brave enough,
tough enough to stay with it. I am proud of that in my
brother.*

Marilyn Hall

*I started working young and helped out the family.
I accompanied a friend down to a radio studio where
she was to audition for a dramatic part. After hearing
her, they asked if I wanted to read, too. I did, and I won.
For some years, in the middle forties, I was one of maybe
three ingenue radio actresses in Canada who got most
of the major roles available to us. At times I made as
much as $140 a week, working with the elite of the busi-
ness. I did not know if I wanted to act all my life. I was
interested in writing, and when the time came, I wanted
to go to college.*

*When Monty and I met, I was going steady with a
boy I had grown up with. We had drifted toward marriage and were almost engaged. But he was out of town
and Monty wanted me to go out with him. I didn't want*

to just sit home, so I started to go out with him. I had
no one to talk to, really, so I talked to Monty. He was a
good listener and a good talker. The first thing we found
between us, and not the least thing, was that we could
talk to one another. He became quite a rock, someone
I felt I could trust and lean on.

Monty says he knew all along we'd get married, but
I sure didn't. When I went away to camp, I left him
easily enough, but then there was an emptiness. I
looked forward to going back to be with him. And when
I went back, I realized I had fallen in love with him. I
was very much at ease with him, and I knew there was
a life for the two of us together.

I was a good student. I could have made a career for
myself in radio or television, if not as an actress, then
as a writer. Monty never discouraged me from it. He
worried I would take on too much, but he was proud of
me and wanted me to make as much of myself as I
could. However, I'm sort of an old-fashioned girl and
my family came first. And when Joanne and Richard
came along I drifted out of acting.

When television came along I lacked the confidence in
myself, but I still tried odd things. I remember I did a
Kraft cheese commercial in which only my hands were
shown on the screen. I ran my hands over some cheese
as seductively as I could, and I made $42 a week for it.

But it was Monty's future I was concerned with. I
wanted him to get ahead. We talked over whatever he
wanted to attempt, but basically I just supported his
decisions. I never even thought about his not making
it big. Somehow I was sure he would. I didn't marry
him for that, but even when times were tough I had
that kind of confidence in him. I'd been in show business
long enough to know times had to be tough every now
and then. It seldom comes easy.

I'm a cowboy. I'll go anywhere and do anything if it's
what my husband wants and it's a new adventure. We

moved around a great deal as he made his way up the ladder—six times in nine years. Often he had such deep disappointments I don't know how he endured them and kept going back for more. But he wouldn't give up, as so many others did, and he got it, as so few ever really do. I was with him most of the way, and I know how rough a road it was.

We fit together. We always could talk to each other and still can. We could always both see humor in life and we laughed together. We always have been able to confide in each other. Our love has lasted. Most couples have times when their marriage threatens to come apart, but I don't think we ever have.

5

THE RADIO SHOW I emceed after my wedding trip was called *The Auctioneer*. We auctioned, traded, and dealt things in much the same way we do now on *Let's Make a Deal*. *The Auctioneer* lasted only a year, but most shows I did then—most shows anyone did then or do now on radio or television—only lasted one year or twenty-six weeks or thirteen weeks. You have to realize that and accept it. Shows flop, but that doesn't make you a failure. No one knows for sure what makes a successful show. They didn't know then, and they don't now. If they did, you wouldn't have so many shows going off every year. You can copy a successful format and put the finest people into it and it probably will still fail.

I learned fast that you try your best, and if it doesn't work, you try your best at something else. In this business you're involved with one show for a while, then another, and then another. That's what makes *Let's Make a Deal* so remarkable. Ten years on the air for one show is a rarity.

In Toronto in those days shows came and went at a rapid rate. I did a lot of different programs for CHUM, but after the sales manager and I had disagreements and he became the station manager, there was a bad situation between us. We both thought we knew it all, and we rubbed each other wrong. I got a few offers from other stations to do other shows, but I decided to free-lance for a while.

For a time I did commentary for the Canadian Broadcasting Corporation. Among other things, I did two special programs. On one I covered happenings in Toronto for the evening news. The other was an overseas broadcast in which I covered happenings in Canada for transmission to the British Broadcasting Company. I also cut some singing transcriptions and made guest appearances on various shows. But I really did not do much, and soon I was just eking out a living and beginning to figure that free-lancing was a hard way to go.

Then Rai Purdy called and asked if I would like to emcee not just one but two shows. It was an unusually good break in this business to be offered two shows at the same time—and they were my first national network shows in Canada. One was a quiz program, and the second was a musical variety show. Both lasted one season. The variety show starred Mildred Morey, who was a sort of Martha Raye or Gracie Fields, a big girl with a big voice and a broad sense of comedy. I emceed, sang some duets with Mildred, and served as her foil in some comedy sketches. They brought in an American writer, Sid Resnick, and he wrote a good show.

I was paid $75 for each show, and the $150 a week I made on top of my other work brought my income up quite a bit. No matter how hard times were, I always managed to make a little more each year in Toronto. I made around $4500 my first year, $6000 my second, and close to $8000 my third year. This was not a lot of money, but it was not a little, either, at that time for a journeyman who was still far from stardom. Marilyn and I had been collaborating on some scripts for a dramatic show, *Curtain Time,* and one week we sold two for $300 each. That same week I cut some commercials for the Canadian Department of Health and got $250 for these. With the $150 I was making from my shows, I was up over $1000 for that week. I sent a telegram home to Winnipeg: "Dear Folks. Am now making $1000 a week. This week. Monty." They got a kick out of it. So did I. It was the first week I'd made that much—and the last for a long time.

Early in 1949, I decided to make a serious attempt to develop and sell new shows through my own packaging house, Monty Hall Productions. At Community Chest meetings, I had met my future collaborator in the hamburger business, Wes Cox, a bright young man who'd been editing a newspaper covering high school activities in the area and doing some broadcasting. I considered him brilliant and enlisted his help. My brother pitched in, too. I hired a secretary who was willing to work whenever there was work to be done and at a very modest salary. The office was my apartment. Several of us worked up show ideas, and I hustled our products from station to station.

I thought we had a shot at success if we weren't shot down by starvation first. I needed a helping hand. Unbelievably, another benefactor came into my life. He was a banker, of all things, and his name was Mr. Houston. I had always thought that bankers were cold, tight-fisted businessmen. But it seems there are bankers and bankers. Mr. Houston was in his sixties when I met him. I had been using his bank, the Imperial Bank of Canada, since I had arrived in Toronto, and I went to him when I sought a loan. I sat down and told him my background. I said I was starting my own production company, had a few employees, and needed money to sustain us while we sought to sell some shows. I pointed out that we had no production companies in Canada at the time, and that there seemed to be a need for one. I explained that the stations were developing their own shows, but they were not specialists. CBC was doing its own things, and the rest were relying on U.S. transcriptions of shows like *The Lone Ranger* and *The Green Hornet*. There was no Canadian origination of shows especially suited to Canadians.

"How much money do you think you'll need?" he asked.

I braced myself and said, "$2500." I had figured that with the secretary making $25 a week or so, my brother $15, Wes $50, and myself $75, and with an office I had found for $250 a month, this much money might sustain us for two or three months. By that time I could be in business. I figured Mr. Houston would fall off his chair when he was asked for that amount. I thought I'd be fortunate to get anything.

He asked me more about the business, however; then he asked me what I had for collateral. I hadn't thought of that. I said, "Collateral?" And he said, "Yes, what have you got to put up to protect your investment in case your plan should fail?" And I said, "Mr. Houston, I don't have anything. I don't own anything of value. My business has no inventory. All I've got is what is here in my mind and here in my heart. I have ideas and ambition and a willingness to work hard to make this business work and enough experience in the field to know it can work. And I am an honest man. I have never defaulted on a debt in my life."

He seemed to be studying me as I made my plea, which I hadn't prepared and which surprised even me. When I was done, he was silent. Then he smiled and said, "Maybe it's not the best business for a banker, but bankers are human. We have to take chances on people from time to time even if they don't meet all our standards for loans and such things. You meet a man and you make a judgment on him. I believe you have potential, and I feel you are to be trusted. So I'm going to take a chance on you. Only one thing—I won't lend you $2500. I'll lend you $5000 and put it in a special account for you. I want you to be free from worry for longer than a few months."

I was amazed. I thanked him as gratefully as I could and I promised to do my best by him. But he was not through helping me. Many months later he called and said, "Monty, have you noticed your overdraft?" My heart sank. I had not been aware of it. And he said, "Well, you had $5000 in the account, and you have sent checks for $5600." I felt terrible and I said, "I'm sorry. We've been careful, but we haven't had any money coming in yet, although I think we are on the verge of big things." Very quickly he said, "Hold on, I wasn't calling you to put pressure on you. I called because I was concerned that you might be upset about it." I said, "Well, I certainly am now." He replied, "Well, don't worry. I have confidence in you and I'm standing behind you. We'll just say the loan was a little larger than originally planned."

So there it was. I had only dreams, ambition, and who knows how much ability? And here was this man who, like other men before him, was willing to be my benefactor. Looking back on it, it is hard to believe. But I can tell you that there are people like this in the world if you are fortunate enough to find them—and you can never repay them enough. I repaid the loan in full, incidentally, but I don't know if I ever made this man realize what he meant to me, to my career, to my philosophy of life, as others, beginning with Max Freed, had meant to me.

We moved into an office that consisted of one large room and four smaller ones in a building owned by a chiropractor in downtown Toronto. We took on two more writers: Leonard Starmer, who was to become one of the top men in the variety field at the CBC, and John Ellsworth, who later teamed up with Frank Peppiatt to form one of the better writing and producing teams in the United States, turning out all sorts of things from *Hee Haw* to Frank Sinatra specials. There were a lot of talented young people around who were hustling for a chance. We couldn't afford another writer, but Ellsworth was willing to come on without pay just for the opportunity to create a product that might make it. Len also doubled as a bookkeeper—as if we had any accounts. We were thinking big, anyway, which is the way in this business.

At the start we put together a program called *Who Am I?*, on which I gave clues in rhyme about a mystery person and the audience mailed in their guesses. We kept adding clues until we opened an envelope with the correct answer on the air and the prize was given away. We convinced CFRB to put the show on the air for a short time as a test, but it was understood that if it was not sold to a sponsor it would be taken off. I went to a friend, Clare Appel, who was in charge of advertising for the Odeon Theater chain, and convinced him to take a partial sponsorship to encourage the station to keep us on while I sought full sponsorship. This kept us going for a few weeks.

One day I played the show for McLaren's Advertising Agency. That evening Hugh Horler, head of the agency's radio department, called and said, "We're taking the show. People's Credit Jewelers is going to sponsor it." Marilyn and I whooped with joy and went out that night to celebrate with a steak dinner. We weren't eating much steak in those days. First thing in the morning, however, Horler called to say that the owner of the jewelry company had a change of heart, they weren't going to sponsor the show after all. Suddenly we were sunk into depression. I remember thinking, well, at least we had the steak dinner and a few hours

of happiness. These things were very important to us.
This was my life. After weeks and weeks of trying to
sell the show, then finally selling it, then having it un-
sold overnight—it was disappointing to say the least.

I decided to try all the advertising agencies in Toronto. I got the idea to simply take a telephone book,
turn to the advertising agencies, start with "A," and
work my way right through the alphabet if necessary.
Well, I went from "A" to "G" and got two appointments,
neither of which led to anything. Then I reached "H"
and what I shall call the Hennessy Agency. Hennessy
went for the show and came up with the idea of selling it taped to a national network made up of any stations that would buy it.

The CBC was the only real network in Canada, and
they wouldn't use game shows with giveaway prizes.
Other shows had been transcribed onto records and
sold to various stations around the country for use
whenever each station wished. But ours was the first
show to be taped and sold for simultaneous airing across
Canada. So we formed the first tape network in our
nation's broadcasting history.

We used two cities as a test market—Toronto and
smaller Sarnia, not too far away—to see what sort of
response we received. It was tremendous. We signed
up fifty-six stations, and Colgate agreed to sponsor us
nationally. The show was a success right from the start,
and more stations signed up. I had my first hit—for
which Hennessy paid me the grand total of $300 a week,
which came to $15,600 a year. Out of this, I had to pay
all salaries and expenses and get by myself, but I had no
choice. Hennessy had created a network for the show
and was in control. Either I worked for him at his price
or I didn't work.

Hennessy also had me do other shows for him, including the *Colgate Carnival*, which was a quiz show, a
Colgate sports show, and *The Roy Rogers Show* for kids.

I did them because I thought they would lead to more money. Some of these programs didn't last very long, but there were always others to take their places. After I had begun to do a lot of these, I suggested to Hennessy that we ought to reach some sort of agreement. "Yes," he said, "I'm going to sign you to a contract which will guarantee you $20,000 a year and you can do *Who Am I?* and these other shows." I said that would be fine, but I never got the contract.

When my first weekly check came, it was for $300 instead of the $385 or so it should have been. "There must be some mistake," I told Hennessy. "I'm still being paid at my old rate instead of the $20,000 you promised me." He said, "I've changed my mind. I just took one of the four shows off the air so I don't see any point in paying $20,000. I'm going to keep you at $15,600 until we see what develops." I should have walked out on him then and there, but I was in debt and desperate for the guaranteed income. I could have called him on his promise, but I was afraid. And no matter how many more shows I took on for him, I never got any kind of an increase.

Hennessy, a smallish, red-haired Irishman, was the toughest, roughest boss I've ever known. I was not rough and tough enough to stand up to him, not then. No matter what I did, it never was enough. He never gave anyone any credit, and he demeaned his employees in every way he could. He was always threatening to fire us, and he was always agreeing to do things for us and then changing his mind. He was the sort of boss you avoid as much as possible, the kind you dread having to deal with. He made my life miserable. I worried and suffered and developed intestinal problems. Nevertheless, I was working regularly and paying off my debts. And *Who Am I?* continued to grow yearly, increasing my national popularity. Eventually it ran 1875 performances over more than ten years.

We had a couple of young, mischievous engineers we called the Katzenjammer Kids—Bill Bodington and Francis Van Rassel. Hennessy built his own studio and installed a sound system in his office so he could hear everything that was said. All day long he would call down and say that we were doing this wrong or that wrong, and it drove us up the walls. Then Bodington and Van Rassel figured out a way to reverse the wires so they could hear everything that went on in his private office, too. The Katzenjammer Kids enjoyed these private broadcasts enormously. As much as I might have wanted to join in this private escapade, I put an end to the eavesdropping. It was an invasion of the man's privacy, and it could have cost us our jobs.

When our second child was born in 1952, Hennessy, in a burst of generosity, decided to give us a present. He knew we were living in an apartment and asked me if we had a washing machine at home. When I said we didn't, he said we soon would have. I was surprised and I thanked him. And after it arrived, my wife sent him a note thanking him again. The machine, however, proved to be the cheapest one on the market—we were giving it away as a prize on one of our shows and Hennessy may have gotten one for free—and Marilyn was disappointed that it wasn't the new automatic type. I called an appliance store and arranged to trade the old-fashioned wringer machine in on an automatic model.

Then Hennessy came to dinner. He just came right out and asked me why I didn't invite him over some time so he could meet my wife and see my children. So, of course, I had to ask him right away. Just before he arrived, Marilyn remembered our new washer and realized that when we showed him our small apartment he might notice that the machine was not the one he had given us. But there was no way out. It was like a silly situation comedy. We gave him the grand tour, physi-

cally twisting him away from the washer to show him
something on the other side of the room. Every time
he went near the kitchen, we headed him off. At one
point, my wife did a sort of matador's flourish with her
apron to conceal the washer. We got away with it, and
afterward we collapsed with laughter.

I worked hard for that man and I had to keep cater-
ing to him to hold my position, which left me with
little pride. After Rickey was born, Marilyn and I decided to take our long postponed honeymoon. I was
producing or performing in all sorts of shows at the
time. I was weary and wanted a break. I informed
Hennessy in advance that I had vacation time coming
and that I'd get ahead in my schedule as much as I
could. He raised no objection, so we planned a trip
through Montreal, New England, and New York.

The week we were to leave, Hennessy sent word
through his secretary that I couldn't go. I told his secretary, "You tell Mr. Hennessy I'm going." She returned
with his message: "If you go, *Who Am I?* goes off the
air and you're finished here." I sent back word, "It's
OK with me." And when I told Marilyn, she said, "It's
OK with me, too." So off we went, scared but determined. I was frightened enough to tell Hennessy that
I'd fly back for a few days in mid-vacation to record
some additional shows, which I did. But we did have
our honeymoon, though my nervousness spoiled a lot of
it. When I came back, nothing was said. *Who Am I?*
remained on the air and I continued to work for Hennessy, turning out show after show. I guess I should have
stood up to him more often. But I was an insecure person at the time.

It soon became clear, however, that I had to get away
from Hennessy. I had learned a lot from him. I had
learned that a dime is not worth a nickel to you if you
pay too much for it. I had learned that no shot at success is worth failing as a person when going after it. I

learned that no work is worthwhile if you dread doing
it day after day. I was determined never to suffer abuse
again—ever! Somehow I would manage to feed my family, but I would never do anything that degraded me
again. If I didn't have my self-respect, I didn't have
anything.

I had a home. It was small, but splendid. It had cost
only $16,125 to build it in a tract of similar homes. And
I needed $5000 for the down payment. Even with what
I made from Hennessy, and having paid back my debts,
I did not have that amount. So I asked Hennessy if I
could have the money as an advance on my salary to be
paid back $100 a week through the year. And he said
OK. But then, after I had signed the papers, he
changed his mind, he said he'd decided against it. "I
just can't see my way to such a large advance at this
time," he said. So I was on a spot. But then my mother-
in-law came through and loaned me $2000. And while
Mr. Houston had retired, his replacement at the bank
loaned me the remaining $3000 on the strength of the
good credit rating I'd established. And I repaid them
both. It was just another little thing which turned me
out of my rut. I had to screw up my courage and get
away. It took years, years I'm ashamed of, years when
my career drifted instead of rising. I'm left with a souvenir—stomach trouble that remains to this day.

It was at this time, too, that I almost acquired a less
desirable benefactor. After working as emcee at a benefit baseball game for the Variety Club, I walked under
the stands of Maple Leaf Stadium to get a Coke before
the game began. A heavy-set man approached me, and
in a voice that resembled a steamroller going over
gravel, he said, "Kid, you know who I am?" I certainly
did. He was a prominent gambler and underworld character from Winnipeg, and I stammered out my recognition. He grabbed me by the shoulders and said, "When
you talked about dem crippled kids tonight, you turned

my spine to jelly. You got to have lunch with me tomorrow, you and the missus."

Since one did not say no to this person, Marilyn and
I showed up for lunch at the Horseshoe Tavern the
next day. The gambler spent an hour telling me how
great I was; then, edging closer, he said. "I want to
do something for you." I could only imagine, as he
reached for his wallet, that he was going to slip me a
couple of thousand dollars, and in my desperate financial circumstances, I am sure I would have accepted.
But the problem proved academic. He reached into his
wallet, pulled out a card, wrote something on the back,
and handed it to me.

I didn't dare look at the card until lunch was over.
After saying our goodbyes, I drove two blocks away,
pulled the car over to the side, and immediately fished
out the card with trembling hands. On one side it said,
"Margaret Rose Tea Room," with an address in Winnipeg. And on the back, he had scribbled, "Good for two
free teacup readings." I was so incensed that Marilyn
had to restrain me from returning suicidally to the restaurant to hurl abuse at the character.

I tried to branch out into television, which by then
was coming in and replacing radio. In the early days of
television in Canada we did not have independent
stations or networks to approach. The CBC controlled
the medium, so I laid seige to the CBC. I had made a
name for myself in radio, and I felt I could make it on
camera, too. I was full of ideas and high hopes. It was
like starting all over again, but it was the medium of
the future and had to be conquered.

I started doing my first TV show, *Matinee Party*,
on the CBC. I developed an idea for a late-night talk-
and-talent program based on *The Tonight Show,* which
Steve Allen was hosting at that time on NBC-TV in
New York. My idea was different enough to be original.
I wrote a sample show and got money from the CBC

for a pilot. Drew Crossan produced and directed a kine-scope with me as host and with a trio and a girl singer as well as guests. I was called in by Don Hudson, a top executive at the CBC. Hudson said that the CBC had its own writers, directors, and producers and wasn't interested in my package. But, he said, the show might work anyway, and if they decided to do it I could audition to be the host. When I objected, he offered me $200 royalty. I said, "You won't let me do anything but audition to emcee my own show, but you'll give me $200 a week royalty for it?" He said, "Not $200 a week. I said $200 period." I said, "Forget it," and left.

Angry, I went to Hudson's superior, Harry Boyle, the head of programing for the CBC. Boyle said it was Hudson's decision. Later the CBC went ahead and made their own pilot of my show, using my material, the same trio and singer, but a different host, and started to show it around. When I found out, I rushed back to Boyle, but he shrugged his shoulders and said there wasn't anything to be done about it. What he meant was there wasn't anything he dared do about it. He'd been a big man when radio was king, but now television was in control and he had lost his power. (After almost fifteen years in limbo he regained a top position.)

I went back to Don Hudson and told him, "You can't do this with my show." And Don Hudson told me, "We at the corporation can do anything we want with any show that is presented to us." It was very much like a commissar in Moscow telling someone "You better like it, buddy boy, or it's Siberia for you." This is not a bad parallel, because the CBC always has operated like a powerful state organization that is accountable only to itself. Its building on Jarvis Street in Toronto is called "The Kremlin."

The men who rose to power there had civil service-type jobs that did not pay much money but put them in positions of power and provided them immense security. They could push writers, performers, producers, and directors around like so many pawns. They could make or break a man's career with a snap of the finger.

Of course, story ideas are always being lifted in broadcasting. There just isn't any way to prove someone else's show was really your brainchild. Sometimes just a part of an idea is lifted. Sometimes your idea may not have been drastically different from their idea in the first place, and they just found a little something of yours they could add to theirs.

Mine was an extreme case of total theft, however, and I screamed bloody murder, which didn't help my standing at the CBC. I was not only doing the show *Matinee Party* but had been approached about a new quiz show. Shortly after my debacle with Hudson, the quiz show idea was dropped, and so was *Matinee Party*. From three shows on the network, I was down to none. I started knocking on doors—on what seemed to be a revolving stage. Everyone was evasive. I remember lower-echelon officers at the Kremlin saying, "Maybe somebody up there doesn't like you," and those in the upper echelons saying, "Somebody down there doesn't like you, I guess." After Stewart Griffith assumed a position of authority in the corporation, he gave me an appointment. I got to his office on time but was kept waiting outside almost forever. When I finally got inside, he immediately left. I waited a half hour before he came back. When I finally got to talk to him briefly, he said, "Is it possible that somebody out there doesn't like you?"

I have never forgotten Griffith's rudeness—or that of others like him. People in positions of power in the entertainment business tend to have enormous egos, and many of them are among the rudest people on earth. I have a pretty big ego, myself, but I remember when I was demeaned, and as a result I may be the easiest person in television for someone else in the business to speak to on the phone or see in person. I am courteous to everybody and try to help anyone I can.

I remember all too well how it was when I went hat in hand begging for a hearing in Toronto and later in New York. I hadn't yet made my move to New York, but I was fast being driven to it.

The middle fifties were tough times for me in Toronto. *Who Am I?* endured and sustained me along with other shows and jobs I picked up from time to time. At one point I took a Variety Club vaudeville show on tour around eastern Canada. The star was George Formby, a great figure in English music halls and motion pictures, and we had solid supporting acts. I emceed, sang, and did a little bit of everything.

After the show appeared in Ottawa, Ernie Bushnell came backstage to see me and invited me out to lunch with him the next day. I'd stayed friendly with Ernie and played cards with him many times at the Variety Club in Toronto. But then Ernie moved to Ottawa and became the top man in programing for the CBC. I knew he had influence, and I went to lunch wondering if I could make use of any of it. Right away he said, "Gee, it's wonderful seeing you, Monty. My wife was saying at the show last night that it's certainly good to see Monty Hall performing again. And she asked me why we didn't see you on television. And I didn't know what to tell her. Why don't we?"

I looked at him and said, "Ernie, you've got to be kidding. You're the head man. If you don't know why I'm not on television, who does? Did you think I'd retired? I'm a bit young for that. I've been trying to get a show from your people in Toronto without any luck." I told him about the show I'd created and how it was taken from me. I told him how I'd raised hell about it and wound up being blackballed. I added that I was thinking of leaving Canada and trying New York.

Ernie listened sympathetically to the whole story and said, "I'm very distressed to hear all this. I've been a booster of yours for years and I believe you belong in radio and television in this country. Canada desperately needs performers of your caliber, and I'm going to look into this situation and see what can be done about it." Well, he certainly boosted my spirits. As busy as he was, he kept the luncheon talk going for three hours and filled it with praise of me and promises for the future. I left him with my feet hardly touching the ground.

Very soon afterward I got a call from Fergus Mutrie of the CBC in Toronto saying that he'd heard from Ernie Bushnell and that he wanted to meet with me as soon as possible. We went to lunch and he asked me for details, so I repeated the whole story. He said, "I promise you, Monty, I will look into this, and I'm going to find out why you haven't been able to get work." Again I left buoyed with new hope.

Then, about ten days later, Mutrie called me a second time. "Monty," he said, "I've investigated the whole situation and I've found you haven't been treated any differently from anyone else." I was stunned. I asked, "Did you talk to the people who stole my show? Did you talk to the people who wouldn't give me the time of day? If you did, what did you expect them to say?" He said, "I talked to everyone and they all agreed they have treated you just as they treat any other talent seeking employment. They just have not had anything suitable for you." "Are you telling me I don't have the talent?" I asked. "I'm not saying that," he replied, "but I am saying our people simply feel they have found nothing suitable for your talent." So I said, "Well, I'm sorry," and he said, "I'm sorry, too." I left, and that was that.

It was a dead end, after all. I was convinced then I had to get away from Canada and the CBC. I didn't know what sort of talent I had, but I knew the CBC didn't know either. I had tried and been turned away. I had to go to where there were greater opportunities. Now was the time to try New York.

6

THERE REALLY WAS no strong reason for me to believe I could beat the odds and break into big-time television in New York. The facts were that I had left Winnipeg without having established myself as any sort of sensation, and though I had made something of a name for myself in radio in Toronto, I had failed to make it in television there. Frustration was forcing my move. Having been beaten up a bit by a couple of contenders, I now felt qualified to take on the champion. Chalk it up to youthful enthusiasm—or desperation. It was a rough, tough fight, I'll tell you. I kept getting knocked down, but I kept getting up swinging.

I made my move on the first of July 1955. Marilyn and I had agreed I would spend at least two months in New York to see what would develop. She was willing to remain behind with our children, who were five and three, and bear all the responsibilities of our home and family. Otherwise I never could have attempted the venture.

I rounded up a couple of other Canadians who were bound for New York—Albert Shea, who was in the research business and planned only a short stay, and John Drainie, a fine radio actor who also felt he had reached his limit in Canada—and we made the trip in my car.

We had not arranged for a place to stay in the big town, and on our arrival I looked through some ads and was struck by one for the Shoreham Hotel on West 55th Street. We could have a one-bedroom apartment with twin beds and a kitchen for $360 a month. That was a lot, especially at that time, and Shea chose to stay elsewhere. But there were benefits, such as a telephone answering service, and I figured it would work out. Drainie and I agreed to share all expenses, and the adventure began.

We each had lists of people we wanted to see, and every morning we would call some and seek appointments. After a time we were batting the same—zero. We simply could not get interviews with most of the people we wanted to see, and those people we did see were not especially interested in us. We pounded the pavements and took a pounding ourselves.

I wasn't surprised. Naturally, it was discouraging, but I had expected it to be tough and I planned to keep at it until it worked. But Drainie's discouragement began to depress him after a few weeks. He was a superb radio actor with a thousand voices, but he had a bad limp, and that didn't help his chances in television. He began to figure he was beaten.

One day I was reading a story in *Life* magazine about Sylvester "Pat" Weaver, the president of NBC, who had been stirring up television with his daring innovations. On radio he had created *Monitor*, the weekend program, and *The Weekday Show*. In television he started *The Today Show*, *The Tonight Show*, *The Home Show*, which Arlene Francis hosted, and

many others. The story said that Weaver was a man
with a feel for the unusual. I was struck with an inspiration. I would try the unusual; I would send him a telegram pleading my case.

As I started to compose the wire, Drainie asked me
what I was doing. I said, "I'm composing a wire to Pat
Weaver at NBC." Drainie was amused. "Why not send
one to General Sarnoff, too?" I said, "Nothing else has
worked so far, so I can't lose anything by trying this."
The wire went something like this: "This may be a daring and presumptious thing to do, but, according to
Life magazine, that is Pat Weaver's sort of thing, and
if it's good enough for him, it's good enough for me.
My name is Monty Hall. I am an emcee and producer
from Toronto and I think I have a lot to offer, but I
haven't been able to impress this on anyone. I have been
trying to see the executives at NBC, but can't get past
their secretaries. Anything you can do to help me see
them will be deeply appreciated. I will be grateful to
you for your consideration. . . ."

I read it to Drainie; he roared with laughter. I took
the wire to Western Union; the operator read it and
started to smile. "Are you sure you want to send
this?" she asked. "Just tell me how much it is and send
it," I retorted.

I went back to the Shoreham and tried to forget it. A
few days later Drainie answered the telephone. "It's Pat
Weaver's secretary," he announced. He laughed as he
said it because he must have figured somebody was
putting me on. I grabbed the phone, and it really was
Pat Weaver's secretary. She said that Mr. Weaver was
quite taken with the telegram and would very much like
to meet the man who sent it. Could I see him Friday
at three? I assured her I could. She added, "Incidentally,
I'm sorry it has taken us so long to get back to you, but
Mr. Weaver just returned from the West Coast." I told
her I hadn't minded the wait at all.

The few days to Friday passed slowly. Now that I'd talked myself into an interview with one of the great men of the industry, how could I back it up? I showed up at Weaver's office early, waited, and just before three an aide grabbed me by the arm, exclaimed, "Now!" and hustled me into an enormous office. Weaver looked at me and said, "Your wire was great. But I only have ten minutes now before I have to catch a flight, so please tell me everything you can in that time." He listened to everything I said, and at the end of ten minutes he turned to his assistant and ordered, "See to it that Mr. Hall gets to see everyone he wants to see here and then give me a full report on the interviews." Then he jumped up and left. The assistant took me out to his secretary. We drew up a list of the people in power at NBC, and she made me a series of appointments for the following week. I walked out wide-eyed and phoned my wife the news.

Of course, the natural ending to such a tale is that the doors of stardom opened to me. They did not. I saw everyone who was anyone at NBC. Everyone treated me courteously and heard me out and promised to get back to me—but not one of them ever did. There was nothing whatsoever, not one single nibble. I didn't even get to audition for a job.

The telegram remains famous in the industry. Almost everyone assumes that it gave me my first break, but it didn't give me anything except a good story to tell later.

Drainie's wife came to visit him one weekend, and I moved out to give them some privacy. She soon went back to Toronto, and Drainie was lonely without her. Shortly thereafter he gave up and returned to Toronto. I didn't give up, but I was tempted to many times. Each morning I would make about ten or twelve phone calls requesting appointments. Then I would wait to get calls back. I'd be lucky if I got one or two calls, and luckier still if I made any appointments at all. Sometimes the

*Hall studies
preparations for the
taping of two
Let's Make a Deal
shows (left), discusses
a bit of business
with partner Stefan Hatos
as announcer
Jay Stewart looks
on (middle), and confers
with writers (bottom)*

Potential contestants on Let's Make a Deal *line up (facing page, top and bottom) and wait sixty to ninety minutes to see which will be chosen for the "trading floor." Ushers (middle left) clear a path for the writers who will make the selections. When they appear, would-be contestants try to capture their attention by shouting and waving signs (below)*

*Alan Gilbert
points fateful finger
at one of the
"chosen" (left),
and a lucky member of
the trading floor reacts
with excitement (below)*

Those who aren't selected remain outside the studio (right and below). They will view the shows as the nonparticipating audience.

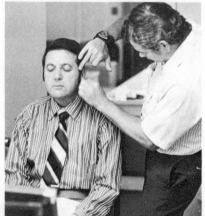

Monty naps (above)
before dressing for
the taping and
getting made up for
the camera (left)

The range of emotions is wide as contestants win and lose.
The contestant in the bottom photo is actually a big winner.

(All photos in this section by Wen Roberts, Photography, Inc.)

phone would not ring for hours, and I would sit staring at it. If I did get an appointment, I would walk to it, even if it was ten or twenty blocks away, because I couldn't afford to spend my dwindling money on taxis. It was midsummer and dreadfully hot, and by the time I arrived, I was barely presentable. Then I had two minutes to tell some executive all about myself. He would say he'd let me know, and that would be the last I'd ever hear from him. If I had another appointment, I'd go home to shower and change because I had to look presentable even if I couldn't afford dry cleaning and laundry bills. Then I'd walk to my other appointment, get another two minutes that came to nothing, and return to my apartment. If there were no messages, I'd sit by the phone and wait and hope.

For the performer the telephone can be an instrument of torture. He is afraid to leave it for fear of missing out on a call that may mean a job, maybe the best of his career. I had an answering service backing me up. Still, it made me nervous. What if the service missed a call or made a mistake? What if I got back too late to reach the caller that day and it cost me a job? To this day I am unable to ignore the ringing of a phone because this built-in fear has become part of me. I can't break a habit as strong as this. You answer your phone. You had better be there to answer your phone. When you're there, it never rings. The minute you go out, it always rings.

The nights were lonely. I had a few friends and relatives in New York and I visited them occasionally. Their family life made me even lonelier. I missed Marilyn and the babies badly and called them every other night. My only income was from the tapes of *Who Am I?* that I cut in New York and sent back to Toronto. Baseball was a blessing. There still were three teams in New York at the time, and they televised all their home games and some of their road games. Sometimes I watched three games a day. Afterward I went to bed and waited for morning—when the whole routine of making calls and hoping for appointments began all over again.

During this time I saw agents who didn't want to handle me and producers who didn't want to cast me, and all sorts of executives who had no interest in me. I would call up some bigwig and ask his secretary, "Is Mr. Smith in?" And she'd ask, "Who is calling?" I'd say, "Monty Hall." She'd say, "Marty who?" I'd say, "No, not Marty . . . Monty . . . Monty Hall." And she'd say, "You're from Montreal?" And I'd say, "No, my name is Monty Hall and I'm from Toronto." I would almost be in tears by this time. She'd say, "Does Mr. Smith know you?" And I'd have to reply, "No, but I'm a performer and a producer and I'd like an interview for a job." And she'd say, "Well, Mr. Smith is busy right now, but if you'll leave your name and number I'll give him your message. Now that was Marty who?" I became known to my friends as "Marty who."

Often when I did get an appointment, I'd go in and find that it had been made for a Marty Hull from Montreal. Then I'd have to explain my name all over again. At first, I had to wait anywhere from fifteen minutes to an hour and a half beyond my scheduled appointment. One thing I am, and that's an independent cuss, job or no job. So when I was kept waiting longer than twenty minutes, I would rear up and tell the secretary or receptionist, "I'm sorry, but I can't wait any longer. If Mr. Smith is not going to see me in the next five minutes, please let me know so that I can leave and come again another time." Some people feel they have to make other people wait; they feel they have to impress the little guys with their power. By keeping you waiting, they wield some power. They put you on the defensive.

Executives have many tricks, and I saw a lot of them. The executive's chair is almost always higher than the visitor's chair. He is looking down on you and you are looking up at him. He is a king, and you are at most a member of his court and at worst merely one of the rabble. And the executive swivels. He has a swivel chair and you do not. He swivels around looking at everything but you, while you have to follow him with your eyes, locked in your place. The executive fiddles with papers on his desk. The more papers, the more important he is supposed to be. Often he takes a lot of telephone calls while you are in the office. The more calls he gets, the more important he is. The executive seldom cuts off his calls or apologizes for taking them. He just interrupts the conversation and ignores you. In a ten-minute interview you are lucky to talk for two minutes, and that comes in starts and stops. You have no reason to believe the executive is listening.

One executive who received me was decorating his new office. The whole time I was with him, he was busy examining the pictures he wanted to hang on his walls. He never looked at me once or said a single intelligible word. He'd grunt "uh-huh" and keep on studying his pictures. When I was done, he finally spoke to me. "Which of these do you like best?"

Years later I was selected emcee of the CBS show *Keep Talking*. After our premiere, Lester Gottlieb, an executive of CBS, toasted me at a dinner at Danny's Hideaway. He told of how he remembered this kid from Canada coming into his office and telling him cockily how he was going to lick this town, and now, by golly, here he was heading for the top. What I remembered as I sat there listening to him was how terribly nervous I had been at our first meeting, how I sat in his office crushing my hat between twitching fingers. Yet now, in the flush of success, he was picturing me as "cocky." So what was the point of his story, and what was its meaning for me? Simply that when you are on the way up, everybody "discovered" you, and everybody has anecdotes, almost always apocryphal. To further prove my point, eight weeks later, when *Keep Talking* did not obtain high ratings, I was fired. A friend of mine met Gottlieb in the halls of CBS and asked him why I had been dismissed. Gottlieb's answer was, "Oh, him and that damn Canadian accent of his!" Gottlieb is not a bad guy; and, in fact, I was always fond of him and still am. But I tell the story to demonstrate that there is one kind of story for the guy going up and another kind for the guy going down.

Keep Talking was my first big network television show in the States. Up till then I had been a replacement for others. I was crazy about the format and loved being a moderator, especially because the show had a great inventive comedy flavor. When I got a few laughs myself, Herb Wolf, the producer, took me aside and said: "I've had a complaint from one of the comics on the panel. He told me to tell you that he'll get the laughs and you just stick to moderating." Being practically a freshman in the bigtime, I heeded the advice and played it straight. I shouldn't have. If I was going to go down, I should have died as a lion, not as a lamb.

I was replaced by Jackie Cooper for a couple of weeks, and then Carl Reiner, for the balance of the season. The show changed networks and used Merv Griffin as the host, but it never got a rating. It was just too sophisticated for the audience. My only consolation was that the change in emcees never added a point to the ratings. Two years later Mike Dann of CBS hired me to do *Video Village*. He sent me a note which said: "We may have been wrong when we let you go from *Keep Talking*, but I know damn well we're right this time!" I appreciated that.

Show business is at once the best and the worst of businesses. If you are on top, it can be the best in almost every way. If you are not, it can be the worst in any way. It is referred to as a profession, but it is not a profession.

A profession is a skill you have learned and can prove. If you study to become a doctor and get your license, you are a doctor forever. You can put M.D. after your name and hang out your shingle and wait for patients to appear. Anyone in the entertainment business has no letters to prove his profession and no shingle to hang up. Instead of waiting for people to come to him, he has to go to others for work. And he is only a professional while he is working.

You go in to executives and say, "I'm a director." But you can prove it only by things you've directed. If you haven't had any experience, you're not a director. A director directs. A writer writes. It's only when you sell something that you are proving yourself. And it only lasts as long as the thing you've sold lasts. And nothing lasts forever in this business. Jobs come and go. Your profession is unemployment marked by periods of employment. Most people in show business—even stars—are out of work most of the time.

You live in fear. I have never met one single person in this business who has not been afraid at one time or another. They wouldn't all admit it, but they all showed it in one way or another. There aren't any of us who are any bigger than the show we have going at the moment. If the show fails, we are failures. We have no guarantees there will be another show. It doesn't matter how long we've been on or how successful we've been, today is all that counts, and our world may crash around our shoulders tonight.

Jerry Lewis is big in movies, but has failed several times on television. Vince Edwards had one of the most successful shows in television history, *Ben Casey,* but when it went off, he dropped out of sight for years. It had nothing to do with how good he was—only with the fact that he had not come up with another *Ben Casey.* Milton Berle was "Mr. Television"—until television forgot him. Sid Caesar, Red Buttons, and so on—the roll

call of great talent ignored in the shuffle is almost endless.

Even the biggest names suffer for fear it will end
tomorrow. It's in the nature of the performer. The contract I had with Hennessy to do the Colgate show, which
was sustaining me in my early days, was like a lifeline.
I took everything the man dished out, because the job
was all I had, and the thought that I might lose it
turned my insides into jelly. I've never seen the fear on
my own face, then or since, but I know it has been
there.

I fought fear through those dreadful days and lonely
nights in New York. I hated the city. It terrified me. I
wanted to go home to friends and family a hero. In the
mornings I'd make fifteen calls and fourteen wouldn't
answer, and the fifteenth would see me and reject me.
And another day was done. The struggle is worse than
most realize. And the ending is usually unhappy.

7

IF MANY PEOPLE were cruel to me in those months in New York, many more were not, and I must be forever grateful to them. One was Sam Rosenwasser. He was a cousin of my mother's and lived in Brooklyn. When I arrived in New York for my first visit in 1946, he was out and I left a message and went to bed. The next thing I knew, he was pounding on my door at the Edison Hotel, dragging me out of bed, pushing me into some clothes, and taking me to the Carnival nightclub to see Milton Berle. Sam was my father's age, but we became true and devoted friends. In the summer of 1955, when I was walking the streets of New York looking for work, and long after that, Sam and his wife, Ada, took me into their home and their hearts. Sam's usual way of handling me was to call from Brooklyn to ask, "What are you doing for dinner?" When I said I was free for the evening, he would say, "Be in front of your hotel in an hour." Dinner with Sam and Ada always consisted of too much food (they must have thought I was starv-

ing) served amid a barrage of solicitous questions:
"Who are you seeing?" "What can I do for you?"
"Where do you want to go?" "How about a Broadway
show?" There wasn't anything that this magnificent
man wouldn't do for me. And to this day, there isn't
anything in the world I wouldn't do for him.

Sam was a relative, but there were friends who were
closer than relatives could be—like Eugene and Emily
Grant. Marilyn and Emily had been close girl friends
in Toronto; and after Emily's marriage to Eugene, all
four of us became close. It was only natural that I
would spend a lot of time with them in Mamaroneck.
They gave me moral support. Gene became like a
brother to me. When Marilyn and the kids joined me
in New York, we settled in Westchester County just to
be near the Grants. And today, though we live three
thousand miles apart, we still fly back and forth to be
with one another on happy occasions and for just plain
visits.

I met Deke Hayward, who was a writer for Garry
Moore at the time. Deke introduced me to Bill Bratter,
his lawyer, and Bill and I took to each other immediately. Bill offered to represent me for free in any contracts or legal matters, saying, "I'm going to represent
you now, and someday you're going to be big and I'm
going to make a lot of money off you."

Through my contacts with Colgate in Toronto, I got
to see the Colgate people in the New York area. They
were in Jersey City, and they set up an appointment
with me to meet Walt Framer, who at the time was
producing *Strike It Rich* and *The Big Payoff*. Framer
was a busy man, and he conducted other business the
whole time I was in his office. He apologized for it,
however, and he let me stay a long while, talking to
me between calls. He invited me back for a second
visit, and then he and his wife took me to dinner at
a fashionable New York restaurant. I have always

thought this was an extraordinarily nice thing for him to do. He had no work for me at the time, but he had plans for other shows, and I got the feeling he might have plans for me. At that point an occasional good feeling was about as much as I ever had.

For eight weeks I did not see Marilyn. We decided she would come to visit me on my birthday, August 25. About that time, Hurricane Hazel struck the Northeast and floods devastated Connecticut. Jerry Danzig, an NBC executive I'd talked to, asked me if I would emcee a telethon in the Hartford-New Britain area to raise funds for the flood victims. I said I'd be delighted. Unfortunately, the telethon was to run from late the night of August 24 to early the evening of the 25, when my wife was due in New York. Danzig said he would arrange for a private plane to fly me from Hartford to New York and a limousine to drive me to the hotel for my meeting with Marilyn. I was dying to show somebody what I could do, so I readily accepted.

The telethon starred Raymond Massey, Robert Strauss, Eddie Fisher, Lanny Ross, and other performers. I served as emcee for eighteen long hours and felt I did very well, and we raised a lot of money. Danzig was impressed with me, but at the time he had little power at NBC. Norman Lear, creator of *All in the Family,* also saw the show. Norman had gone home to Connecticut to help his mother bail out during the floods and had watched the telethon for many hours. Years later I met him in the halls at NBC, and he told me of this incident from eight years before. He said, "The funny thing about it was that I always remembered this Canadian kid doing a sensational one-man show all night and all day long; but when it was over, I never saw him again, and I wondered what had happened to him." So much of this business is timing. You can impress the right people at the wrong time, and the wrong people at the right time.

I left the studio exhausted but exhilarated. I'd needed that opportunity to perform. I was driven to a private airfield where the plane was ready but the pilot was not. His son, a youngster of sixteen or seventeen, said, "My dad is busy, but I'll fly you." I said, "Can you?" He replied, "Sure, I've been flying for years." The man who had driven me to the airport appeared worried as he told me, "Listen, you don't have to go if you don't want to." And I said, "I want to. My wife is waiting. I haven't seen her in eight weeks. If he's willing, I am." We walked to the plane—and my heart sank. It resembled a large orange crate with wings attached.

The kid started the engine, we bumped down the runway, and suddenly we were aloft. We flew at altitudes of 500 to 1500 feet, which was like driving a little high off the road. He kept glancing at the instrument panel with a worried look, and I was too concerned about my own discomfort to ask him what worried him. My knuckles were white from gripping the door handle, and I kept saying improvised prayers in my mind. It was a short flight, and finally we reached LaGuardia Airport, coming in right through the telephone wires, it seemed. We made it, and I blessed the boy silently. The limousine was waiting and got me to the hotel before my wife arrived.

Marilyn's plane had ridden the tail end of the hurricane into New York, and she was pale and nervous. We clutched each other, cried and kissed, and then she ran to the bathroom to throw up. She couldn't eat that night, I couldn't sleep, though I had been up for forty-eight hours straight. It was not a particularly romantic reunion. The next day was much better, but then it was over and time for her to return to Toronto and our children.

I knew we couldn't go on this way, but we also decided I shouldn't give up on New York. We agreed that after Labor Day I would return to Toronto and then start commuting—one week in Toronto, one week in New York—and we would manage the money somehow. So she went back and I started to wait for the Labor Day weekend, while continuing to make the usual useless rounds. God, how I missed those children!

When the appointed weekend came, I decided to drive the car back. Leaving late on Friday afternoon I drove hard until around midnight, when I sacked out in a motel. Early the next morning I resumed my drive. The closer I got to Toronto, the more anxious I became, and before I realized it, I was driving ninety miles an hour. On the Queen Elizabeth Highway between Hamilton and Toronto the four-lane highway suddenly becomes a divided highway. The change makes a driver come unexpectedly upon a divider with a heavy stanchion at its foot. I had forgotten about the road and was thinking only of my family when suddenly I was speeding directly at the divider. I swerved, missing it by inches.

The near accident scared hell out of me, and I slowed down to a sane speed. I reached Toronto and drove to my house and up the driveway. Six or seven boys and girls were playing on the grass. But after ten weeks without them, I wasn't sure which of the children were mine. Then two of them came running toward the car crying out, "Daddy! Daddy!" and I was so shaken I could not even get out of the car. All the love I had stored up in New York welled up in me, and I just sat there with tears streaming down my face. I finally got out of the car and clasped the kids to me. Marilyn came out of the house and started to cry watching daddy with his daughter and his son.

I had my reunion with my family and my week at home, and then it was time to fly back to New York for my week of telephone calls and pounding pavements and making office calls. It became a regular routine. I

did my shows in advance in Toronto and on Sunday I'd
fly back to New York for five days; on Friday night
I'd fly back to Toronto and wait by the telephone for
the next week. September passed, and October, and November. Through Danzig I was offered $600 a week to
do a show in Chicago. Well, I wanted the money, I
wanted the show, but I didn't want Chicago. From
Toronto to New York is a vertical move; from Toronto
to Chicago is a lateral move.

To keep up my contracts, I hit upon the idea of sending a mimeographed news sheets of my doings, "A Memo
from Monty," to those network and agency folks I had
met—even briefly. To my surprise they actually seemed
to enjoy them. Once I missed a weekly mailing, and
Steve Krantz, program director of WNBC in New York,
asked me "What happened to the latest 'Memo from
Monty'? I missed it." I laughed and said, "I guess I was
too busy, although I don't know what I could have been
doing." "Are you too busy for lunch?" he asked. I was
not, and we went.

Krantz told me he was having trouble with a show,
The Sky's the Limit. "You seem to have some good
ideas," he said. "I want you to watch the show and tell
me what you think is wrong and what can be done to fix
it up." I watched the show every day for a week, and
I found a lot wrong with it. At the end of the week I
wrote a long dissertation, touching on the show's structure, production, personnel, prizes, everything. I mailed
it to Krantz and forgot about it.

Shortly thereafter Colgate-Palmolive stopped sponsor-
ing my show in Canada, and I was cast adrift. What
else did I have? Early in December, I was sitting at
home in Toronto wondering what to do when my world
turned around. The date, I remember, was December 7,
1955. Steve Krantz called me from New York. "Monty,"
he said, "Your report on the show was brilliant. I think

your ideas will work. I'm ready to make you an offer to start work immediately as both producer and emcee of *The Sky's the Limit.*"

Finally, my first chance had come. Excitedly, I said, "I accept." Then I added, "I really don't know if I'm ready to handle the dual role of producer and emcee." And he said, "Well, take a day or two and think about it and then we'll negotiate." "Fine," I blurted. I hung up and danced Marilyn around the room.

Again the phone rang. And again it was long distance from New York. I couldn't believe it. It was Walt Framer. "Monty, Warren Hull is taking a vacation from *Strike It Rich*, and I thought maybe you'd like to do the show for a few days while he is gone." "You bet I would," I told him. When we hung up, I turned to my wife and heaped this new bit of heaven on her, and we went on dancing around the room.

Less than an hour later the phone rang a third time. It was Gordon Keeble, who was working with an independent agency in Toronto. "Good news," he said. "I've sold *Who Am I?* to Canada Packers. It can go right back on the air because they're ready to back it immediately. Let's lock it up." I was overwhelmed. One hour earlier I had nothing. Now I had a New York show to do, a stint on U.S. network, and a new sponsor for my radio show in Canada. After all that time, good fortune had struck three times on a single day.

I called my friend Bill Bratter in New York, told him the developments, and admitted that I had not even thought of asking what sort of money was involved. He advised me, "Just take whatever they offer at this stage. We'll worry about more later. But don't sign anything until I see it." "Fine," I said. And from that time Bratter was my official representative. I got $500 to do the Hull shows and $450 a week on *The Sky's the Limit* and $300 a week for *Who Am I?* I wanted to start paying Bratter, but he said, "Forget it for now.

You've been starving too long, and I'm not in need. When you catch up and get ahead, then I'll start taking fees from you. You're going to make a lot of money. I'm not going to lose out on anything."

I decided against taking the producer's job on *The Sky's the Limit*. I wanted to be free to do as many other things as possible. We set December 30 as the date for my first show. In the meantime, I did the three *Strike It Rich* shows, and everyone seemed to think they went well.

I was at the U.S. Immigration Office in Toronto getting a resident alien visa so I could work in New York on a steady basis when my wife phoned to tell me to get in touch with Bill Bratter. I wound up on a three-way conference call with Ed Wolf, a New York producer and packager, who was in Phoenix at the time. He had seen me on *Strike It Rich* and wanted me to host a new national show called *Twenty Steps to a Million*. I told them I was certainly interested.

If I could add a regular national show to my local New York program, I'd really be on my way. Scheduling conflicts would have to be worked out, but that wasn't an immediate problem. *Twenty Steps to a Million* was only in the formative stage, and I went over to Wolf's office whenever I could to help shape it up. Almost everyone in the office was a relative of Ed's, and I was quickly accepted into the "family." Meanwhile, I did *The Sky's the Limit* five days a week and worked hard to dig it out of the hole it was buried in. Its ratings had gone way down, and we had to attract a new audience, which is difficult with an old show.

One sidelight: Steve Krantz said I could do pretty much what I wanted to do to improve the show. I had taken over for Gene Rayburn as emcee, and I wanted to replace the lovely young lady who was assisting him on the air because I thought I could work better with a lively male announcer, as I do now with Jay Stewart on

Let's Make a Deal and as Johnny Carson does with Ed McMahon on *The Tonight Show*. I hired Bill Wendell, and he worked out well. The lady I fired to make room for Bill was Hope Lange, who was to become a most successful movie and television actress.

It was great to be working—especially now that the other show was in the works, too. Every Friday afternoon I'd leave the studio and fly home to Toronto for the weekend to be with my family and to tape *Who Am I?*

This schedule was very tight. Each week the same cabbie rushed me to the airport. I never had time for lunch and he was kind enough to pick up a carton of milk, a couple of hardboiled eggs, and some bread and butter from a local beanery, and they would be waiting on the seat for me.

On Sunday evening I'd catch a plane back to New York in time to get a night's sleep before beginning the new week's work on Monday, but I was weary of being apart from my family for so long. And Marilyn was starting to say that my visits were like having a soldier home on forty-eight-hour pass. It certainly seemed time for me to move the family to New York. So in May 1956, when Joanne finished kindergarten, we made the move. We sold our home in Toronto, but I was wary of buying a house in New York right away. With the help of the Grants I rented a three-story house in suburban Mount Vernon.

Our house in Toronto had been small but new and modern. The Mount Vernon house was large but old-fashioned. It had heavy drapes and heavy furniture, and everything creaked. Marilyn was excited as I drove her and the kids to it for the first time, then obviously disappointed when she saw it. She said, "When you told me you'd found a house in Mount Vernon, I thought it was the Mount Vernon where George Washington lived. Now that I've seen the house, I wonder if George is still living here." Well, we had lived apart

for almost a year since I embarked on my mission to
Manhattan, and old house or not, at least we were to-
gether. Soon we began to get postcards reading, "Dear
Alien. Classes in English will be taught at Mount
Vernon High School. Please attend."

The day we moved in to our new home *The Sky's
the Limit* was canceled. Some timing. The show had improved, but it was just buried too deep to be saved. A
few days later Ed Wolf sadly informed me that Raleigh
Cigarettes, which had all but bought *Twenty Steps to a
Million*, had decided against it at the last minute because CBS would not give them a better time period,
and finding another sponsor seemed unlikely. Suddenly,
I had nothing again. I had moved my family to New
York, and now my only job was back in Toronto. Tough
times loomed ahead.

Then Mort Werner called me from NBC to say the
network was pleased with my work on the local show
and was interested in putting me on a network program. Steve Allen's *Tonight Show* was doing well
Monday through Friday nights, he said, and they
had a similar show planned for Saturdays. They needed
a fresh personality like me to do it; the producer
should meet me, more as a formality than anything
else; and it was all but set. I was thrilled. I had become
a specialist in game shows and I enjoyed doing them,
but this was a chance to host a variety-talk show, and
I thought it would be perfect for me, the kind of show
I wanted to do more than any other—and still do.

When I walked into the producer's office, he asked,
"What can I do for you?" I said, "Mort Werner felt I
should meet with you. Didn't he tell you I was coming?" And he said, "Well, he told me you were coming
in, but he didn't tell me what for." When I told him it
was about the Saturday night show, he drew back and
his eyes narrowed. "What about the Saturday night
show?" I was surprised and I stammered, "Well, he said

he wanted us to talk about my emceeing it." His expression turned hard and hostile. "I don't know anything about that. I do know you're not anywhere in my plans." I couldn't believe I had been sent on such a wild goose chase. One moment I was a star, the next moment a piece of dirt. How often we ride a rollercoaster in show business, up and down in seconds.

8

It WAS BACK to the telephone and the streets and the
offices and making the rounds one way or another.
But now there was a big difference. I was known and
I could get in to see people, even if there wasn't much
for me. I did manage to land part-time work on
NBC's *Monitor*, pinch-hitting for fellows who for one
reason or another were absent. Occasionally I'd do a
few bits on my own, but it wasn't anything I could
count on, and the pay was uneven.

One day Mort Werner, who clearly cared, called me
in again and assured me that NBC had high hopes for
me as an emcee, which made me feel better, and wanted
to put some eating money in my hands while waiting
for the right opening to develop, which made me feel
even better. He said, "You've been pinch-hitting on
Monitor. I'd like you to be a regular. That will pay
$161.60 a week. And then we're putting on a Saturday
morning cowboy movie. We want you to dress up in
a checked shirt and host the show. I realize it's not a

prestige thing, but it will pay $500 a week. Add that to your *Monitor* pay and you have $661 a week. Does that sound like eating money?" It certainly did. With the $300 from my Canadian show, and with an odd job here and there, I averaged around $1000 a week for a time.

Monitor presented news, music, and a lot of special features, including live on-the-scene broadcasts and interviews with personalities. Originally the program stressed these live segments, but as time passed they started to tape a lot because it was easier to insert taped segments whenever they wanted instead of constantly disrupting the schedule by shifting to live reports.

The original idea was better. It packed more punch. In the early years we always tried to make things lively. Occasionally we tried too hard. One time NBC sent Merrill Muller and Jinx Falkenberg to cover a visit of Queen Elizabeth and Prince Philip to Ottawa. Morgan Beatty and I were co-hosting the show from New York, and Murray Burnett was producing. Burnett got a call from Muller asking, "How would you like an interview with the Queen?" "Fantastic," Murray said, and told me to announce to the audience that shortly we would be presenting a live interview with Queen Elizabeth. "Murray," I said, "you're kidding. The Queen doesn't grant interviews." Murray replied, "If Muller says he can get one, he can get one." "Look, Murray," I protested, "I'm a Canadian and I know about the protocol of British royalty. There is no way Muller is going to get an interview with the Queen." At which point Murray told me to do as I was told.

So Beatty went on with the show and every five or ten minutes I came on to announce that shortly we would be having an interview with the Queen. Twenty minutes passed, then forty, and still no interview. The switchboard began to light up with calls from listeners wondering what had happened. Meanwhile Muller and Jinx were broadcasting the reception ceremonies in Ottawa, but without the interview. Then Murray got Muller on the phone. "Don't worry," Muller said. "I'll get to her any time now. Just play records and tapes and fill in until I can get it." Apparently, someone had told him he could get to the Queen, but as I expected, it wasn't happening.

An hour passed. By now everybody up to General Sarnoff was calling us. The network executives who had been listening in were worried, and worrying Murray, who was starting to sweat heavily, but I kept making the announcements and telling Murray I had told him so. Which, of course, endeared me to him. Jinx described the Queen's entrance into a ballroom. I couldn't resist making a suggestion to Murray: "Tell her to grab Philip, and say, 'Hey, Prince-baby, how about a few words?'" And Murray replied, "A few more words from you and your head will roll." Then Muller called and said, "I understand the Queen has gone to sleep. I guess there won't be an interview." Murray just stared at the phone in disbelief.

Desperate, his job at stake, Murray was suddenly struck with an inspiration. Urgently, he huddled with Beatty and wrote something out for him. Then he told me to introduce Beatty and the interview. I was dumbfounded but did as he asked. "And now," I said, "here is Morgan Beatty to bring you Merrill Muller's interview with Queen Elizabeth from Ottawa." And Beatty said, "Ladies and gentlemen, we have Jinx Falkenberg and Merrill Muller on the line from Ottawa and Merrill has Queen Elizabeth with him for an interview. Hello there, Jinx. Jinx? . . . Jinx? . . . *Jinx? Are you there Jinx? . . . The line is dead!*" He was reading it slowly, like a child reciting aloud. "I'm sorry . . . ladies and gentlemen . . . the line to

Ottawa must be down . . . We cannot continue our conversation with Merrill Muller and the Queen of England in Ottawa . . . If it can be repaired in time, we will return to it . . . And now . . ." The show went on, but not with me. I was laughing too hard.

Murray Burnett was quite a character. We used to broadcast a harness race from Roosevelt Raceway every Saturday, and Burnett started to book our bets. Since most of us knew nothing about trotters, we each bet a different horse. If one of us won, Murray would pay off the price announced by the track, but he always came out ahead. This went on for weeks. One night I came in with a tip on a hot horse. I told the others, and we all put our money on the same horse. Murray was surprised by that and not sure he liked it. When the horse finished first, he was sure he didn't like it. When we went to collect, he refused. The payoff was $8 or so, but with all the winners, he owed us a pile. He said, "Nothing doing. You guys ganged up on me. I'll refund your bets, but I'll be damned if I'll be taken." So he stopped booking bets and we stopped betting.

When I began *Cowboy Theater*, I met with the producer and we discussed my background. He wanted to westernize me, of course, and he was delighted to learn I was from cattle country in western Canada. I told him how my grandfather had practically ridden the range and how my father and uncle had helped him. I told him my uncle owned a string of horses and wild west ponies and at one time led parades at the Calgary Stampede. He sent all this information to the publicity department, which worked up some exotic releases. Then he took me to a specialty store on Fifth Avenue and bought me some expensive cowboy-style shirts.

There I was, Mr. Wild West himself. I didn't have to wear cowboy pants or boots on the air because I was seen only from the waist up. The studio was not much

bigger than an outhouse, and they paneled the walls
and hung up some guns and portraits of wild geese in
flight. I'd sit there and announce the movie, which
usually was 1930's vintage and starred Charles Starrett
or Buck Jones. I got pretty damn tired of the chase
scenes—but it was a wonderful show, nevertheless,
with that son of the Old West, Monty Hall, sitting
there in that Old West outhouse telling everyone what
they were watching and making pitches for a toy company every five minutes. An actor couldn't make a fast
draw before it was time for another commercial. He'd
be half way through the draw, and I'd throw in a commercial; he'd complete the draw, and I'd throw in
another commercial. I was at the peak of my profession,
all right. But then I guess Ronald Reagan did much
the same thing as host of *Death Valley Days.*

The show started in September, and about a month
before Thanksgiving a member of our sales department
called me and said, "Monty, great news. We have just
made a deal with Macy's. Guess who is going to be
the number one man in their Thanksgiving Day Parade
and ride the horse right at the front? Monty Hall,
that's who! You're going to be grand marshall of the
parade." "You're kidding," I said. "Who could be more
natural than Monty Hall?" he replied. "Star of
Cowboy Theater, descended from a long line of horse-
men and ranchers? What a boost it will be for you
and the show." I said, "Look, there's something I have
to tell you. I've never been on a horse in my life."
There was a long silence on the other end of the line.
It was his turn to say, "You're kidding." "What made
you think I had?" I asked. "Your publicity," he said.
"Oh, that," I replied. "Well, it was true as far as it went.
But as for me, I never rode a horse outside of a
carousel. I never rustled a steer or did anything like
that." He said, "It would be such good publicity."
I said, "I think it would be bad publicity to have old

Cowboy Monty thrown from his horse while it was standing still in front of the parade and in front of millions of people. There is no way I am going to make a fool of myself by trying to ride a horse for the first time at the head of a parade." "No way?" he asked. "No way," I answered. And he never spoke to me again.

The show lasted twenty-six weeks, which was routine, and when it was over I was out the $500 a week and back looking for a new show while living on my paychecks from *Monitor* and *Who Am I?* Despite the ups and downs, we had bought a house in New Rochelle, figuring it was foolish to pay rent when we could be building up equity in a house of our own. So now I had a fairly fancy place, but I didn't have the jobs to support it in style. So we took a Florida vacation. In this business the only time you have for vacations is when you're unemployed. A tan means you're "at liberty."

In some ways the period I entered into next was the worst of my professional life. I was known and should have been able to make it, but I couldn't. There was nothing for me. I came close to a few things, but I missed out. Walt Framer once called me in to meet Bess Myerson. They had been working together on *The Big Payoff*, and it had gone off the air. He was trying to come up with a new show for her, and he wanted a man to be emcee. Bess, of course, is a former Miss America, a beautiful woman—and tall, more than six feet in high heels. I'm a little under six feet, and when we met I looked up at her. I talked to her on tiptoe for a while. Finally I laughed and said, "Bess, if we do this show, you're going to have to work in your stocking feet." She looked down at me and replied, "No chance. Bess Myerson does not work in her stocking feet." That was that.

Though I didn't have anything to do, I kept going

into New York every day anyway. As the saying goes, Marilyn had married me for better or worse, but not for lunch. I had seen all the people I had to see, and they all knew I wanted work. Marilyn saw that hanging around the house was torture for me. So she threw me out, and I was glad to go. She urged me to get on the commuter train and ride into the city every day and visit people and keep in touch and let them know I was still around. And so I put in a nine-to-five day in the city just like all the working people. I'd check in with Marilyn a couple of times a day to see if there had been any calls. There never seemed to be any.

I'd go into the RCA Building and go up to the NBC studios and walk through the office and kibitz with the *Monitor* production staff. Or I'd go up to Ed Wolf's offices, because I felt like a member of the family. Ed had a sister on the switchboard, and a nephew, a son, an uncle, and a brother-in-law on his staff. He always had people around because it was a comfortable place to be. I always was welcome in whatever meeting was taking place, and I sat and listened and once in a while made a suggestion. When they had lunch, I was always invited. I was treated wonderfully. No one there ever put me down or said anything about my situation. I guess they realized I had to have some place to go, some place where I felt I belonged, at least on the fringes.

As the weeks went by, it got harder to endure this existence, and the rejections got harder to accept. I remember Mort Werner one day saying, "I think I've got something for you. We're going to revive the *Bride and Groom* show, and we're thinking of you as the emcee. I want you to go and meet the producer, Roger Gimbel." All this sounded sadly familiar to me, but what choice did I have? I made an appointment and went to see Roger Gimbel.

I had never met him. His office walls didn't reach the ceiling, and from where a visitor waited by the receptionist's desk, you could hear some of the talk coming from inside. I was on time but kept waiting, as usual. He was with someone else, and his secretary hadn't even announced me when I caught part of his telephone conversation: "Yes, we're trying to revive *Bride and Groom,* and we need an emcee. But the toughest thing of all is to find an emcee. Every time I start looking for one, the program department always sends me the same five or six old names—Bill Cullen, Bert Parks, Dennis James, Monty Hall, Bud Collyer. . . ."

I sat straight up, almost in shock. What the hell was this? How many shows had I done? Had many weeks had I been on the air? How could I possibly be classified as one of the same old names? I had never even met the man, much less auditioned for him or worked for him.

"Yeah, the same old names. They never find me anybody new and that's what you need—someone new. The public is tired of the same damn faces all the time."

I was new, even if he didn't know it. Nationally, the public had hardly seen my face. I was being damned for having been around a while looking for work, even if I seldom got any. As I listened to him, I got madder and madder.

Finally, his visitor left and his secretary told him his next appointment was waiting. She neglected to say who it was, however. He looked at me, and he obviously didn't know who I was. I said, "You don't know who I am, do you? Well, I'm one of those old faces you're getting tired of having suggested to you for your shows. I'm Monty Hall and I'm number four on your list. . . ."

I had caught him off guard, and he apologized. "Look, no offense meant, but every time we do a show, the program department sends us a list of names; and although

I've never met you, I guess, seeing your name on that list all the time, I automatically put you in the same category as the others."

Maybe his embarrassment turned to anger at having been embarrassed. In any event, I never heard from him again. Robert Paige, the former movie actor, was brought in to emcee the show, but it went off after a short run. I have no idea whether I could have made it a better or more successful show. Naturally, I feel I could have. In this business, if you don't think you can, you can't. You need confidence. A good-sized ego is almost indispensable. You have to sell yourself, your personality, to the public. But first you must sell yourself to the network or the agency.

I won a lot of auditions and lost a lot of shows because I wasn't a big name, or the producer preferred a friend. By God, I was good at this, and I had proven it. But I couldn't get a chance then, and it was tough to be shut out for the wrong reasons.

I feel for all the good actors who are always out of work. There are talented performers tending bar or running liquor stores or selling shoes or real estate or insurance all over Hollywood. You run into these familiar faces all the time, and it embarrasses you and makes you feel sad for them.

I was deeply depressed. I stopped going into the city and sat home. My brother wrote me. He had established his legal practice during the time I had gotten next to nowhere in show business. He knew I was struggling again. "You've got it," he wrote, "but they don't seem to want it, so why suffer their refusals and insults? Why is it so important to be a performer? It's time you gave your family some security. My practice is going well. Why not join me? You're still young enough to go back to school. Together, the Hall brothers will be invincible."

I thought about it for months. I knew I would make

a good lawyer, and I would enjoy practicing with my brother. I would have a profession that no one could ever take from me. I would never have to face long layoffs and uncertainty, and I would never again have to sit at home waiting for the phone to ring. I thought about it for a long time. It was the only thing that made any sense—but I couldn't do it. I was a performer and I had to perform.

9

I WASN'T STARVING, of course. With *Monitor* and *Who Am I?* and an odd job here and there I was making around $500 a week, and we were able to live well on that. But I didn't have anything solid and I wasn't getting anywhere.

One day in late 1957 Steve Krantz said to me, "I've an idea for a show, and I want you to emcee and produce it. We're going to play Bingo on television, with the home audience. People at home will use the digits in their telephone numbers. We'll pull numbered balls out of a machine in the studio until we get calls from winners whose telephone number matches what we pull. We'll take the calls on the air, check out the numbers in a telephone book, and award prizes. Channel Five is interested in it as a local show, but if it works I think we can syndicate it across the country." I wasn't refusing any reasonable offers so I told him to count me in.

Through Bill Bratter, I had managed to get MCA,

the biggest talent agency in the country, to represent me. Dick Rubin became my personal representative and he got me $600 a week from Channel Five, with a year guaranteed, and 10 per cent of any syndication. The program was called *Bingo at Home* and went on the air early in 1958. Our first show must have jammed every switchboard on the east side of Manhattan. We hadn't realized how many thousands of people might get to a winning total at the same time. The next morning the telephone company came up and ripped out every line to our studio. That was the end of the telephone game. We had to improvise a new form of Bingo by that afternoon. We still used phone numbers but decided to do it by mail. We'd limit the amount of numbers on each show, wait for letters or postcards from winners, check them out, and reward them. We still had thousands of winners each show.

It was a terrible program, boring as could be, and I hated it. But it caught on. Not that anyone at the networks realized it. The ratings showed no one was watching. Still, we were getting 200,000 postcards or letters a week. You have to live by ratings in this business. There is no real replacement for them as a measurement of your show's appeal to the public. If ratings are good, you believe them. If they are bad, you doubt them.

Bingo was the lowest rated show in its time slot, but the mailmen were bringing us bundles of mail daily. We made all the papers and *Life* ran a full-page picture of me holding a numbered ping-pong ball. But the show died of its own devices. There were too many prizes. We couldn't keep up with them. Also, scores of people complained that we hadn't responded to their winning cards. Finally, we surrendered.

Before Bingo went off, I landed two important network shows. I was asked to substitute for Jack Barry on *Twenty-One,* which was the number-one

rated program in the country at the time. Game show
or not, this show, along with *The $64,000 Question*,
had a tremendous following of fans who wanted to
see whether an average person could answer awesome
questions on the way to wealth. I did well, and the
Barry-Enright office called to ask me to replace Barry
for a few weeks while he went on a night-club tour.
Later they asked if I'd be interested in taking over
full-time because Barry wanted to continue in his new
career. I almost knocked them over accepting. It was
worth $1000 a week to me, and it put me on coast to
coast.

At the same time, Ed Wolf had made me emcee of
Keep Talking on the CBS network. That was worth
another $1000 a week. Suddenly, I had two national
shows, a local show, and a Canadian show. Monday
nights, I did *Twenty One*. Tuesday nights, I did
Keep Talking. Every afternoon, Monday through Friday, I did *Bingo*. Saturdays, I did *Monitor*. Sundays, I
did my Canadian show, *Who Am I?* I was a busy guy
that month and in the $150,000-a-year bracket. That
month.

Keep Talking wasn't getting good ratings and after a
few weeks I was fired. Herb took some of us to lunch
at Longchamps and broke it there. "You know how it
is, kid," he said. "The show's in trouble and we got
orders to shake it up—new emcee, new panelists. Nothing personal, you know, but we got to let you go." And
I smiled and said, "Oh, hell, I know how it is. Don't
worry about me. Right after I enjoy these oysters
Rockefeller, I'm going to commit suicide." I put up a
big front, but I wasn't fooling anyone. It was a kick in
the ego, and it hurt.

Then I received another blow. I had been subbing for
Barry on *Twenty-One* and was about to take over for
him permanently when a report hit the newspapers
that the show was fixed. A former contestant named

Barry Stempel said that he had been offered a job with the show if he would lose and clear the way for a more popular contestant. He said he lost but didn't get the job. So he went to the D.A. He also charged that the contestants were given answers in advance. *Twenty-One* was not alone. Other big-money shows, such as *The $64,000 Question*, *The $64,000 Challenge*, and *Tic Tac Dough*, either already had been accused of fixing or were soon to be.

I couldn't bring myself to believe the charge. I never had knowledge of any such set-ups on any show I'd emceed, including *Twenty-One*. If it had been done, it had been engineered without my knowledge. Maybe they wouldn't have wanted the emcee to know about it so his reactions would be real and he wouldn't do anything to make anyone suspicious.

In any event, the Parkson Advertising Agency called me in and said they were sorry, but Barry was going to have to take over again at once because it was felt it would look bad if he wasn't on the air while investigations were taking place. The fix scandals spread and the big money giveaways folded fast. Some leading men in the business, including Barry, were out of work in the industry for many years.

I do recognize that the guilty seriously abused the public trust. Still, I think people like Barry were dealt with harshly. No one was really hurt. It was a deception, but so are wrestling and roller derbies, all done in the name of entertainment. The punishment didn't fit the crime. I'd have put the guilty on probation. Bank robbers and muggers usually get second chances, and often a lot faster than the Barrys.

In the wake of those scandals the shows I work on now have built-in safeguards. The networks police the shows closely. Producers and employees are liable, and the rules are followed to the letter. In the case of our shows, we would not jeopardize our position and success by any kind of hanky-panky, and I am sure that this holds for the entire industry today.

When *Bingo* was bounced, I suddenly was left without a show in America again. But the Channel Five producers had been pleased with my work, and Bennett Korn, the general manager, asked me what sort of show I'd like to do in that same one P.M. time period. When I suggested an interview show, he created *By-Line: Monty Hall*. It was a sort of *Tonight Show* in the afternoon. Every weekday I sat around a coffee table with actors, scientists, ministers, politicians—people from almost every field—and discussed their work and the world around them for a half-hour. I pride myself on my wide interests and ability to talk to people on any subject, so this was a tough test for me. I feel I passed even if the program did not. Our ratings showed no one was watching, although our mail showed many were. The letters called the show "an oasis in the desert of daytime television." But the sponsors were dissatisfied with the ratings, and we went off the air.

As I have said before, I have made many compromises in my career, and experiences like *By-Line* only reinforce my belief that before one can become a patron of the arts, he had better get himself some wherewithal. In other words, the first step toward becoming a philanthropist is to earn some money. At this stage of my life, that seemed to be the paramount issue.

With the demise of *By-Line* I was willing to do any kind of show at all to take its place. I had a contract with Channel Five to fulfill, and I did anything they wanted me to, including announcing wrestling matches.

The wrestling was a farce. I broadcast these shows every week from Sunnyside Gardens in Queens. I just did them straight and didn't hoke them up the way others did. It was a job. Every match was scheduled to be the best of three falls, but we had arranged that every match would go the limit. That way we could get in more commercials.

The fans were frightening because most of them believed in it, although the fakery was transparent to anyone with eyesight. A friend of mine, Dr. Abe Kroll, a dentist and man of many talents and much intelligence, was hooked on wrestling. He used to plead with me to take him to one of the shows. I kept saying that if he did go he would see how phony they were and be disappointed. But he didn't want to hear about the phoniness, he just wanted to go. So one night I took him. I showed him the briefing room where wrestlers were getting their instructions. I told him exactly what would happen. I let him sit near me at ringside to see it happen exactly as predicted. We ran far overdue on a commercial and I signaled to the referee several times before he finally simply disqualified both contestants to give us a break. The good dentist saw it all. As we drove home, I said, "Abe, I'm sorry, but now you must see it for what it is." And Abe said, "What it is is the most exciting thing going. I don't care about the side stuff. I enjoyed every minute of it. I want to go again." Well, there is one born every minute.

I heard there was a job open with the New York Rangers as color man on their hockey broadcasts. Les Keiter of WINS was impressed enough with me and my knowledge of the game to hire me without an audition. Because of my other commitments in town, I could only work the home games. This made it pretty tough on Jim Gordon, the play-by-play man, because he had to do both play-by-play and color on the road. I got a fast fifty a game for my Wednesday and Sunday nights in Madison Square Garden. But as a Canadian I had come to love the game, and I might have gone on for nothing if asked. I did the games for two seasons, but had to resign when I started *Video Village*.

My strongest memory of this show was when I got
the team's coach, Phil Watson, fired. I had Watson on
between periods of one of the Rangers' worst games
and asked him why the team was playing so badly.
Phil, a fiery fellow, told me why right out, ripping
each player in turn. He started out, "Well, take Worsley
[the goalie], with that beer belly on him. He couldn't
stop a barrel from rolling into the net." He went on
from there: this player was selfish and another was
lazy and that one had no ability and another was
wasting his energy chasing broads. Muzz Patrick, the
Ranger general manager, was listening, and as soon as
we were off the air Watson was no longer coach.

That summer I got a job telecasting International
Soccer League games from the Polo Grounds over
WPIX. There were teams from Germany, Italy, Hun-
gary, Yugoslavia, England, Scotland, Brazil, and so
forth, but despite New York's enormous ethnic population from countries where soccer was the top sport,
no one came to the games.

I enjoyed these play-by-play telecasts because they
required fast thinking and apt description. I have never
believed that a play-by-play announcer should relate
only what is happening on the field, but as a reporter
should try to convey to the audience the nuances:
"What is the strategy now? What is the manager thinking of? What would you do in this situation?" This
draws the listener or viewer into the action and gives
him a chance to be an armchair quarterback. So I never
missed an opportunity to interpret an action. For example, soccer players have a marvelous tendency to
showboat. When injured, they swoon and lie on the field
immobile. After eliciting the crowd's sympathy, they
jump miraculously to their feet and resume two-way
action at top speed. Accordingly, when I saw a player
go into a Sarah Bernhardt, I couldn't resist saying:
"Keep your eyes on Stanislaus. He's lying there like

dead, but I guarantee he'll be on his feet in sixty seconds." And he always was.

Among the incidents I recall is one that arose when
the Yugoslavian team was playing Brazil. Before the
game could start, we had to have first the United States
national anthem, followed by the national anthems of
the two visiting countries. After "The Star Spangled
Banner" and the Brazilian anthem, the Polo Grounds
public address system started on the Yugoslavian anthem. The very courteous audience in the stands was
appalled to see the Yugoslavian team break ranks and
start to kick the ball around. They booed the athletes
for their disrespect. Knowing there had to be a reason,
I surmised over the air: "The only thing I can think
of, folks, is that these players are all Titoists, and the
only record we have here is the national anthem that
was played under Mihailovich." After the game, I found
I was right.

I received some great compliments for my soccer re-
porting. The president of the Scottish team Kilmarnock
wrote a letter to the soccer league saying that I was the
best soccer announcer he had ever heard. A *Cue Magazine* critic called me one of the best play-by-play men
he'd come across in any sport. It may be hard to forget
criticism, but it is easy to remember compliments.

About this time I gave up *Who Am I?* It had been on
the air for ten years, but I couldn't continue without
returning to Canada. As that show went off, my bank
account began to shrink. A Channel Five executive
called to remind me that the station had a contract
with me calling for $800 a week until the end of the
year and that they wanted me to do something to earn
it. I agreed that was fair enough.

He said they wanted me to do a children's show.
My blood ran cold. If there was one thing I didn't
want, it was a children's show. He said, "You'll tape
the show during the week and it'll play for three hours
on Saturday mornings." To me it was like the end of

the world. I ran cartoons and educational films and I played games with the kids. I sat around and talked to them and felt like a fool every minute. After four or five weeks I quit. No weekly paycheck was worth that to me.

I don't remember the name of the show, and neither does Marilyn. I don't want to remember. That was the ebb of my career, worse even than doing the wrestling.

An odd blessing emerged, however. I used to have the cameras pan across the faces of the children in the audience and linger on a closeup on each one, figuring that this would be a thrill for their relatives. After the show had been off the air a while, I met a woman at a party. She said, "I want to thank you for the warmest moment of my life. My mother was in the hospital dying of an incurable disease. More than anything, she wanted to see my little boy, her only grandson, but children were not permitted to visit patients in the hospital. My son was going to be on your show. I knew you put a picture of each child on and prayed you would do so with my son this time. So we brought a TV set into Mother's room. As your show came on, she was in a coma, but the moment you put a picture of her grandson on screen her eyes opened. She saw her grandson, smiled, and died hours later. Thanks to you, my last memory of my mother is with a smile on her face."

Performers occasionally have a frightening emotional impact on the public, and it is a large responsibility. I hated that show, yet in a few seconds I gave two women something almost supernatural. And it may be that those moments make it all worthwhile.

During that period, Bill Bratter died of a heart attack. When I got word of his death, I went to the funeral parlor in Manhattan to pay my respects. There I saw grown men sit and cry, for he had helped others as he had helped me. I could have used a Bill Bratter in my life during the tumultuous times that were to come.

10

WHILE I HAD *Twenty-One, Keep Talking, Bingo, Monitor,* and *Who Am I?* all going at once, I heard that Jack Paar was going to take a week's vacation from *The Tonight Show.* I asked my agent if he could get the week for me. He looked at me as if I were crazy and exclaimed, "You!" That was a great boost to my ego.

Some agents are marvelous. When you need them, they could care less. When you don't need them, they care. I remember sitting in the office of an MCA agent who was handling Red Buttons. Red had been big on TV for a couple of seasons, but his show had gone off. A secretary buzzed the agent to tell him Red was calling. The agent said, "Oh, for Christ's sake, get rid of him. Who needs him?" Then he turned back to me. He didn't need me, either.

In the 1950's Bill Bratter had talked MCA into giving me an agent on a three-year contract. The agent didn't do a thing for me, and I'm sure he didn't even try. He never called me. About three years later I

186

figured I'd try to get someone else, and I called the
agency to find out when my contract was up. The
secretary said, "You've been finished with us for three
months." That hit me pretty hard. They hadn't even
bothered to call or send a note. I had been removed
from their roster, from the face of the earth.

My morale really hit rock bottom when all my
shows went off the air. For a time my friends and I
tried to develop ideas for shows in hopes that we would
hit the jackpot. One of my co-workers at *Monitor*
was Bernie Kahn. He had a friend, Nat Ligerman, who
ran a laundromat in Greenwich Village to keep body
and soul together. Nat had a sign in his shop that read:
"You don't know what you're missing until you use my
laundromat." And to prove it, every one of his customers missed something. Nat had three sons at the
time, and keeping them in clothing was difficult. His
customers made unscheduled contributions. Among his
clientele were such stars as Anthony Franciosa and
Jason Robards, Jr. To this day they don't realize that
their underwear was being worn by assorted Ligerman
children.

Bernie and Nat used to bring me ideas, and I would
reject them. Nat wanted to be in show business even if
it meant sweeping up after the elephant in the circus.
He operated his thirty-two machine laundromat only
because it brought in a buck. It also brought in television people who lived in the area, and he could try
out ideas on them or ask them for jobs. He used to send
ideas and scripts to the network executives, and he
called himself Nat Ligerman Productions.

One day Nat answered the phone with his usual bark:
"Laundromat!" The caller turned out to be a partner at
Doyle, Dane, Bernbach advertising agency. One of Nat's
submissions intrigued him. He asked, "Incidentally, did
you say 'laundromat'?" Nat immediately changed direction: "No, no! I said, 'Ligerman Productions.'" At that

moment washing machine number 16 started spilling suds, flooding the store. Nat's only assistant, a Puerto Rican boy by the name of Chico, was in the back of the shop sorting out the stolen socks. "Chico!" Nat screamed, searching desperately for someone to help him, since he could not and would not dare leave the telephone. He turned back to his caller for a moment and then again desperately shrieked "Chico!" At the third summons a head peeked around the barrier and answered, "What ees eet, Nat?" Ligerman, having a prospective client on the phone and unwilling to reveal the true nature of his predicament, shouted, "Camera 16's gone crazy!" The man on the other end was stunned. "Sixteen cameras?" he asked. Nat regained his composure. "I got thirty-two!" he said proudly.

The show didn't sell, but Camera 16 was fixed so it stopped flooding. One day Nat and his buddy Bernie brought me an idea, but I didn't go for it and had to reject it. As they were leaving, Ligerman paused and asked, "What's the first thing you'd say if I said the word 'black'?" I said, "White." Ligerman said, "Yes, but maybe someone else could say 'cat' or 'dark' or 'night.'" "Come back in here," I said. He returned, grinning. He said, "I wanted to try that on you because maybe there is a show in free association." And that was the beginning of a program we called *First Impressions*—and, for that matter, several other shows.

I spent weeks developing the idea, and came up with a two-part program. In the first part the audience would be shown key words, and contestants came up with answers based on clue words. In the second part married couples would answer the clue word separately, and if they matched them in free association, they would get points toward a winner's prize.

A friend of mine did some art work and I arranged an appointment to discuss the show with Oscar Katz, head of daytime programing at CBS. Nat Ligerman, desperate to get into show business full-time, called me nightly from the laundromat to see what progress we were making with the show. When he heard I had an audience with a CBS executive, he begged to go along. I said, "No, Nat. You have no experience in television or in meetings like this. You're overanxious, and you're liable to say something that will screw us up." He said, "No, I won't, I swear it. I just want to tag along. I've got a good suit. I'll shave. I'll sit in a corner and never open my mouth." Reluctantly, I agreed.

The next day we went to 485 Madison Avenue, and I made the presentation to Katz. Nat, true to his word, sat silently in a corner. Oscar was interested and proposed what is called a "step deal." He said, "We'll give you some offices next door at 501 Madison and we'll give you some money to prepare an audio tape. If it looks good, we'll shoot a pilot. If that works, we'll go on the air. To begin with, we'll give you, let's say, $8000 as work-up money."

Nat, who never in his life had heard of so much money being given out at one time, jumped out of his seat and shouted, "Eight thousand dollars!" Oscar Katz, who was really interested in the show and thought my partner was outraged by the size of the offer, leaped from his seat and shouted back, "All right, make it $12,000."

I couldn't believe it. "Sold!" I yelled, and hustled Ligerman out of there before Katz found out what had hit him. I said, "Damn it, Nat, you almost blew it." "Did I?" he asked. He wasn't sure what had happened. I told him, "Hell, no. You got us four grand extra."

We produced an audio, but CBS didn't buy it. I took it to a friend, Bob Stewart, who worked for Goodson-Todman, the game show people. He took it down the hall to show Mark Goodson. When Stewart returned, he suggested some changes. I went home and worked on it, came back, and talked over the changes with Stewart. He went down the hall and talked them over with Goodson. Then he returned with more refinements. This routine went on for weeks. I was never permitted to see Goodson. Stewart would suggest changes. I'd go home, work on them, and bring them back. Then Goodson would always suggest still other refinements.

Stewart finally talked Goodson into trying our idea out on *I've Got a Secret*. Garry Moore, who was the emcee at that time, told his celebrity panel, "I'm going to try an experiment on you. I will say something to you, and you give me the first thing that comes to mind." I forget the words involved, but it worked well under the circumstances. But it didn't seem to sell Goodson and I got tired of my trips to see Stewart and his invisible boss, so I gave up on that end.

Another friend, Perry Leff of the Frank Cooper agency, put me in touch with a New York producer named Art Stark, who took a shine to the show and suggested we try to work out a format that would use a celebrity panel. By that time I was willing to try anything, so I invited Art to be my partner in the project. We started to develop the show along new lines and soon we arranged a run-through for CBS.

Stark was working on a show called *Who Do You Trust?* with Johnny Carson as emcee. We got Carson, columnist Murray Kempton, and some others as a panel. They had to identify celebrity guests through free association of words and hints. Joan Fontaine, Jan Murray, and Louella Parsons were the guests. On the day of the run-through New York was hit with one of the biggest snowstorms in its history. It looked as if we were lost, but we hired bulldozers to dig people out of the suburbs and somehow got Oscar Katz and other executives to the studio. Only Jan Murray, in Scarsdale, couldn't make it, so we did his bit by telephone. The show went off all right, but nothing came of it. That was not unusual. Most television series take a lot of selling, because no one is sure what will succeed. Even if a network or a sponsor falls in love with a show, they aren't sure that the public will.

In September 1960 something solid turned up at last. One day Alden Schwimmer of the Ted Ashley agency was driving me home from the golf course when I saw my wife and my car going the other way on the parkway. "What is she doing?" I wondered aloud. I found out twenty minutes later when Alden dropped me off and Marilyn returned. She had been searching for me desperately. I was wanted as a rush replacement for a show in New York.

When I returned their call, they said, "Thank God we've reached you. You've got to do this show tomorrow morning. Can you do it?" Without hesitation, I said, "I'll try." Then I said, "What show?" They said, "Video Village. Do you know the show?" "I have to be honest," I admitted. "I've never even seen it. You show me how and I'll do it." They told me to come on in, so I drove into New York.

That summer CBS had bought a show called *Video Village* and made Jack Narz emcee. Narz, however, was having domestic difficulties. He had a wife and a home in California and a five-day-a-week live show in New York. His wife wanted him to stay home. He had asked CBS to shift the show to California, but they had not agreed. Now he had suddenly gone back home to talk matters over with his wife, and someone had to be found to do the program the very next day.

The show was like a Parcheesi game. It was laid out on a large board and the contestants moved up and down the board by rolling dice. The show's originators, Heatter and Quigley, laid out the board in a hotel meeting room, and we went over and over it. The next morning at CBS I did a couple of rehearsals. We went on the air at 10:30, and it worked. I saved the day. The Heatter and Quigley people poured praise all over me. They were very grateful and I was elated.

That afternoon Narz called and said he was giving up the show to save his marriage. I was asked to carry on for a few days. After those programs went well, they asked me if I would be willing to do it permanently. I said I would, and they went to the CBS brass and asked permission to make me the permanent emcee.

Jim Aubrey, then the big boss at the network, was leaving for Hawaii. He said he had someone else in mind for the spot, an old friend from California named Red Rowe. Heatter and Quigley argued that I'd pulled them through in a pinch and deserved the job. But Aubrey insisted on his man, and Rowe came in and worked a couple of shows.

But Perry Leff, who was representing me, and Heatter and Quigley were persistent. They went to Larry White, head of daytime programing, and said, "Tell Aubrey we want Hall." White courageously made the decision while his boss was away. Aubrey returned and apparently gave in. I suppose he had done what he felt was the honorable thing for his old friend, and then had decided to do what was best for the show. So I got a national network program, at $1250 a week, with my name up in lights on the marquee outside Theatre 52 just off Broadway.

Several ironic twists followed. Despite his return to California, Narz's marriage ended within months. Then in February CBS decided to move the show to California as Narz had wanted them to do originally. I decided to go along with the show, since it was becoming clear to everyone in the business that the bulk of the television production was shifting to Los Angeles. Anyway, aside from *Monitor*, I had nothing to give up. Marilyn agreed.

Then, just before I was to leave for the coast, Bob

Stewart called me for the first time in months and invited me to lunch at the Stage Delicatessen. He said, "That idea of yours, *First Impressions*, is still the best idea that's come across my desk in a long time, and I've finally got Mark Goodson interested enough so that we can go ahead and start working on it together." I told him I had already made a deal with Art Stark, was going to California, and it was too late. "Well, that's too bad," he said.

In March Marilyn and I left the kids with a sitter and went west. It was warm when we arrived in Los Angeles, and we were wearing heavy winter coats. When I stepped off the plane, I took off my coat and said, "That's it. No more coats. I'm staying." We fell in love with sunny southern California right then. Once I got there, I never wanted to leave. You live better— it's that simple.

We didn't feel secure enough to buy a house right away, but we rented a lovely place in the hills of Laurel Canyon for $600 a month. It was like living in the country. I had to do five *Video Village* shows and one *Kideo Village* show, a Saturday children's version, weekly, but we started to tape and wrapped them up in three days. The rest of the time I lay around the pool or played golf. It was such a different way of life, half vacation all the time.

I remember the first day I went to work in Los Angeles. I rented a little Corvair and drove up to the CBS gate in a line of large cars. Right ahead of me was the producer of *Video Village* in a Rolls Royce, the director in a Jaguar, and my assistant, Eileen Barton, a prominent singer, in a Cadillac. As each pulled up to the gate, the car was waved right in. When I pulled up in the Corvair, I was stopped and the guard asked who I was. I said, "Look, buddy. You waved all the others in without asking that question. But I've got news for you. If you don't let me in, Corvair or not, there's no show today!" After he found out who I was, he let me in. I get in easier now.

I always have enjoyed studio work. It may be the same old show, but every time you do one it's new and offers something different. I enjoy the cameraderie of the crew. I have never had an argument of any kind with anyone on the floor of one of my shows. We may not agree on how everything should be done, but we work it out. I'm not temperamental. It takes a lot of people doing many jobs well to make a show successful. Any one of them can mess it up, but most of them don't. There are a lot of pros in television who work hard but who do not get rich or famous, and I appreciate them.

In the summer of that year, I began to have severe abdominal pains. The doctor whom I consulted said I had an infection and needed surgery, which he later performed. But after six months I was so little improved I went to another doctor. He discovered that the surgery had been a waste of time. My problem stemmed from a slight perforation of the small intestine, and as long as the intestine leaked, the infection would re-form. Just when it seemed that more surgery was needed, almost miraculously, the perforation sealed and the infection drained away.

I continued to have severe stomach distress from time to time, however, and further examination by a gastroenterologist revealed that I had ileitis. Because of my stomach trouble and the problems I've had with my back, some have labeled me a hypochondriac. But I have missed only twenty shows in ten years on *Let's Make a Deal* and none on *Video Village* for two years.

That first winter I worked in constant pain, but I tried not to impose my discomfort on anyone else. At Christmas time a very nice thing happened to me. The producers and performers always throw parties or give gifts to their crews. It's a custom, and crews expect

it. They are never expected to respond in kind, and
they almost never do. One day I was lying down in my
dressing room during the lunch break when there was
a knock at the door. I asked who it was but couldn't
make out the name. Wearily, I got up and opened the
door.

There standing before me with wide smiles on their
faces were fifteen or twenty members of the CBS crew.
They handed me a box, and some of them shouted,
"Open it up . . . open it up." I opened the package
and there was a tall, handsomely carved wooden pepper
mill with a crown on it. "Read the card . . . read the
card," they yelled. It had been specially prepared by
the art department, and it read, "To the King of Television from all his Crew." They had all signed their
names to it.

I was deeply touched. One of the old hands, a little
guy who always wore a hat, said, "Son, this is an important thing we just done for you. To tell you how
important it is, we've only done it once before, and
that was for Jimmy Durante. So I wanted you to know
this is kind of important to us as well as to you." He
didn't have to tell me.

I had never really given up hope on *First Impressions* and still hoped to sell it somehow. Shortly after
my surgery, I read an item in the trade papers that
Mark Goodson and Bill Todman were starting a new
show called *Password* on CBS. It sounded suspiciously
like what I had been trying to sell them earlier. My
lawyer, Roy Blakeman, who had taken over my affairs
after Bill Bratter died, was also the lawyer for Goodson-
Todman, and I asked him about the new show. He
said, "I knew you'd read the item and wonder about
it, but it's absolutely not the same thing you showed to
Mark. Don't get excited about it. Call Bob Stewart
first thing in the morning."

I called Bob Stewart. It was one of the most painful

telephone calls I've ever experienced. He said, "Yes, Monty, what can I do for you?" I said, "Didn't Roy Blakeman tell you I was going to call?" He said, "No, he didn't. Why are you calling?" I said, "I'm calling because I heard about *Password*." And he said, "Monty, I knew you were going to call about that. I knew it would upset you." I was getting very upset.

"Look," he said. "I'll level with you, but it's just between us. When I had that last conversation with you and you told me you were no longer interested in working with us on your show, I reported it to Mark. He said, 'Well, we're going to go to work on this idea anyhow.' We changed it and worked up a sale. I said, 'Don't you think we ought to cut Monty in on this because he brought the show to us in the first place?' And he said, 'No, Freud was with us long before Monty Hall.' So that's it. I wanted you to know how it is. But I will not repeat it publicly. I'm sorry."

I'm sure he was, for Bob Stewart is a decent fellow. He was, in essence, telling me where his loyalties lay. I couldn't blame him. Show business is a jungle. Survival of the fittest.

I called Blakeman back and told him what Stewart had told me. He said only that he was headed back to New York and would look into the matter there.

A few days later he called me and said, "Mark wants you to come to New York." I said, "Well, that's more like it." "Wait a minute," he said. "He wants you to come to New York to prove to you that he had this idea long before you brought it to him." I replied angrily, "You mean he wants me to go all the way to New York just to tell me I'm wrong?" Roy said, "Yes, he says you're wrong. He claims that he had the idea before you ever entered the office."

"Well, then, I'm going to sue him," I said. Roy pointed out that he also represented Mark and would have to withdraw from the case. I told him I'd get another lawyer. And I did.

Meanwhile, NBC started another Goodson-Todman show called *The Match Game* in which three contestants wrote down their reactions to a word and if they matched with one another they received points toward prizes. Since this procedure was outlined in the second half of my original show, I figured I had a second lawsuit to file. And now NBC would be involved, too.

However, Larry White at CBS told me, "Look, you're working here as an emcee on our network. It wouldn't look good for you to be suing another packager on our network and to be biting the hand that's feeding you."

But then, right in the middle of the controversy, NBC turned around and bought my own program, *First Impressions*. I was delighted but perplexed. Some of my friends said I should go ahead with the suits. People at the networks obviously urged me not to. An idea is an idea, they said. We all have them. You can't prove one belonged to you. If you want to keep working in the business, you can't sue people.

In the end, I did not pursue the lawsuits. I was a little man in the business, and I would have been bucking the big shots. I could never have gotten ownership of the shows; the most I could have gotten was some money, perhaps royalties. I wanted to get ahead, and suits would have alienated people.

I am not unfamiliar with suits myself. Since becoming a successful producer, I have had countless people pounding at the door to show their ideas. As a favor to some friends, I have met with a few. Nothing has ever come of it. But as soon as a new show is started, inevitably a phone call comes from a lawyer, saying, "You stole this from my client!" "What on earth did we steal?" I ask. The lawyers answers, "Well, his show also has three panelists!" Such suits are always dropped. A dentist who came to visit me one day insisted he had the greatest panel show of all time. He explained that three celebrity panelists tried to identify a man's occu-

pation by interrogating him. I looked at him with up-
lifted eyebrows. "That's it?" I asked. "That's it," he replied. "Haven't you ever heard of *What's My Line?*" I
queried. "What the hell's that?" he shot back. I said,
"Well, it's only been on CBS Sunday nights a dozen
years or more!" The dentist was furious. "The hell you
say," he muttered, taking up his portfolio and leaving
the office in a huff.

Three shows developed out of the idea of a free
association game. *Password* has been a great hit and
remains on the air to this day. *Match Game* had its
success, and so did *First Impressions.* Selling it was a
thrill, though the experience was diluted by the heart-
break of all that went with it. After I flew back to
New York, Art Stark and I signed the contracts, and
I had made my first major sale in this country. Since
the show was to be done in California, we offered to
move all those who had helped us put it together in
New York. Bernie Kahn came out as a writer. Nat
Ligerman wanted to go more than anyone, but as
what? "As anything," he said. "I'll sweep the floors. I'll
run messages. I just want to get out of the laundry
business and into show business, and this is my chance."
So I told Nat to come out. I made him a production
assistant and later an associate producer. He's been with
me ever since.

We took offices in the NBC building at Sunset and
Vine and set up shop in November 1961. The title of
the show was changed to *Your First Impression* because
First Impressions is a subtitle of *Little Women,* and the
network, like all networks, was nervous about anything
that could cause any complications.

There were problems with the show from the start.
Among those who had come with us from New York
was Fred Stettner, who was a brother-in-law of Dan
Enright—and thus involved by association in the quiz
show scandals of 1958 along with Barry and Enright.

Some people at NBC remained determined that none of these people would ever work in television again. However, I would not fire him. An hour before the first show was to go on the air, we got a call from an NBC executive in New York telling us not to use Stettner's name in the credits or the show would be taken off the air.

I told Stettner and he said if his name were removed, he would sue. I knew he had a case. I asked him to let it go for now so we could get through our first show and I'd fight the good fight for him the following week, but he refused. He was fighting for his life—and I was fighting for my show. In desperation I got on the phone. It was past quitting time in New York, and I had to track down NBC executives at their homes, but I did obtain permission to use the credit.

Afterward I was angry with the NBC executives who had posed this problem in the first place, and I was angry, too, with Stettner, for not backing down briefly. He was and is a friend, but I still think he was wrong in this case. In this business, the show is the thing. What the hell does principle do for you if you screw up the show? Putting on these shows is a team effort, and we all have to pull together. This was opening night. And it damn near was closing night at the same time.

The incident goes to show how this business bends you. I admire men of principle and have fought for my own. Maybe I was wrong to ask Stettner to lower his fists even for a minute. But we all run scared in television. He was. And I was. We didn't have positions of power; we had few weapons; we were desperate for survival. It's easier to fight when you're not afraid, when a failure doesn't threaten to finish you.

Your First Impression started off struggling. The format wasn't working right, and there were personnel problems. Art Stark started to telephone every day to offer advice. Then Bob Aaron of NBC started to call from New York with his own daily observations. Somehow we got through the first thirteen weeks, and our option was picked up for another thirteen weeks, but I knew we were in trouble. I flew back to New York to meet with Stark and Aaron, and I laid down the law. This was my show and I was not going to see it destroyed. They could call and make suggestions, but as long as they were in New York and I was in L.A. I was not going to spend all my time on the phone with them. I told them I was going to make the final decisions, I needed a new producer, and I was going to change the format: the first half of the show would have celebrities as usual, but the second half would have ordinary contestants.

I wanted Stefan Hatos as producer. Hatos had produced *It Could Be You*, with Ralph Edwards, which had been in our time slot before we took over. (Our emcee, Bill Leyden, had come from that show.) I met with Hatos and he struck me as a shrewd, sharp, no-nonsense man with great experience. But Stettner was still on staff as our producer. I explained the problem to Hatos and offered him the title of consultant and a position of responsibility. He accepted, and I then made it clear to everyone on the staff that he had a lot of authority. Hatos smoothed off all sorts of rough edges. For instance, he saw that all the work and advance interviews were finished on time and that there were scripts for each show. Up to then we had been working from notes made on the backs of envelopes.

Stettner soon was dissatisfied with his diminished stature. He was handling administrative details, while Hatos had taken over the creative function. NBC still wanted Stettner out, but I stuck with him. I offered to give him my own title of executive producer, but he saw this for the gesture it was and finally quit. I watched him go with mixed feelings. I loved the guy and liked his work, but he wasn't right for this show, and it hadn't worked with him.

There are shows and shows and performers and performers, and none of us is right for all of them. Leyden wasn't right for *Your First Impression*. Bill, who died of a brain hemorrhage a few years ago, was a friend and a fine performer. He had done *It Could Be You* for six years, and everything focused on him. He worked with the audience, he was on all the time, and he did beautifully. But on *Your First Impression* he just sat in the emcee's chair and funneled the free association flow among contestants. He had no chance to express himself and he didn't like it. He didn't work well with our celebrity panelists. I was a referee more than an executive producer.

The game wasn't simple enough, and was ahead of its time. It was psychological and revealed a lot about those who played it. We asked people to respond instantly and to really let themselves go. When they did, it seemed to stir up storms.

One day Cathy Nolan of *The Real McCoys* came on in a mean mood. She completed one phrase, "I wouldn't walk a mile for . . . any man," and another, "The problem with this country is . . . President Kennedy." We got 7000 letters from those two lines alone. The country wasn't ready for such frank irreverence. Another time Joanie Sommers threw the network censors into an uproar with "I won't . . . go to bed with every Tom, Dick, and Harry." Unfortunately, few were as free with their feelings.

We also had a mystery guest. The panel was shown five pictures of celebrities and told that the mystery guest was one of the five. They then had to guess which one by the responses the guest made. When Hugh O'Brian was the mystery guest, the late Inger Stevens was a panelist. She took his answers and made a brilliant but brutal analysis. She said something like, "Well, whoever he is, he sounds to me like a man who needs the love of a woman badly. He must be a bachelor. He refers to living alone with his dog and enjoying the company of the dog. He plays baseball with the boys. I think the kind of person who lives this way must be Hugh O'Brian. And if he is the kind of person I think he is, I would like to be the person to give him what he needs." Well, instead of taking these remarks as a compliment, Hugh was insulted and demanded the tape be destroyed. We were in no position to throw away shows, so it went on as it was.

On another occasion, Dennis James, a member of our panel, said of the mystery guest, "I don't know who she is, but she sounds over the hill." Nina Foch emerged from the booth and threw a punch at him.

Some guests were gracious. Joan Crawford was our mystery personality on one show, and Archie Moore, the light-heavyweight boxing champion at the time, was also on the show. When Archie found out she was there, he said he was a great fan of hers and asked to be introduced to her. Warily, I promised to try to arrange it. After the show, I went to Joan's room and asked if she would mind waiting around to meet Moore. She said, "Why, I'll do better than that." Finding that he was on the next floor of the studio, she bounded up a flight of stairs and swept into his room with a wide smile and outstretched hand. He was surprised and delighted.

Richard Nixon was a guest on the show when he was running for governor of California. He had lost his bid for the Presidency to John F. Kennedy two years earlier, and he was waging a losing battle to beat Pat Brown. He was highly, explosively nervous, and we had to lay everything out for him very carefully. He was worried about his television image, which had been criticized in his campaign against Kennedy, and he was worried he would say something he shouldn't. But he got through the program all right. He even came up with a clever line: "I wish that I . . . had become a P.T. boat captain." That wowed the audience, and he was very pleased with himself.

NBC, however, felt we had to cancel that show rather than show favoritism to one of the candidates. When I telephoned Nixon to tell him, he got quite upset and went into a tirade against the network. He really wanted that guest appearance to go out over the air. Later I thought about his outburst when he lost the election and told the press on camera, "Well, you won't have Richard Nixon to kick around any more"—and again when he became President and Vice President Agnew began to blast the media. His *First Impression* show did go on, however, because Pat Brown appeared on another broadcast.

Your First Impression stayed on the air for two and a half years, but never got super ratings. We just got by, slipping from a 30 per cent share of the audience to 28, to 27, to 26; and twenty-six weeks into the 1964 season, the show was canceled. The share is the percentage of the viewing audience that is watching television at that time, as contrasted to pure ratings, which show the number of people who are watching out of all television households available.

But as an owner and co-producer of the program, I had finally made enough money to get some security for myself and my family. In September 1962 we had bought the Spanish-style home we still occupy on a quiet street in Beverly Hills. And I was turning a corner toward bigger and better things. Stefan Hatos and I had become partners, and we were dreaming up shows and packaging them. For me, this was an old story, of course, but this time it had a happy ending. Hatos and I were concentrating on a new show I would emcee. It was called *Let's Make a Deal.*

V

A LADY CAME *on* Let's Make a Deal *dressed as a little girl holding a baby bottle. Monty Hall took away her bottle and said, "All right, for $200, show me another nipple." There was an instant of stunned silence. The lady blushed, he blushed, and the audience exploded into laughter.*

Hall has made mistakes on the show, but not many. It is unrehearsed and he is out in the audience ad-libbing with the contestants, but he has almost always kept his wits about him and avoided saying the wrong things.

He knows in advance which wallets, boxes, and so forth contain which items, and he guides each bit accordingly. There have been times when no item or the wrong item was revealed and he had to improvise as he went along. No one noticed because he is so smooth.

Once there was a big buildup for a prize in a box, which when Monty opened it contained nothing at all.

The lady contestant could not believe it. Neither could Monty. The box was supposed to contain chicken feathers, but no one believed it, no matter how hard Monty tried to convince everyone.

Another time a contestant turned down a box in favor of a bag. The box supposedly contained a $1650 watch. As Monty opened it, he said, "And here you could have won, worth one thousand, six hundred and fifty dollars, a. . . ." The box was empty.

Swiftly he said, "All right, Blair—Blair's our prop man—where's the watch?" And he looked in the direction of the curtains as the audience laughed. They cut to a commercial while everyone searched for the watch without finding it. They came back and Monty said, "Our prop man, Blair, has gone home, He locked the watch up in a safe, and our other prop man doesn't know the combination. But backstage in a safe is a watch worth $1650—one thousand, six hundred and fifty dollars! And at home somewhere is a prop man worth about twenty-five cents at this moment." The audience laughed.

But Blair wasn't to blame. The watch had been stolen. Valuable small items usually are locked in the safe until showtime. Guards are posted to watch them once they are removed and packaged for the show, but someone had stolen this watch right out from under the guard's nose. It never was recovered.

Nevertheless, the cars, boats, and beagle puppies usually are there when their hiding places are revealed. Tires, wheels, and hubcaps have been stripped from cars, however. Some of these cars are especially made for the show and are called "zonks." One lady took home a zonk and displayed it in her backyard.

Except for the animals, the contestants must take the prizes they win. They have to pay the taxes on them, too. Producer Stefan Hatos once tried to have the show *pay taxes on a needy contestant's prize, but the contestant had to pay a tax on the money given him for his taxes, and it turned out to be an endless cycle.*

The show will not buy back prizes or make substitutions. Even the companies that provide prizes are not permitted to repurchase them.

The contestants may sell their prizes to others, of course, or they may keep them. They seldom keep the animals. But one lady who took home a lion cub called up the show a few months later to ask if it would take the lion back because it was eating up her furniture.

A school teacher won a heifer worth $1000, but not worth a nickel to him. Since the show does substitute gifts for animals, he was offered a color television set, which he accepted. However, before it was delivered, friends convinced him he should have gotten a substitute closer in value to the $1000 value of the heifer. He called up the show to complain, saying he didn't want the set. He wanted a $1000 value or the heifer. An assistant said he would discuss it with his bosses. When the school teacher returned to his apartment that day, there was a truck outside with the heifer in it. The heifer was unloaded and presented to the man with the comment, "You want the steer, you got the steer." He rushed upstairs to call the show to ask if he could have the TV set, after all. He got it.

As much as $28,000 in prizes has been given away in a single show. Of course, everyone can't win big or winning big wouldn't seem big. Whatever they win, the contestants seem happy. Even the losers seem happy. Monty says he has seen ladies make bad deals, perhaps trading a $3000 car for three young pigs, and still kiss him. The men do not kiss him, but some hug him. He has had men grab him and throw him straight up in the air. This scares him because he worries about his back, which goes out on him constantly. He goes backstage complaining, "Oh, my back."

Few women miss the chance to kiss him. He says he is the only person in the world who comes home from work with lipstick on his collar and his wife asks him if he had a hard day at the office. This is one of his favorite jokes. Another is that when he comes home without lipstick on his collar his wife is suspicious and asks him just where he has been and what he has been doing.

Requests for tickets come by the thousands from all over the country, and there is now at least a two-year wait. Those who are selected have no guarantee they will get on the trading floor, much less on camera. They dress up in their costumes, and they show up as squirrels or trees or nuts, and they wait in line for hours and a couple of writers walk up and down the line and pick potential contestants by pointing at them and that's it. The rest retire to the audience. Then, on the trading floor, Monty points at someone and he or she suddenly is on camera, a contestant.

A fish, or at least a man dressed as a fish, trades a can of sardines for a car. He jumps a full foot off the carpet, claps his hands excitedly, and reverts in age for a moment from fifty to fifteen. The audience cheers as if it shared in the winning. A can-can dancer calls the cost of five items within pennies, and wins a car. Cheers. Another contestant goes through the stages of agonizing decision and ends up with a $1500 ring.

But, wait, it is not the final triumph. At show's end she has another step to go. She is asked whether she will trade her $1500 ring in for what waits behind one of three curtains. From having watched the show, she knows great prizes wait behind two of the curtains, the grand prize behind one, but she also knows a "zonk," a surprise worthless or worth little, waits behind the other. Will she gamble? Will she risk the treasured ring? The audience shouts advice. She looks appealingly to her husband for his advice, but he will give her nothing. He wants no part of such a critical decision. He will

*help decide every important matter in their life except
this one. What will she do? The suspense mounts. "Yes,"
she screams, "I'll go for a curtain." Suddenly she is
Bankroll Bernie. She hesitates betting two bucks at a
race track. Never in her life would she wager a ring
worth $1500. Except now. She picks her curtain. Another
contestant picks hers, risking her prizes. Her curtain
slides back to reveal a houseful of furniture worth $8000.
More cheers. More tears. Another hug and another kiss.
She shakes from the thrill of it all, her face ecstatic.
One of the other contestants has swapped a fur coat for
a trip around the world and cash for expenses. She
shrieks. She hugs her husband. She kisses Monty. She is
a working lady. Her husband is a working man. How
can they take time for a month-long trip around the
world? They have kids. Who will care for the kids? No
matter, they will manage. They will go.*

*A lady says after losing, "It's not so bad, not winning.
You can't count on winning, you know. You want to win.
You hope to win. Watching it at home, we want people to win and we don't even know them. It's all for
fun. It's fun to be on and fun to watch. You feel sorry
for people who lose, but you know some of them have to
lose. If you lose, it's all right. It really doesn't matter
that much. It's not important. It's not the end of the
world or anything like that."*

*A man says, "Greed doesn't enter into it. Everyone
wants something for nothing. That's human nature. On
this show, if you get on, you've got a chance. But it's the
spirit of the show that counts. If we weren't willing to
let our hair down and just have fun, we wouldn't be
dressed like this, not for anything, not for any prize."
He is dressed like a cave man. He holds a club in one
hand. In the other he holds tightly to a key to a new
camper.*

*A lady dressed like a frontier woman, who did not get
on, says, "I'd have picked the right curtain. I had a feel-*

ing about it. I'd have dressed like Tarzan to win that camper. I waited two years to get to the show and then I didn't get on. It's all right. I don't mind. I enjoyed the show. I always enjoy the show. I always watch. I wanted to be on once, though. Just once. I told everyone I was going on. Oh, well, it was fun being here. I guess I'll write for tickets again. I can wait two years. I'm not going anywhere. What do you think I should wear next time?" Smiling hopefully, she walks away into the night.

11

Even while Stefan Hatos and I were turning out *Your First Impression*, we were trying to create other shows that could be sold to the networks. I emceed some of his run-throughs and asked his advice on some of mine. It was only natural that we would get together to try it as a team. In Hatos-Hall Productions, we became equal partners.

One of the shows which did not sell, but which should have, was *Three of a Kind*, in which teams of three butchers or three truck-drivers faced teams of three school teachers or three waitresses in battles of wits. Another was *Chain Letter*, which eventually did sell but did not last long. (Incidentally, *Three of a Kind* led us to *Split Second*, which sold in 1971 and is a smash destined for a long run.)

Another show was *Let's Make a Deal*.

I told Stefan about *The Auctioneer*, which I had done in Canada. I worked directly with many members of the audience in this show, not just with contestants or a panel. Although I'd never been able to convince a TV executive, I thought there were possibilities for a format in which the emcee operated in the arena, right out among the people.

On *The Auctioneer* I asked members of the audience for articles such as postage stamps or silver dollars, and I offered $5 or $10 for each item they happened to have. On another part of the show we auctioned off a mystery item. Both features were enormously well received, and I told Hatos I thought they would work in a TV game show.

He worked on a show called *Ladies Be Seated*, in which the emcee, Johnny Olsen, bought items from members of the audience and offered to trade the contents of a box for the cash. This show had stemmed from one called *Super Market*, in which contestants had to guess the retail price of items. Steve felt both these procedures would fit our new program.

We felt we had something, and we did. Eventually we incorporated these and other stunts into a format that concluded with a "Lady and the Tiger" trick in which two contestants got the opportunity to trade what they had won for whatever was behind one of three curtains, at least one of which was sure to conceal the largest prize on the program.

As we practiced it on ourselves and others on our staff, we sensed that there ought to be a fair amount of excitement as the contestants proceeded through various stages. They always had to risk something to get something, maybe nothing. Originally it was determined they would have to bring something, anything to trade to get into the game.

Acting like a carnival barker or a commercial pitchman, I'd say things like, "I'll tell you what I'm gonna do. I'll offer you fifty bucks for that. Is it a deal? Let's make a deal. I'll trade you what's in this box for that watch."

We agreed that *Let's Make a Deal* was a great title. It was Steve's idea. I think he had used the term "zonk" on a previous show to represent some sort of booby prize, and that's what we called our "losers." It did not occur to us to ask the contestants to come in costume. That aspect developed spontaneously. As the people brought in things to trade, some began to dress the part. A man bringing a pig would dress as a farmer. It caught on and added enormously to the informal appeal of the show.

We didn't realize how good a show we had at first. We decided to work up a run-through that we could try out on clubs and organizations that had written NBC asking for group tickets to other shows. We rated them as audiences—good, fair, or lousy. We tried the good ones first. We asked them if we could try out a TV show idea as the entertainment for one of their meetings, and a lot of them invited us to come.

We'd finish taping *Your First Impression* at nine o'clock at night and jump in our cars and get to a meeting at ten or so and perform until around ten-thirty. We didn't use prizes or props or anything. We had cards with the prizes spelled out on them—$200 or a $1000 set of furniture or a $3000 car or a five-cent comb—and the people had to use their imagination.

We played all over the Los Angeles area. I remember we did a show for TOPS—Take Off Pounds Sensibly—in a meeting room on top of a supermarket, of all places. We often had to go in the back door like delivery boys. Some meetings lasted so long we didn't get on until nearly midnight.

But the reaction was the same every time everywhere—a smash hit. Even without props or prizes, the audiences reacted with enthusiasm and excitement.

We couldn't believe how good the response was. We started to play some of the groups rated as "fair" audiences, and again the response was great. So we tried groups that were rated "lousy." Some of them seemed to resent our even taking up their time, but, sure enough, the show caught them and they reacted enthusiastically.

After a while, we decided we were ready to try the big time. First we contacted Armand Grant at ABC, and he agreed to look at a full-scale run-through. So we hired a big NBC studio at Sunset and Vine and invited impartial groups to act as an audience and be called on as contestants. We had a few props, but again we used only pieces of paper as prizes.

It was a sensation. The audience reaction was wild. I finished with these words . . . "and so this is Monty Hall saying as the old traveling salesman used to say, 'caveat emptor—let the buyer beware.' " I bade all farewell and faded behind the curtain to a thunderous ovation with my heart pounding. I knew we had just demonstrated to a network executive a show so certain of success that it would be easy to sell.

Happily, I joined Steve Hatos and our agent, Jimmy Saphier, who were talking with Army Grant and his assistant, Dick Dunn. I was surprised to see long faces. I asked Saphier, "What's the matter?" "He didn't like it," he answered. I turned to Army Grant and I said, "You must be kidding. Didn't you see what I saw out there? That wasn't a rigged audience. They roared. They cheered us to the rafters." And he said, "Yes, that's all right, but what could you do tomorrow?" I replied, "We'd do more of the same thing we did today. And variations of the same thing day after day. That's the way you do any game show. Only the contestants change. And the questions. As far as that goes, what has Bob Hope done for thirty years? Or Jack Benny for

forty years? If it's good today, it'll be good tomorrow."
Army said, "No, you'd just repeat yourself and it
wouldn't be any good. I can't see any future for it."

I walked away in disbelief. Dick Dunn came up to
me and said, "I thought it was sensational. Absolutely
sensational. I'm as surprised as you that he doesn't
like it." I thanked him, but his opinion wasn't the one
that counted. I went off with Hatos and had a couple
of drinks and expressed my rage, sorrow, and frustration. I've done many run-throughs for many people in
my time, and I have done some so badly that I was
ready to beat the buyer out of the room. But when
you do one this good and have it rejected, it is almost
more than you can bear because those moments of
triumph are the ones you live for. We decided there
was nothing we could do differently, except to do the
same show for a different man.

Two months later we set up a run-through for Bob
Aaron, the head of NBC daytime television, and Jerry
Chester, his immediate boss. We did the same show
with another neutral audience and we got exactly the
same great reaction. I walked off feeling this time had
to be it. I walked up to Jerry Chester, and, incredibly,
his reaction was almost exactly the same as Army
Grant's—word for word—"What do you do the next
day?" Steve and Jimmy and I looked at one another in
shock. The same thoughts passed through our minds—
was it possible that the three of us, with our experience
with audiences and feel for the business, were wrong?
Or were they, having emerged briefly from their ivory
towers, out of step with the public? It was easy to
blame the executives. Now, for the first time, our confidence in our judgment was shaken.

I don't think we would have given up on the show.
Certainly we would have tried CBS, although they
were leery of giveaway shows since the scandals.

Monty prepares to board the engine for the filming of the initial sequence in his first television special, **The Monty Hall Smokin'-Stokin' Fire Brigade**

Romping on the beach
with daughter Sharon
before the filming
of a scene
in the television special
(above)
and with the
entire family—Marilyn,
Joanne, Richard and a
clowning Sharon (below)

*Richard and Joanne (above),
and Marilyn and Monty
in 1972 (right)*

*Monty's parents,
Mr. and Mrs. Halparin,
in a late picture taken
before Mrs. Halparin's
death (left).
Monty in Israel
at the dedication
of a public park
in memory of
his mother
(below)*

קרן קימת לישראל
חנייון על שם
זה הלפרין
ג. קנדה

PICNIC and RECRE

IN HONO

ROSE HA

WINNIPEG, MANITO

JEWISH NATION

But this wasn't that sort of show. We had many different contestants, and not one of them won anything unreal. It was the reactions of the contestants that made our show, not the prizes. It was the games they played, which each viewer could vicariously play along with them.

We didn't have to worry. By the strangest sort of coincidence, as Jerry Chester's reaction had been as bad as Army Grant's, Bob Aaron's was as good as Dick Dunn's. And Aaron, unlike Dunn, was in a position to argue with Chester, and he did. Jimmy Saphier went right to Jerry's superior, Mort Werner, and said, "Look, we have a sensational show. Jerry Chester doesn't think so, but Bob Aaron does. We wouldn't tout a show if we didn't feel it was a winner. All we want you to do is check with Bob Aaron as well as with Jerry Chester and then see it for yourself." Mort did and came back and said, "All right, let's get up a pilot so we can really see what you have. We'll pay for it."

So we prepared a pilot. It was by far the best pilot I had ever made for any game show. It worked as well as this show always works. We sent it to New York, and this time Mort Werner, other studio executives, and the advertising agency people who were brought in to see all agreed that it was the most exciting pilot of this kind of show they had ever seen. We knew we had a sale.

The NBC people took an option on the show, and we signed a contract for $25,000 a week for five shows each week. Of that, about $13,000 went to us, and out of it we had to provide prizes and pay our staff, including ourselves. NBC took $11,190 for its studio and personnel costs. The rest went for commissions. This was not a lot for a show such as ours, but it was a start.

We had some problems getting a network time period, but on January 1, 1964, we were finally ready to start. Our show was put in the two P.M. time slot opposite, ironically, *Password*, which was a big hit for CBS. *Let's Make a Deal* worked wonderfully well right from the start, but it had to win a new audience and do it against a show that had a hold on more than half the viewers. We started with a 17 per cent share of the audience and inched up week by week, to 20 per cent and then to 25 per cent. Meanwhile *Password* went down to 50 per cent and then to 45 per cent. We were renewed after thirteen weeks and again after twenty-six weeks. We had knocked ten points off *Password* and made NBC competitive. It was a strain waiting out those thirteen-week cycles. What sort of security is that for a man to live with?

Then NBC moved us to the 1:30 slot, which posed a new problem. This period had been station option time throughout the network, and the individual stations had been providing their own programs to fill the half-hour. Many of these shows had been successful locally for years, and now the stations were being asked to remove them to take our show. They did not have to do it, and many didn't, so we were without a full line-up of stations with which to get viewers. To top it off, we were thrown up against the sturdiest soap opera in television history, *As the World Turns*, on CBS, which had a tight hold on over 50 per cent of the audience. Nevertheless, we went right at them. We added stations and got our ratings up to more than 30 per cent, while *As the World Turns* dropped to less than 40 per cent.

Suddenly, we were secure. If we hadn't whipped the opposition, we had caught up with them and brought NBC up to CBS. Also, our success helped the show that replaced us at two P.M. We were making money for the network, and we continued on that level for five years.

From the time I arrived in California my life had changed around enormously. Although Steve Hatos and I were not getting very rich, we were doing all right because, as the producer and the emcee, we did not have to pay others to do these jobs. Our audience grew yearly. There was no way we could fail. What would we do the next day? We would do better, and better every day after that, too. It was an enormously exciting time.

When we sold the show *Chain Letter* to NBC for $20,000 a week, and when it folded after fifteen weeks, we weren't worried. I had been working too hard, anyway, emceeing *Let's Make a Deal* and producing *Chain Letter* at the same time. I wanted to enjoy the fruits of all I had put into getting to the top. My only annoyance was that NBC was not properly appreciative. They acknowledged the success of our show and how it had boosted their daytime schedule, but it seemed to be beneath their dignity to praise a game show. They were getting $7400 per commercial minute and were sold out. Critics panned the program. But the people loved it. I asked Herb Schlosser to renegotiate a new and better contract for us and he refused. He said, "We expect you to live up to your present pact for the full five years."

In 1967, Proctor and Gamble canceled a show in the eight P.M. Sunday slot and wanted us to fill in while they were readying a new program. NBC didn't want to broadcast game shows at night, no matter how much larger the audience they might reach than dramatic or variety shows, but they didn't want to lose P&G. We did the show for buttons—and against awesome opposition—*The Ed Sullivan Show* on CBS and *The FBI* on ABC. Sullivan had more than a 40 per cent share of audience, *The FBI* more than 33 per cent, NBC less than 28 per cent. At the end of our stint we had the lead, 32.9 to 32.7 for the *FBI* to 31.5 for *Sullivan*. It was an astonishing upset, although almost no one noticed. NBC didn't even say, "Nice going, fellas." When I think of the top people who had flopped opposite Sullivan, such as Steve Allen, it irks me that they shrugged off our success, but they did. P&G did congratulate us, however. An executive told me, "We are absolutely delighted with your success this summer. We're sorry to see it go. If we weren't committed to our new show, we'd be happy to continue with you." They should have.

Later in the fall, *My Mother, the Car* turned out to be a disaster, and NBC asked us if we were prepared to put *Let's Make a Deal* on at night again in January. By now we were a proven nighttime entry, and we felt we were entitled to more money. We asked for a $6000 raise. NBC said to forget it. They bought *Hollywood Squares* instead. We were hung out to dry—and damned disturbed.

So we moved into 1968, the fifth and final year on our NBC contract. Now five years is a tremendous run in television, even for a daytime show, and we had proved we could do the job at night, too. We knew that we would be renewed and that we'd have to negotiate our new contract by the fall since our old pact would expire in December 1968. We decided we wanted $28,000 to $30,000 total per week daytime, for five years, with two years guaranteed, an opportunity to prove ourselves again at night at about $30,000 a week, and some fringe benefits.

Early in the year, NBC said they would like to start discussing the possibility of a renewal. We said that was fine with us. In the spring, a negotiator met with Steve and me in Jimmy Saphier's office. He came in, smiled, opened up his briefcase and said, "Well, gentlemen, have you given some thought to what you might like to ask for?" Saphier said, "Yes, we want $30,000 a week." The negotiator stood up, snapped shut his briefcase, and said, "That's impossible. There's no point in opening negotiations at that figure. I'll return when you decide on a more moderate figure." And he left. We had mentioned only the daytime figure, none of the other things we wanted, but we knew how these people operated and weren't upset. He came back a month later and asked us if we had come to our senses yet. We said that we felt our figure was sensible, and he left again. By then we had begun to be disturbed.

In June, the day after Bobby Kennedy was shot, the negotiator returned for another try. We were in no mood for any more nonsense. We were entitled to a large raise. Other game shows were getting $30,000 and even $40,000 a week. NBC had not even pitched a proposal at us. "What do you really want?" the man asked. We said that we wanted just what we asked for. "Well," he replied, "then I have no recourse but to go back and tell Larry White [the vice president for daytime programing] to find some new program for your time slot for next year." I said, "Fine, you do that." And, as he got to the door, he turned around and said, "You certainly have my regrets," as though he were a doctor giving the last bad news to the widow. Angrily, I wheeled on him and snapped, "Save your regrets for someone who needs it. There are more important problems in the world today than the fate of this show."

We began to think about switching to another network. We had had feelers from ABC, which, of course, had turned us down originally, and also, rather surprisingly, from CBS, but we hadn't taken these too seriously. Most feelers are just talk. One network wishes it had some show another network has, and from time to time one of its executives may say, "Hey, if you'd consider coming over to us, you call me, right?" And the owner of the show will say sure. But nothing much usually comes of it. I knew NBC wasn't worried about any feelers we'd had. They knew CBS wasn't taking on any prize shows, and they figured ABC was so far behind that an owner of a successful show would have to be insane to bury himself over there. But we weren't so sure. We had faith in our show and felt it would work anywhere.

Elton Rule, who had just become the head man at ABC, invited me to come to New York to talk to him. He wasn't personally negotiating for his daytime programing, but he wanted to meet me and perhaps probe the possibilities of my shifting our show. I met with him in July. He said, "We know we can't open formal negotiations with you until ninety days before the expiration of your contract, but I want you to know we are definitely interested and my checkbook is open and I am ready to write in some interesting figures." I said I would certainly consider it.

I did not keep my visit to New York any secret. When Larry White at NBC learned about it, he immediately arranged a luncheon to be hosted by Don Durgin, one of the network's top executives, in the executive suite. I had been with the network on and off for many years with many shows, small and large, but this was the first time I had been given this sort of treatment. In addition to Durgin, many other executive superstars were present and ready to romance me. I wasn't given a key to the washroom, but I was served first and the small talk centered on Monty and his show, good old Monty, one of the oldest and most valued members of the team. My advice was asked on everything from problems of industry to the Vietnam war. Everyone hung on good old Monty's words of wisdom. I was sparring with them. I wasn't going to be a sucker for their trap.

Eventually, Don Durgin turned to me and said, "I understand that Jimmy Saphier was not happy when

we did not sign *Let's Make a Deal* as a midseason replacement for *My Mother, the Car.* You realize it was
economics, not program content that dictated that decision. We could get *Hollywood Squares* for very little
money, and your price had gone up. We were
forced into making a decision that upset Mr. Saphier."
I looked at him, and I said loud enough for the others
to hear, "Because of the proprietary interest that Mr.
Saphier has in *Let's Make a Deal* and that which I
and my partner have, let's say that Mr. Saphier suffered
only ten per cent of the hurt."

Durgin stopped the preliminary sparring and moved
into the main event. Larry White had quarterbacked
the team to this point and now the coach was taking
over. Durgin declared elegantly, "I hope we will have
no argument when it comes to re-signing *Let's Make
a Deal* for another five years." I said, "Well, of course,
this is a matter for Mr. Saphier to negotiate. He is
our agent and he does our negotiating. I am not going
to negotiate at lunch. We have let NBC know the
sort of money we want, but your negotiator declined
to discuss it. There are many things we want and have
not been offered. I would suggest that if things are to
work out for us next January, a better attempt be made
by NBC to go into these matters. And for now I prefer
to leave it at that." The lunch was over.

Going down in the elevator, I found myself next to
Larry White. He whispered, "You're a son of a bitch,
but a brilliant one." I followed him into his office and
asked him what he meant by that. He smiled and said
that it was the coolest performance he'd seen. Then he
said, "Now, just what in hell do you want?" "Look,
Larry," I replied, "you know your man hasn't treated
us well at all. He hangs around only long enough to
open and close his briefcase and offer us his sympathy.
We've been dealing like enemies."

He sighed and said, "Suppose I gave you thirteen

weeks of nighttime, would that close the deal?" I told him that wasn't the main point. We wanted a large increase in our weekly money, at least twenty-six weeks at night, some rerun rights, and ownership of our tapes. I said, "Why don't you get together with your people and see how much you can give us and then meet with us instead of all this nonsense." He answered, "I'll do that. I'm making a trip to Europe in September and I'd like to see this settled by then." I said, "It's up to you." And I left.

After my return home, we began to get calls from NBC executives in California assuring us that everything would work out. Then the offers began to come in. Every week, someone from NBC in New York called to offer us a thousand dollars a week more than the original offer. By the end of the month we were up $4000, but still $5000 to $7000 short of what we wanted. And they still were offering only thirteen weeks nighttime. I discussed every step with Steve and Jimmy, and we were in absolute agreement about standing firm.

Then NBC sent us a new negotiator who said, "Let's start from scratch"—which, of course, was absurd. Jimmy Saphier told him that we would continue from where we were and suggested that instead of trying to nickel and dime us to death they get serious: time was getting short. He also reminded him that we could begin negotiating with another network ninety days prior to the expiration of our contract.

Larry White, about to leave on his trip, called to remind me how *The Price Is Right* had failed after switching to "that other" network. I told him I didn't care what had happened to any other program. I had faith in the show, and if we could get a better contract from another network, I'd have to consider it. I told him, "You have yet to begin to negotiate with us on a reasonable level. Let me put it to you this way: If you're not getting any loving at home, then the hussy across the street is going to start looking better to you."

And off we went to negotiate with ABC. Their first offer was, if I remember correctly, around $25,000 a week for the five daytime shows, twenty shows a year cleared for reruns, one nighttime show a week for twenty-six weeks guaranteed at $20,000 each, and ownership of all tapes. The contract was to be for five years, with the first year guaranteed. It was not all we wanted, but it was a lot closer than NBC had come. And it was straight out. We told them we would think about it.

We thought we might have a shot at CBS, too. Fred Silverman, their vice president of daytime programing, had taken Steve and me to dinner and said he wanted us very much and would go high to get us—thirty to forty grand a week—if he could get his superiors to rescind a rule that limited a contestant's winnings to $500 on any single show. He couldn't, however, and that took care of CBS.

ABC went up to $29,500 daytime and $30,000 nighttime. NBC inched up but still wasn't that high, and time was running out. One week I flew to Montreal to be the guest of honor at a United Nations dinner. When I got back to L.A., we were right up against the deadline. I was surprised when I was met at the airport by Steve Hatos instead of the usual limousine driver. He said, "We've got things to discuss." It was all very dramatic—it was our future.

Steve told me that Saphier had been on the phone from New York. NBC had come up to the same sort of money ABC had offered. "What about nighttime?" I asked. He said, "No, they're still at thirteen weeks." I said, "What about reruns?" "No," he replied. I asked, "What about ownership of the tapes?" "No," he answered. "Well," I concluded, "it seems to me we're still a lot further apart from NBC than we are from ABC." Hatos said, "Jimmy feels that if the daytime offer is equal we should stick to NBC." And I said, "The nighttime may not mean much to Jimmy, but it means a lot to you and me in professional standing as well as in our bank accounts. And I think the other things are important too." And he said, "I agree with you 100 per cent."

We got to my house late in the morning. We telephoned Jimmy to tell him that Steve and I agreed the other factors were too important to ignore. He tried to talk them down, but we stuck to our guns. I knew he had tried for a two-year guarantee and been refused by both networks, but I suggested now was the time to tell ABC that if it guaranteed us the two years —104 weeks daytime and fifty-two weeks nighttime— it would seal the deal. Saphier said he would try. He called back in a little while to say Elton Rule might go along but that Rule needed the approval of the board of directors and they were not all available and would have to be reached. Steve and I sat back, ate tuna sandwiches, drank coffee, and waited while our fate was being decided across the country.

About an hour later, Jimmy called and said, "The board at ABC has accepted. What do we do?" Steve and I smiled at each other and in unison said, "Sign!" Jimmy asked, "What about NBC?" We said, "Tell NBC we're sorry, but we've signed with ABC. They had plenty of time to satisfy us and didn't try very hard. Their last offer was topped by a lot." And Steve and I shook hands and toasted each other with coffee.

Just before quitting time that day. Jimmy signed for us with ABC. Before he could call NBC, NBC called him. He was asked to lunch with Robert Sarnoff, chairman of the board, and Bob Stone, president of the NBC associated companies. "For what reason?" Jimmy asked. "It's time to finally put this *Let's Make a Deal* thing to bed," said the NBC man. Jimmy replied, "It was put to bed at five yesterday afternoon. We signed a paper with ABC. We're moving." There was stunned silence, followed by flustered roars of upset. It hit 30 Rockefeller Plaza hard. The rest of the day I got more phone calls than I've ever gotten in one day. The executives from NBC moaned, "How could you do this to us?" And I said, "I'm sorry, but you did it to yourself." The performers I worked with chortled, "You fired a network. You've struck a blow for all the underdogs."

Herb Schlosser called and said, "You've made a mistake. NBC will kill you. You'll be left with nothing." I replied, "Maybe and maybe not, but the two years we're guaranteed will be enough to take care of us for a long time." He insisted we hadn't been fair to them, but later he called back and said, "I want to apologize. I talked to the people in New York, and I know now they did not treat you right. I had been assured over these past months that everything was being done to satisfy you, but I now know otherwise. We here in California were told to sit back and let New York take care of it. Well, we did, and I'm sorry we did. You played fair. Jimmy Saphier negotiated in good faith. I admire you enormously. I wish you the best of luck with your new network, and I hope some day you'll be back on NBC." He was a damned good sport. I thanked him, and sincerely, too.

Our negotiations had been headlined in *Variety* for weeks. When a top program threatens to switch networks, it's a big story in show business circles. We became even more newsworthy after we went on ABC. ABC had six shows opposite us while we were on NBC. They came and they went. They had a 15.5 per cent share of the audience when we went on. We doubled that within a week and then shot up to 35.2 per cent. NBC lost everything it had gained with us, dropping back into the 15 per cent range. First they tried a soap opera, then Art Linkletter, then a game show, then some other things, but they never recaptured what they dropped when they lost our show. CBS held fast.

But our success went much deeper than that. A popular show pulls up programs that surround it because viewers tend to turn to the channel of a show they want to see and leave it there, especially in the daytime. Even at night, there is not as much dial switching as is commonly thought. In our case, we hoisted the ratings of the show preceding and the two following us. The emcee of one of them told me, "Thanks for the ranch you got me." *Let's Make a Deal* solidified the entire ABC daytime picture and projected the network into a virtual daylong tie with NBC and CBS, a situation that holds to this day. *Variety* reported that ABC made so much money that it was in a position to pull up to the two other networks at night, too. Instead of dying, we were more alive than ever and so was ABC.

On January 29, 1969, *Variety* reported:

DEAL THAT SHOOK UP DAYTIME
ABC GRAB MAKES
CBS THE LEADER

Seldom has a top network suffered from the defection of a single show as has NBC from the loss of Monty Hall's *Let's Make a Deal* daytime strip to ABC. And along Gotham's video row the wisenheimers are claiming that NBC would have saved itself grief aplenty had it made a deal to keep Hall.

As it is, the subsequent ratings skid since *Deal* lammed the net have shrouded the 30 Rock citadel in gloom. For in the weeks since CBS has forged in front (while ABC has moved right in behind).

Though nighttime prime-time is the glamour arena in Nielsen points, more true anguish attached to daytime numbers . . .

For acute evidence of daylight billings impact on a web, take ABC where the 1968 profit and loss statement showed an approximate $1.8 million loss due to news operations. What's interesting is that the week-long nighttime deficit was estimated at $8 million, but was almost offset by a like profit from the daytime zone, which now is where a net has to make it.

. . . One of NBC's keystones in its surge up . . . was *Let's Make a Deal*, which had climbed to a 30 share plateau in its slot and, equally important, was pumping adrenalin through the whole of the net's afternoon ratings. *Hidden Faces*, the serial that replaced *Deal*, has yet to rise above the 12 or 13 share level and, worse, has had a predictably deflationary effect on most of the NBC lineup behind it.

Though CBS is the beneficiary of Hall's move it appears to be because the NBC slippage has been picked up by ABC. At 2 P.M., for instance, NBC's *Days of Our Lives* soaper still owns the time period but is down to a 32 share, while ABC has moved way up.

The three web stake in daytime billings is figured to reach some $350 million.

Others were enriched, too. For instance, NBC became determined to hang onto everything firm it had. *Hollywood Squares* was holding up its morning lineup, and when they asked for a contract renegotiation, they got a tremendous raise. Later, the show's emcee, Peter Marshall, called me and said, "You're probably the best benefactor I ever had. You have made me a rich man." People I'd never met thanked me for making them more money because NBC raised them rather than risk losing them. And NBC could have kept us so easily! Well, we live and learn.

As I write this, in our fifth year on ABC and tenth year on television nationally, *Let's Make a Deal* remains at a peak of popularity, with an estimated twelve to fifteen million viewers daily.

And how quickly the five years have gone by! By the time we had to face ABC in negotiations as we had NBC, conditions had changed, and many people had become wiser. We had no difficulty making a new deal with the network. We got a very large increase on our daytime show, a deal for making several pilots for daytime, more reruns, generally making *Let's Make a Deal* the hottest property in daytime. On top of all this, our deal is firm for three years, noncancelable. You don't see many contracts like this one around. For Monty Hall personally, it was also a good negotiation. I contracted to do one major variety special a year in prime time and two weeks of the late show *Wide World of Entertainment* each year. The network also offered us a chance to develop prime-time series of a non-game sort with their funding—all of which makes us most happy clients, and I am sure, as far as the network is concerned, the feeling is mutual.

Nighttime was another story, though we were just as solid there. ABC launched us in February 1969 at nine on Friday nights opposite *The Name of the Game* on CBS and *The Friday Night Movie* on NBC, which were both successful. We started with a 20 per cent share and rose to 25 per cent. Then we were shifted into the 7:30 slot opposite Don Adams's *Get Smart* on CBS and *High Chapparral* on NBC, and we lifted our network's rating from 18 per cent to 28 per cent, and *Get Smart*, which CBS had just picked up from NBC, died. So ABC switched us again, this time to Saturday night at 7:30 against *The Andy Williams Show* and *The Jackie Gleason Show*, and we lifted our slot from a 22 per cent to 31 per cent, and Williams's show went off.

Most of the television critics said Gleason killed off Williams, but a fast study of the situation will show that Gleason's ratings remained the same, while ours went up and Williams's went down. So we did it, even if we didn't get credit for it. Li'l ol' David and his slingshot. ABC switched us once more to Monday nights at 7:30 opposite *The Red Skelton Show* and *Gunsmoke*, and we took the slot from 21 per cent to 28 per cent, and Skelton skidded toward cancellation. The critics said *Gunsmoke* did it, but *Gunsmoke* didn't. In fact, it lost and fell from the first five for the first time in years. We went up while Skelton went down. Again, the situation wasn't seen for what it was.

I do not totally delight in all of this. Some of the shows that lost out were performed by the greatest talents in the business. But the name of the game is ratings, and I am proud of the way our show stood up. No one could admire Don Adams, Andy Williams, or Red Skelton more than I do. All enjoyed long-running success on television—but so has *Let's Make a Deal*.

Our reward for beating the big boys time after time was to be bounced around like a poor relation. Game shows lack prestige, you see, especially at night. In the early part of 1971, the Federal Communications Commission ruled that the networks had to return a half hour of prime time nightly to the local stations. It was an effort to stimulate local programing and provide a new market for the independents, but it has not worked. For the most part local stations filled the period with syndicated shows on tape produced by the prime packagers. But the regulation remains. All networks had to drop three and a half hours a week. ABC

decided to give up the first prime period, the 7:30 slot,
such as we were occupying. However, we were assured
by various ABC executives that they would find
another time for us. A day or two before the new
schedules were to be published for the fall, Jimmy
Saphier called ABC to double-check and he was told,
"How can we keep you off?" The next day the schedule
came out without us. It was a shock. Unproven shows,
such as *The Bobby Sherman Show* and *Nanny and the
Professor,* had been purchased and were on the schedule, but not us.

We couldn't believe they would dismiss us so easily,
but there it was. We telephoned people. We saw people. Everyone said they were sorry, but we'd been
squeezed out. Yes, our ratings were good, but something had to go and in a pinch all the networks had
removed most of the game shows because they weren't
prestige items. But even after the *Sherman* show and
Nanny bombed and were canceled, we could not talk
our way back on as replacements. We asked for the
Monday Night Football slot after the football season
ended and were refused.

To salve my wounded feelings, Michael Eisner, still
in his twenties and the new vice president for daytime
programing, offered me eight to ten summer variety
shows at $60,000 each. I was hesitant. Few shows make
it to the fall lineup off the summer showings, and
$60,000 was insufficient to do an hour show right. It
would be an opportunity for me to make it as a variety performer, but the show would have been an
unfair exchange for a regular nighttime spot and I
turned it down.

Steve and I decided we should syndicate the nighttime show, but ABC owned the rights to it and would
have to release us. They refused. We met with Saphier
and our attorney, Leo Ziffren. Angrily, we agreed to hit
ABC where it would hurt the most. Either the network

would restore us to a nighttime slot, or release us for syndication or we would stop producing our daytime shows. We lacked legal grounds, but we felt this was the one way we could force the issue, regardless of the risk. Again, this is the business. Talent is treated roughly and sometimes it must respond in kind. If you win, all is forgiven. If you lose, forget it.

I decided to approach Leonard Goldensen, chairman of the board, and a personal friend. I explained the situation to him, and he seemed sympathetic and asked how much time he could have to look into it. I said, "You can have a week, until next Wednesday." He said fine. I didn't threaten him with our plan to halt production.

I waited until Wednesday morning without hearing from him. I called him and he was out to lunch. Quitting time in New York came and went. An hour and twenty-three minutes later, Jim Duffy, president of the network, called and said, "Monty, we have had a meeting and we have something that will make you happy." It turned out they had agreed to release our show for nighttime syndication. It did make me happy. With this almost eleventh-hour decision, we did not have to test our threat. I feel we would have gone through with it.

The network did ask that its own division, ABC Films, be given the right to syndicate the show. That was fine with us. Most of the ABC affiliated stations that had shown us so successfully before no doubt would buy us now. We were bought by 131 stations, an enormous number for a syndicated show. We were bought by stations in ninety-two of the one hundred largest cities. Now we are in different time slots in different cities and our ratings vary from city to city, but our average 35 per cent share of the audience is the highest of any show in syndication and has made us the "number one prime-time-access show in the country." Our success in some cities is startling. We have had 62 per cent of the audience in New Orleans, 52 per cent in Philadelphia, 51 per cent in Cleveland and Cincinnati, 48 per cent in Atlanta, 46 per cent in Salt Lake City. *Variety* called us "the one unqualified rating success in the field."

We sold ourselves cheap. The various stations that bought the show were raking in huge sums for their own spots. ABC Films charged according to the size of a station's market, and they soon realized we were getting about half what we were worth. Our rates were doubled for the 1972-73 season. Several stations protested. Our Cleveland outlet, for instance, had been paying roughly $1000 a week and was asked to pay $2000. They offered $1500. In the stalemate, they protested to the Wage and Price Board on the basis of the freeze. They lost their case.

Meanwhile we remain on the network afternoon schedule and our ratings are as high as ever. Steve Hatos and I also developed, packaged, and sold *Split Second* to ABC. Emceed by Tom Kennedy, it has become by far the most successful new show in daytime television and is seemingly assured of a long and prosperous run.

So this is success. It took a long time coming. Polls have named Monty Hall the best-liked emcee in television, topping stars I respect enormously. In August of 1973 my star was placed in cement on the Hollywood Walk of Fame alongside the greats of motion pictures, television, radio, and the music world. Hatos-Hall Productions has hit the top as a packager of game shows, which remain indispensable to the television economy. I have made and am making more money than I ever dreamed possible. It was certainly a struggle and often it still is, but the old fears do not dog me today.

VI

DON RICKLES LAY *on a couch backstage at the Riviera Hotel in Las Vegas. He said, "I don't know why the hell Monty wants to play our game. We couldn't play his game. I'd die trying to handle his show. And he's liable to get killed doing our shows. When you're the best at something, and he's the best at his thing, the dummy should be satisfied. He's a nice guy. Good talent. But he seems to have suicidal tendencies."*

Monty Hall sits by the pool outside the condominium in Palm Springs that his family sometimes uses. It is a clear day and the mountains are a magnificent backdrop. The sun burns down bright and hot. His daughter Sharon is playing in the pool while Marilyn sits reading and watching her, wearing a wide-brimmed straw hat to protect her fair skin from the sun. Monty lies in a lounge chair, grateful for the break in his schedule. He speaks of the television special he is planning.

"I had a commitment to do a special for the network," Monty Hall said. "I wanted to do a variety show with music, but I did not want to be surrounded by superstars. I didn't want anyone to say later that I just stood

237

*there and introduced those performers. I wanted to come
out of it a new man with a new image as a star who
could make it on another stage. But I couldn't figure
out how to do it. I discussed it with top producers and
writers but they all suggested things that someone else
had done. I wanted to be different. ABC kept asking me
if I was ready and when could they expect the show?
Finally they said they were holding a spot for me on
June 5—a Monday night at eight. I had about decided
to let it go rather than do something I wasn't sure of
when the William Morris office asked me to speak to
Art Fisher and Neal Marshall, two young men who were
starting as a production team. Artie had never produced
a show before, but he had been acclaimed for his direction of the Sonny and Cher television show, which was
successful and imaginative. They worked out an idea I
liked and their enormous enthusiasm for the project
convinced me to take a chance on them and go ahead
with the hour."*

Before the taping, Monty was excited about the prospect. "We've been promised $250,000 to do it," he said,
"and I'm prepared to spend every available cent on the
show. ABC wants more hour specials, so this first one
can be a pilot for a series of hours. Or it can just stand
by itself, and we can try other things with the other
hours.

"On this one we're going to put me with the people
of California in their natural settings. We'll do segments
all over the state. We might do a segment in San Fran-
cisco's Chinatown, another in a fishing community
around Monterrey, or on a real ranch in cowboy country,
in an Indian community in the desert or a Mexican
town near the border.

"I'll talk to the people about their lives. I'll dance and
sing and fish with them. I'll participate in any traditional
festivals they may do, and I'll stand aside and let them
do the things they do best, too. We'll have some guest
stars, a singer maybe and perhaps a singing and dancing

*group, but no one who will overshadow me. It will be
all class with no slapstick stuff. We'll call it* Monty Hall:
Of, For and By the People. *I'm tremendously excited
about it.*

"*We have six weeks. I'll be busy with* Let's Make a
Deal, *and I have some appearances to make in Chicago
and Florida. After that, I'll have three weeks free for
taping. For the first three weeks, Fisher and Marshall
will have to work things out themselves. But I'll try to
stay on top of it.*

"*I'll judge the show's success by the ratings, the reaction of network executives, the critical response, and
my own feelings about it. We have to get a 30 share or
better. Of course, that depends on how much the network promotes and advertises it and on the lineup of
stations. If it's successful, we'll have a ready-made audience for the next one.*

"*This is very important,*" he admitted. "*If it's successful it will open up whole new vistas for me. I've had
popular success. Now I want artistic success, too.*"

*In Los Angeles, Artie Fisher is Monty's guest at a
Variety Club luncheon that salutes Monty as "Mr. Variety Club, a man who has done more for charitable
causes than anyone in Hollywood." Fisher, youthful-
looking, his hair resembling a Chico Marx fright wig,
wears a brown polka-dot shirt under a brown jacket. He
comes across as a sharpie—clever and confident. He
talked about his own prospects. "What does this show
mean to me? It means a good deal of money." He laughed.
"Since it's my first producer-director deal, it means a
chance to impress the important people in this business.
When I tell people I'm producing and directing my first
network special, they ask me who it's starring? I'd love
to say Frank Sinatra or Barbra Streisand. But I have to
say Monty Hall. People ask what can he do? I don't
know. Yet. I know he does the most successful game
show ever. But we're not doing* Let's Make a Deal.

"*I have to find out what he can do. Let's Make a Deal stars the people. This special has to star Monty and me, in that order. We'll find his strengths and play to them. I know his weaknesses. But I'll keep that to myself.*

"*The format will work if we dress it up. Some day we'll take this show to Bar Harbor, Maine; Eagle Pass, Texas; Savannah, Georgia. This time we'll take it to Japanese Deer Park in Buena Park, Olivera Street in downtown L.A. . . . You thought we were going all over California? No—we can't afford to go far afield. The network only came up with $225,000 instead of $250,000. That cuts out travel.*

"*We've got Cass Elliott, the Mike Curb Congregation, and Fred Smoot. We'll do some slapstick stuff to liven things up, but it'll be different than Deal. This isn't going to be any freak show. We're not going to have any oddball people. We'll have a beautiful show. The camerawork will turn up lots of color which we'll splash all over the screen. I got ideas dancing in my mind.*

"*I did The Monkees Special. That established me. I created a show so bizarre they stood up and took notice. I did it out here. I flew back to New York, and got a call to return to L.A. to do an Andy Williams Special. Did that so well I wound up doing his series for two-and-a-half years. The thing they like about me is that I get unusual ideas and put 'em on the screen. And I'm the fastest in town. I do a lot of homework before I show up for work. We don't waste time shooting. I did the Wow Special, which was a smash. Now it's Sonny and Cher— a director's show. Cher suddenly is a sensation. Well, I handle women well.*

"*Monty Hall is something else. He's scared, and I'm aware of it. I'm not scared, but I'm not in front of the camera. I have to work it so his fear doesn't show on screen. He's a real mensch. He wears a coat and tie. He won't let me dunk him in a mud puddle on camera. He wants to come across with class. All right, I'll work it out. It's my show. The producer and director have to*

be in charge. *They have a list of ten or twelve guys they
consider producers in this business. I want to be on that
list. It just takes one winner to get on and then you can
stay on forever, even with losers. You risk riding a loser
while you're looking for that one winner."*

*Monty went on his trip, but he called up every day to
find out what progress Fisher and Marshall were making. They kept telling him he had nothing to worry
about. He pressed for details, and again they told him he
had nothing to worry about.*

*Once when he phoned, Neal said, "Don't worry, The
Monty Hall Smokin'-Stokin' Fire Brigade will be a
smash." Monty was stunned. He said, "What's that?"
Neal said, "That's the new title of your show." "Why a
new title?" Monty asked. Neal answered, "We're going
to put you on the back of a fire engine and we're going
to race around and get a lot of attention from people.
It'll provide a colorful opening for your show."*

*Monty didn't like it at all. It didn't make any sense to
him. Was he going to be a fireman or was he going to
be a man of the people? He said, "I thought the original
fit perfectly." Neal said, "It had no life to it. This is like
the sound of a fire siren. You stop and look. It'll be ter-
rific. Don't worry."*

*Monty was in Jacksonville and was tired from his
travels, and he figured if they had this much enthusiasm
for a new title, a gimmick, he should share it, not dampen
it. He told himself they knew what they were doing.*

*When he returned home and asked to see the script,
he was told that things weren't ready yet. He asked
again from time to time and kept getting put off. Nothing
was ever brought to him for his approval. Neal Marshall
wrote some comedy material and it was approved by
Art. It called for some cameo appearances and Art
booked Dom DeLuise, Jim Backus, Rosey Grier, and
Jo Anne Worley. Creative control had passed from the
star, Hall, to the producer, Fisher. Hall let it go because*

he was told only half the show would be scripted—the stuff with Fred Smoot, Cass Elliott, and Mike Curb's Congregation—while the rest would be ad-libbed by Monty.

The first location was Zuma Beach, where Monty would ride a fire truck up and down the Pacific Coast Highway for the opening shot of the show. The aide came for Monty and suggested he wear a brimmed cap to shield himself from the sun. Thinking there was one in a closet, he stepped into the dark to pick it out. Unknown to him, a trap door leading to the basement had been left open by a telephone repairman. He stepped into the air, and as he started the plunge, he managed instinctively to throw out an arm and shove himself backward to safety. In a split second he had saved himself from a dangerous eight-foot fall.

Later, at Zuma Beach, he rode the fire engine up and down the highway for hours, hanging on for dear life, scared to death, thinking, "I was saved from that fall because the good Lord meant me to die on this highway." Then everyone adjourned to the beach, where Monty was to stand and sing with a large group around him. There were five hundred persons in the group, and they ran at him hard, so hard that they rammed into him. The shot was redone.

In the evening, after ten hours of shooting on the beach, the scene that would be the finale of the special was shot. The temperature had dropped from 70 to 45 degrees. Bundled in a borrowed jacket, lying on his back, Hall sang to the accompaniment of a guitar, but his voice cracked on a high note. No singer would do this scene without prerecording the number in a studio. At the end of the take, Hall wanted to do it over. Fisher yelled from the truck, "It's perfect!" Hall said, "But I think I can do better." Marshall said, "It's money in the bank. After all, they don't expect you to be Andy Williams." The critics later will pick on this flaw in the scene, whereas in fact Hall has a better than average voice. There was no need to sacrifice him in this scene.

They worked with Indians in Westlake. It was 110 degrees, and everyone was practically prostrate with heat exhaustion by the time they got to Monty's shots. His scenes were always last. They had to rush, and that worried him. "Don't worry," *Artie said. In Turlock, they were at a rodeo and spent more long hours shooting another fire engine running up and down the coast.*

"Can't I talk to one cowboy?" *Monty asked.*

"There isn't time," *Artie replied.*

"But the idea is for me to talk to people," *Monty said.*

"We don't have it set up here. We have an old lady for you to talk to in Watts," *Artie answered.*

At Japanese Deer Park, Monty was made up in a mobile truck parked outside the main entrance. A Japanese-American woman brought her little girl through the gates. The girl was to be one of the dancers and was in traditional costume. Another little dancer asked, "Is this a commercial or somethin'?" *An aide answered,* "No, it's a Monty Hall Special." *One girl said,* "Hey, Mommy, this is a Monty Hall show." *The mother said,* "Ah, Mon-ty Hall. Maybe we win lots of money."

Monty, made up and wearing a kimono, sat off to one side, signing autographs for some dancers. Cameras and other equipment were all over the place. Artie Fisher ran here and there giving orders. Someone asked Monty how it was going. He squinted, made a face, and said, "I don't know. By this time it's impossible to tell. We're really rushed. We're expending lots of energy but I don't know where it's going. I'm really getting tired. After the beach business they had to rush me by helicopter to the studio to tape two* Let's Make a Deal *shows. The pace is starting to tell. My back is really beginning to bother me."*

In his first scene at Japanese Deer Park, he played with a little girl. He sat down next to her and smiled softly at her and began to engage her in conversation. At first she was shy and silent. Gradually, he drew her out, and she started to giggle. She took his hand. He sang "If I Were a Rich Man" *from* Fiddler on the Roof *to her and she was fascinated by it. He kissed her and she kissed him back. (This sequence, lost in the ending, never appeared on screen.)*

Monty spent five hours a day talking to television editors across the country in quest of publicity for the show. He suggested that his future lay with programs of this sort, not with Let's Make a Deal. *As the days began to run out, he called Art and Neal and said he wanted to help with the editing. "We're doing fine," they told him. "We don't need you. You do your thing. We'll do ours. The show will be sensational."*

Four days before the show was to go on the air, he saw the editing. He had been getting more and more uneasy, hanging on to the hope that when the show was cut and pieced together in final form, there would be more continuity than there seemed to be when they were shooting it. Now he knew better. "It's not good," he said to Art. "You're wrong," Art said. "It's so good it should be put in a time capsule." "Maybe," Monty replied. "If it's buried deep enough."

Two days before the show, Monty screened it for Jimmy Saphier and the people at the William Morris Agency. They watched in depressed silence. As it went along, there were good things here and there, and they said something nice about it. But when it was done, they agreed: The first half was terrible, the second half wasn't bad, but it wasn't great either, and by then the whole thing was lost. It wasn't the show he had planned.

Jimmy Saphier said, "Your big mistake is you let other guys take over for you. Bob Hope tells everyone how he wants everything. He supervises his own cutting. That's what you should have done." The William Morris agents agreed. Monty said, "Now you say it. All the time you saw what was happening, and you didn't say it. Why do you guys always give me good advice too late?"

He went home deeply depressed. It was too late to change anything. He lay in bed with Marilyn and stared at the ceiling and told her how disappointed he was. She tried to console him but there wasn't anything she could say.

On Monday the big ads appeared: HOP ABOARD "THE MONTY HALL SMOKIN'-STOKIN' FIRE BRI-GADE"! IT'S A BELL-RINGING ROMP. *But those who read the advance reviews learned that it is not much of a show. Morton Moss wrote in the L.A.* Herald-Examiner: *"What seems to have been sought by Art Fisher is an air of the spontaneous. You do get a feeling of an enter-tainment that appears unstructured . . . it loses shape. The burst of colors . . . is typical of Fisher, who seeks to turn the screen into a bath of sensuousness. We thought the concept of celebration a good one, but not entirely fulfilled. Certain particularities we liked. . . ."*

Monty Hall waited for the show to go on, knowing it would not help him at all. It was, he said, like knowing an accident was going to happen to you when you couldn't do anything about it.

The show went on. The fire engine screamed down the coast, Hall hanging on. A Mexican dance began delight-fully, then was destroyed as Smoot moved in to parody a bullfighter. The slapstick intruded. The first half of the show was terrible, and dials must have been switching all over the country. But the show got better. The con-trast between the Japanese dancers and the rock dancers was striking. Monty's conversation with an aged lady in Watts was a pure delight. The bonfire scene on the beach for the finale was lovely. The second half, in fact, was pretty good.

The best things were those that were done as Hall had said he wanted them done originally. The worst were those that were added and changed. The bursts of color dazzled, but the special did not show off the host, Monty Hall.

The critics were lukewarm. The ratings were good but not great. Few network executives called Hall to comment on the show. Those who did said, "Well, Monty, there were some good things in it. . . ."

It was done. Standing in the cool night, Hall said, "I think it could have been saved. Had we replaced six minutes of that dreadful slapstick comedy with six min-

utes of human comedy. Had I talked to more interesting people like that wonderful woman in Watts. Had I insisted on this or that being done. But right from the time I let them change the title and take control from me, the show was lost. I don't blame Art Fisher. He has great talent and got the show he wanted—the movement and the color. It just wasn't the show I wanted. It wasn't any good for me. I blame myself. I should have been stronger, tougher, more insistent on my rights as the star and owner. I know what is best for me.

"In recent years, I've let others take over too much. It's worked out with Let's Make a Deal *because Steve and I have the same concept of the show, because we respect each other's talents, and we have a team that knows it inside out. But the two biggest failures of my life— Vegas and this special—came because I let others run the show and run me. The biggest successes of my life came when I ran my own shows and did what I felt was best for me. Well, I've either got to revert to this or get tougher, or I've got to quit trying these things.*

"I think the original concept of the show was good and would have worked for me," Hall said later, "but I just don't know anymore. I know that wasn't the show we did. And I don't want any more of these disappointments. I'm not sure what my next move will be."

He sighed and continued, "Well, I can't kick. Life has treated me well. I lead a good life. I am in a position to do what I want to do. I have a fine family and a warm home. I have a sense of satisfaction about the obstacles I've overcome, the work I've done for others, and the children I've raised with my wife. I suppose these are the important things anyway."

VII

In Monty Hall's office on Sunset Boulevard
hangs a sign quoting a magazine story. It reads:
You can learn more about America by watching one half-hour of *Let's Make a Deal* than
you can from watching Walter Cronkite for an
entire month.

Stefan Hatos

I DON'T TALK *to Monty about his excursions into other
fields of entertainment. If he wants to try Vegas or TV
specials, that's up to him. He can sing and dance a little.
I don't know how far he can go with it. I think he has
his limits. But he may go further than I think.*

I don't want him putting down our show, though,

247

which he seems to do when he talks of leaving it. Until the time he really does leave, he shouldn't mention the subject. I've pointed this out to him. I think he agrees with me.

If he leaves, it will hurt the show. He's not irreplaceable—no one is. But it would take just the right talent to replace him, and I'm not sure we can find him or get him. Monty is so closely identified with this show after all this time it would be bound to sag right after he went. In the beginning it could have worked with someone else—and in the end it might, too. But the network isn't so sure. No one can be.

I could care less what the critics write or what some people say. We have a clean show, an exciting show, and it entertains people. If it is not high art it reaches thousands of times the number of people high art reaches. I don't know what the point is if you don't reach people.

I think it is safe to say that Monty and I share equally in everything connected with Let's Make a Deal. *I came up with the title, but we developed the show together. I think the format is as foolproof as a game show format can be. It is incredibly consistent. It played perfectly the first time, and it plays exactly the same today.*

I put the show on the floor, and Monty plays it. We have a large staff working for us. I decide which stunts will be used each show, which prizes will be at stake, and how the show should run. I parcel out the assignments to our writers and merchandizing people. They whip up the details and I formalize them into a final script. Monty takes it and makes it work. He is everything a top emcee should be—handsome, glib, personable, quick-witted. He is very smooth and does not wear out his welcome. He loves people and is able to have fun with them without making fun of them. It is a very tough show for an emcee to operate, and he performs skillfully. But he has a foolproof vehicle.

Over the years, however, Monty has made it his own show. Publicly it has become his show. But I have an ego, too. Privately, I feel it's my show. I feel I make it go as much as he does.

I have fought fights alongside him—and I have had fights with him. We always agreed on what we wanted from the networks and stood shoulder-to-shoulder in every confrontation. But we have beefs. What business partners don't? I don't know if our disagreements will ever drive us apart. It could happen. We have contributed to each other's success, but we see many things from different viewpoints. He is talent, I am production, and there are natural conflicts.

He has a large ego. It's what makes him tick as talent. Most performers must have this sort of confidence. He is a hypochondriac. We all know it and accept it—he has to be babied. His back bothers him—or his stomach. He hates to work. We had one hell of a row when I was working eighty hours a week and he wanted to stop rehearsing his shows. But when he works, he works beautifully. He walks out there into the audience, and when the red light goes on on that camera, he comes to life.

He may have lost some enthusiasm for the program. It doesn't show yet, I don't think, but it could hurt. I suppose it's to be expected. We do more shows than anyone—237 daytime shows and 39 nighttime shows a year. That's a lot even though we limit taping to three nights most weeks. It's a rut, and Monty's tired of it.

But what do any of us do in any job? We do the same things. We sell shoes or we sell insurance or we sell real estate. Monty should realize that if it's not this show, it's going to be some other show. I'll be damned if I know why the comic wants to play Hamlet. And I'll be damned if I know why the best game show emcee in the business sees himself as Sammy Davis. Hell, a man

*should be satisfied to be the best at anything. It's helped
make us both rich.*

*Why is a variety show or a talk show any better than
what we do? I've been in this business a while. I'm an
old pro. I measure the importance of programs by their
returns. I have no desire to do arty stuff no one wants
to watch. If something flops at the box office, it's no
good. If it brings in business, it's good. I could handle
high drama. I'd rather run a good game show at twice
the ratings. It's not that easy, you know. For every one
that succeeds, a hundred fail. It may look easy, but it's
not. It's harder to come up with a game show that will
work for ten years than it is to create a super-duper
variety show that is lucky to last a season or two.*

*I like the life game shows have brought me. I wasn't
born into money any more than Monty was, but I
learned faster how to spend it. He's still conservative
with cash, not for charities, but for himself. I figure
money was made to be used. My wife and I have three
daughters and a nice home in Encino, and we have what
we want and go where we want and go first class. Monty
is more careful about things.*

*In business we're close. I don't have to worry about
offending Monty, and he doesn't have to worry about
offending me, because we say what we think and we play
straight with each other. We don't even have a contract
between us.*

*We don't agree on a lot of things, but we know how
to disagree together, which is important. He had a hard
fight on the way up, and I admire him for making it. I
like him personally. Our office is sort of a fun place.
There's no backbiting. We're riding the crest of a great
wave. If Monty wants to do something else, he can be
my guest. I can walk away from this, too. But personally
I feel this has been a nice thing. It's kept me out of pool
halls for ten years, anyway.*

Jay Stewart

I've been the announcer on Let's Make a Deal *since it started. A lot of us have been with it from the beginning. If Monty leaves, it will be tough to replace him. I think I could handle it, but I probably wouldn't get a shot at it.*

The prospect scares us. In show business you know better than to count on long runs, but after ten years most of us have been spoiled. We're no longer used to looking for work. We've also gotten raises over the years so we're used to more money than we'd make if we were hired for a new show that wasn't assured of success. The new contract makes us all feel good—mighty good.

Some staff people were uptight about Monty's hints that he might leave. They told him he shouldn't try Vegas or specials because he might get hurt, but they're not thinking of him; they're thinking of themselves, and they don't want him to find something which might take him away. It's a touchy situation.

Monty is marvelous to work with. He has chutzpah, which is one way of saying gall and guts. I don't know about the other things he wants to do, but I know he has varied talents and could probably be successful with many things—if he found the right ones. Anyway, he's got what I call screw-you money. He can do what he wants to do. He can afford to take chances. He could retire tomorrow.

Nat Ligerman

I was running a laundromat at Sixth Avenue and

Eleventh Street in New York City when Monty Hall came into my life. When I came out of the Army, I thought I might have a future in radio. On the GI Bill, I went to the Columbia School of Broadcasting. I went to a TV school. No one thought I had any talent. So I got a laundromat in the Village. But I had ideas. Ideas are a dime a dozen. Who knows what's good? I sent in a lot of ideas for shows. Most of them were sent right back. A few were considered and came close. And I did get shows on. The idea for Do Re Mi *was mine. NBC bought it. I had no representation. I didn't know what the hell I was doing. A guy there offered me $50 a week royalty for it. I said it didn't sound like much. He said, "You take it or we'll do it anyway." I took it. I got screwed. You want a list of the screwings I got before I met Monty?*

I begged to be given a job, any job, when Monty went west. He took a chance on me. I've watched Monty get rich. And I've done all right. I've seen him work in pain, surviving on Percodan. I'll tell you, he's a mensch. I mean a real gentleman. He hasn't changed in all the years I've known him. Only gotten wealthier— and even that hasn't changed him much. He lives about the same as he always did.

I'm not sure I want him to leave the show. I'm still paying off a car. Sure, it worries me. What will I do if he leaves the show and the show leaves the air? Write The Godfather? *It's already been written. I could write for other shows. Maybe. But I like this show. After ten years, it's like a treasured old overcoat. Lose it and you freeze to death.*

Dennis James

*I don't want to break out of my bag. If I'm doing a game
I enjoy, it's great. I don't mind being called a game show
emcee. I think Monty minds a little. He shouldn't, but
he does.*

*He's my close personal friend. He kept me alive. He
kept a lot of people alive. There is not a man in this
town who has done more for charities than this man.*

*Monty is tops as a game show emcee, and he's the
greatest dinner emcee I've ever known. I think he's
getting into a rat race with very keen competition, so
keen I wouldn't want any part of it. But Monty wants to
play Hamlet—and he might make one hell of a Hamlet.
He's beaten the odds before.*

Mort Werner

*It's hard to say why I hired Monty Hall. Why did I hire
Johnny Carson? It's a gut reaction. I put Hall to work on
Monitor, and we kept him working after that.*

*You have to give ideas a chance to work. Maybe some
of our people weren't sold on Let's Make a Deal after
a run-through, but the idea just seemed to fit Monty
Hall. I said, "So we blow fifty grand on a pilot, let's get
something to see." The pilot showed we had a hit on our
hands. Of course, you think every show you put on is
going to be a hit, and not many are. This one was.*

*Some parts of our association with Hall weren't so
pleasant. We put on Hollywood Squares instead of Deal
because we felt Squares was more of an adult show that
fit a nighttime, prime-time audience better. I know Deal
is a hit in nighttime syndication now, but it doesn't have*

*prime-time opposition, and syndication selling is differ-
ent from network programing. On the networks ratings aren't the only measuring stick. You want balance
and program flow and content that can catch the best
sponsors.*

Which is not to say I wasn't sorry when we lost Deal.
*I'm only glad I wasn't responsible. As head of program-
ing, my job was to put shows on the air and try to keep
them there. Contract negotiations are handled by others.
Possibly our people were overconfident and didn't pursue the renewal aggressively enough, but I can't say
for sure. Whatever the snags were, they were unfortunate for us. As I observed it, Monty conducted himself
with dignity and honesty and was open and aboveboard
about everything.*

*On a personal basis, I judge him as a very bright,
kind individual, quite aware there are other people in
the world beside himself.*

Ed Vane

I was an executive with NBC when we bought Let's
Make a Deal *from Monty Hall and Stefan Hatos, and I
was an executive with ABC when they switched the
show to that network.*

*The first I saw of the show was the pilot. It was sen-
sational. I know some of the fellows felt it couldn't be
maintained, but we decided to take a chance. You always take a chance anyway. If you can't take a chance
on a sensational pilot, what can you take a chance on?
We took a chance on Monty. He'd kicked around for
years without a big break, but he'd done enough by
then to prove he was a pro. He turned out to be more.*

There are maybe four or five great emcees in the business. He is one of them.

He and his show made a lot of money for NBC. It attracted and held a wide audience. It not only drew top ratings, but pulled its surrounding shows up by the bootstraps. Our daytime picture became as bright as CBS's. ABC wasn't even in the picture. He and his show made millions for NBC and they were not even remotely rewarded in kind.

ABC felt it needed Deal desperately to become competitive. Maybe NBC underestimated the unique importance of his show. We didn't at ABC. The daytime is when you make your money, and we felt Monty's show could make our daytime.

Many millions were at stake, more than the public realizes, and they were very delicate negotiations. Throughout them, Monty operated with total candor with both sides. He is an honorable man who told the two sides what he wanted with complete honesty and did nothing devious. At the zero hour we celebrated a great victory. He and his show turned our daytime fortunes around dramatically. He hoisted the shows on both sides of him. He about matched CBS and destroyed the NBC replacements in his own time slot. Overall, he thrust us up into a three-way battle for daytime dominance for the first time. And he has held his place.

The decision to take him off nighttime was not made hastily. We had to take off three-and-a half hours of shows. His ratings were good, but we felt they wouldn't go higher than 30 per cent. We had to gamble on shows we felt might reach 35 or more. On nighttime you need that. It's true that many of the shows we put on flopped, but they were shows with potential. It's hard to predict which shows will catch fire. Often we've been right. We were wrong on these shows, and we had to go back to *the drawing board and develop other shows that had super potential.*

We want to keep Monty on Let's Make a Deal, *day and night, for a long time to come. Frankly, we fear the show will fail without him. I know he's been interested in doing other things for a long time. I'm not sure why. He's the best at his business. Does Willie Mays complain that all he is is a great baseball player? Is Willie looking to make it as an airline pilot? Monty's aspirations to break into musical comedy or some such thing may be too much for him. His aspirations may outstrip his ability. However, it is possible he has unexploited talent. We want to keep him happy and give him every opportunity. Possibly he could be more valuable to us in another slot.*

Michael Eisner

I couldn't speak to a person dressed like a duck without laughing in his face. Monty has a sincerity and sense of sympathy that enables him to dignify nervous people in costume.

I have no idea if he has other talents. I suspect he does. He feels he can be big as host of a talk show or variety show. We are as interested in finding out as Monty is. So far, however, the evidence is not exactly in his favor. His special was not great, but not bad. The numbers surprised me some. Our show in that time slot the week before got a 19 per cent share. Monty got a 23 per cent share against Laugh-In's 28 per cent and Gunsmoke's 36 per cent. That's all right for the first time out, but the show could have been better.

We want to keep Monty and Let's Make a Deal. *We have tried and will continue to try to make him happy in other areas, too. He's a very smart, aggressive man and drives a hard bargain.*

In any event, we are grateful for what he has done for us. The shift of his show resulted in a gain to ABC that must be measured not in millions, but in the hundreds of millions of dollars. I wonder if the general public can comprehend the impact that this man and his partner Steve Hatos and their show have had on the television industry.

VIII

Marilyn Hall

I AM *Monty's biggest fan. I laugh at stories I've heard for twenty-seven years as though it's the first time they've been told. Not because I'm conditioned to laugh, but because I thoroughly enjoy the man as a performer. The impact of his personality is always fresh, always new to me. Since I know him so well, I also know his stress points, his vulnerabilities; and when he gets into trouble with his craft, I go through agonies for him.*

Vegas was a nightmare. I took a tranquilizer before the show. Monty's one failing is his trust in people and letting them make decisions for him. His stamina and fortitude constantly amaze me, because he is not a robust man. His energy is not physical but comes from some secret well of determination inspired by some driving force that says, "There are people out there who

have come to see a performance, and I cannot fail them."
He can't say no, and consequently he takes on so many
commitments and obligations that I wonder whether he
will survive; but he comes through a winner, and I sigh
with relief over another crisis passed. He has a kind of
divine inspirational confidence that the timing will be
there, the fast repartee, the give and take—and it is,
without fail.

I wouldn't change anything about our life together.
It is true that I hung back for many years as a performer in my own right. But life has brought us so
much, I can't complain. And Monty, more than life,
brought it to us. He fought for it.

Joanne Hall

I can remember living in Canada when Dad was in
New York and in New York when he was in California.
He called long distance every night and talked to us,
and we exchanged tapes. Even when we were apart, he
was with us. We're a very close family, intensely loyal
to one another, and while Dad had to be away from us
a lot all these years, he always made his feelings felt.
He is a very good man. By nature he is a straight, almost puritanical person who believes in home, family,
God, and hard work, and he has always instilled a feeling for these things in us. When I think of my parents'
marriage, I think of warmth and togetherness and understanding.

I wasn't aware for a while of who he was and what
he did. But I did, of course, become aware. When I was
young and I'd meet other youngsters and they'd find
out who I was, or, rather, who my father was, it would
color their attitude toward me, and I didn't like that.

Now I relax, enjoy it, and let it pass. I had been the one to make it an issue, becoming defensive or feeling no identity of my own. But it was all part of adjusting to life, and my life now is so apart from my parents that there is no competition—only love and mutual pride.

I started performing in high school. I love it. I love to act and sing, and the stage attracts me enormously. My life will be theatre. Now I feel that if Dad's name or his friends can help me get a foot in the door, I would be foolish not to take advantage of it. Theatre is a business; and when you are given a good business offer, you accept. In the end, it is my work that will be judged.

It used to really hurt when people slammed Let's Make a Deal, *or when friends would ask why my father didn't do something better. I always stick up for it and for him. I think it's an entertaining show, and it does just what it wants to do. Dad could do more. I admire him enormously his courage in trying other things. I have great faith in him and his talent, and I root for him terribly hard. I feel his disappointments very personally. I don't worry about him in terms of success or failure, though. I worry about the stiff pace he keeps.*

Richard Hall

I remember when I was very young and Dad replaced Warren Hull on Strike It Rich. *A friend told me he had seen my daddy on his television. I was surprised. I thought my dad was only on my TV. I thought everyone saw their dads on their own TV's. It took a while before I realized he was set apart as a TV star, a celebrity. And it took even longer before I understood what sort of life it was.*

I was driving somewhere with my dad and we heard

*on the radio that Walter Alston, manager of the Los
Angeles Dodgers, had just signed a one-year contract.
"One year!" I said. "He's the best in the business and
they give him only one year!" And then Dad said that
his contract was up every thirteen weeks. Of course,
that's not the case now, but it was then. For the first time
I realized the relentless insecurity and pressures he felt
and appreciated what he had accomplished.*

*I used to hate it when I'd be introduced as Monty
Hall's son. People immediately liked me because of my
father. I immediately disliked them because of this. I
resented it, and still do. These people have no idea of
me. It's affected my feelings toward my father and
complicated my search for my own identity. As a teenager I had this almost fanatical drive to be so successful
my father would be introduced as Richard Hall's father.
I don't feel this much any more.*

*I don't think I'm emotionally closer to one parent than
the other. I want to write, which is more like my mother.
But I want to write different things than my mother
does. I want to be a serious journalist. I don't want to
write entertainment. I really don't think I'm too much
like either of them.*

*They feel I never wanted to be a performer? I'll tell
you a secret: I wanted it more than anything in life for
a long time. I envied my father and sister their talents.
Their personalities overpowered me. I didn't try out
for drama or variety in high school because I couldn't
see trying to live up to my father and trying to follow
in the footsteps of a sister who had been the star of the
school shows. I knew I wasn't good enough. I wish I
was, but I'm not, so that's it, and I gave up on it long
ago.*

*Because of his heavy schedule, my father missed a
lot of my growing up. We always talked about going
fishing together and never did it. I guess we missed some*

father-and-son things we might have done together, and I felt bad about it. But I had him on weekends, and we'd play touch football and swim. He was always interested in my hobbies. I had a coin collection, and he helped me. I was aware that Dad cared.

I am still dependent on them financially. But I do have some independence of them. I came home this summer to be with my hometown honey. I saw my parents, too, of course, but I was mostly with her. We had this understanding that they would pay for my tuition and room and books, but that I would earn my own expenses. However, when I went back and was poverty-stricken, there was never any question that they would take care of it. They just sent me the money so I could live decently. There was no point in my starving. Things like this are beautiful between us.

I was very disappointed in Yale. I found a lot of snobs there. They were only concerned with having a good time and later becoming successful. To them success was measured only in money. They thought because I had a similar background I should think as they do— but I don't. I want to help make this a better world for people who are not successful and rich and comfortable. I don't expect to have any great power to right wrong, but I hope I can at least exert some influence for good.

I argue with my father about politics a lot, but we are really not that far apart. He is a liberal; I am an ultra-liberal. He was a Muskie Democrat; I was a McGovern Democrat. But he never put me down for my views; and I honestly think I have influenced him some. I was surprised when he contributed money to the McGovern campaign. His prominence gives him a certain power, and I don't think he has used this power enough politically. He has used his power for good in other ways, though, and I'm proud of him for that. He's given of himself to needy causes much more than almost anyone

I've ever known. I do respect him. He is a man of ideals, and this is rare.

If people bait me about Let's Make a Deal, *I defend it. And if they put him down, I defend him—very strongly. At Yale a professor started to say sarcastic things. I suppose he thought I would have to agree with him. I told him to shove it. When there was a sarcastic article in the Columbia University newspaper, I wrote a very strong letter to them supporting my father and his show. I simply won't stand for a superficial, sarcastic sort of criticism. If someone doesn't like the show or his performance, that's fine, but if they just say what they think they're supposed to say about such shows and their emcees, I get angry—and in one way or another I tell them to shove their superficial opinions.*

Joanne and I worry about Dad. He has emotional toughness, but not professional toughness. He's all alone out there trying to do something no one else thinks he should. I don't think he's realistic about his talents. If he would surround himself with the proper support in the right setting, he would come off fine, but he plunges right in unprepared. He worries too much about what his fellow performers think about him. He's over-anxious to prove himself on an elevated level. I hope he gets what he wants out of it.

Sharon Hall

What do I think of Let's Make a Deal? *I'm bored of it. It's been on as long as I am old. It's OK. OK, it's good. I'm not excited by it. I don't watch the program all the time. I've seen it. When I was two or three, it confused me when Daddy was here in the house and on TV, too. That was fun watching him with him. Now I'm seven and I'm used to him being on TV. By the time I'm eight I'll be tired of it. I'm not tired of it yet. He's not just a daddy to me. He's a daddy on TV. And I like it. And the other kids like me because of it. It bothers me a little. I'm me. Ever since I began camping when I was four years old, the kids would ask me for his autograph every day. Now the kids are used to me.*

I miss him when he's away working. I want to see him more. Watching him on TV isn't the same as being with him. Is he a good daddy? Yes. One thing, I tell him to phone me before I go to sleep when he's away and he always calls me. I'd rather he'd come home. He hollers when he gets mad. He doesn't scream off his head. He doesn't get too mad too much. He's a pretty good daddy. He lets me do what I want. Mommy is always saying don't do this and don't do that. But she's a pretty good mommy, too. Am I spoiled? I don't feel spoiled. My mom forgets to give me my allowance all the time. I can't have all the things I want.

Lots of kids at school, their daddies are on TV, too. Maxine Komack. Her daddy's Jimmy Komack. And Patrick Cassidy. Well, it's not really Cassidy. Her mom is Shirley Jones. And her daddy was Jack Cassidy. Only I don't think he's living at home any more. It gets very confusing in a lot of my friends' homes with all the different daddies. I'm glad I've just had one daddy and one mommy all the time.

What do I think about my daddy's work. I think it's a hard life. Not scary. Hard work. I don't know anything else about it. Would I care if he gave up Let's Make a Deal? No. I'd make him start another show. I always want him to have a show on TV. I'd like to be a performer. But not on TV. I'd like to be on the stage like Joanne. I'd like to act. I don't know what I want to be. But I want to be like my sister. I think she's going to be a star. She lets me comb her hair. I've been around performer people. I met Mama Cass when I was on the special. I just sat there around the bonfire while my daddy sang to me. When I saw myself on television, I thought I looked yucky. And my marshmallow never got roasted. I was nervous at first. Then I felt comfortable. But I didn't do anything. I liked my daddy on it. I like to hear him sing. I'll let my hair grow so I can be a performer, too.

My brother? I like him. He plays hide-and-seek with me. I like my whole family. I like my life. It could be better. I don't like it when we go to a show like the ice show and a great big line forms to get my father's autograph and I can't see. It bothers me. I wish people would leave us alone more. I don't know why they make such a fuss over him. He's just my daddy.

Robert Hall

My brother went through hell to get where he is, and he deserves all the credit in the world. I have no envy of him or his success. I have my own success.

I guess it's a disease of his profession, but as successful as he is, he seems insecure. Which is why he is trying these other things, always wanting to nail down another piece of security. He worries about himself. If he has a weakness, it's that he is hypercritical. He criticizes me, my wife. He sees things, and if he doesn't like what he sees, he has to have his say. I say, "Monty, old boy, you may be God at the studio, but you are just a rich relative here."

I think he has been too tough on our father. Mom was superhuman. You can't compare parents. We all do the best we can. Our father fought for survival, and it made him short-tempered, but he never hurt a soul and always did his best for us.

He is basically a beautiful man, my brother. He is

generous to his family. He gives to others. His charity work is incomparable. And he is a success in his profession.

Maurice Halparin

I wish my son would quit. He's got enough money to sit on. What does he need the knocks for? If he's in it for the green stuff, he'll just give it away. He's got guts. He's got it in his head he can do other things. And he could. But what does Monty need it for? Why does he drive himself so? So the critics can spit on him?

No one could ask for a greater son. Wealth and affluence did not change him. Just gave him the chance to do more good for others. Tears come to my eyes when I think of my family. You should have such a family. Such a pride as I have.

When they moved us here, it was so wonderful. We used to pinch each other to make sure we weren't dreaming. And then my wife died. What a loss. Without her, life was terrible. Monty invited me to live with him, but I like it here. This is my home. He sees that I have every luxury. I am married again now, and things are running smoothly. We have a lot to thank him for.

12

"WHAT TIME IS it?" *seven-year-old Sharon Hall was asked. "It's five minutes to* Let's Make a Deal," *she replied. A child of television, she tells time by shows. Channel Seven was turned on. The shows are taped weeks in advance, but Monty seldom gets to see them when they come on. That evening, however, he was at his beach home in Malibu, a triple-tiered condominium facing the pounding Pacific.*

He sat in a soft chair watching the show. "I shouldn't have worn that suit," he said. Marilyn replied, "It looks fine." "I don't like it," retorted Sharon. Hall made a face.

A man won and jumped high in the air. "There, don't tell me the men don't react as much as the women," Hall said. "Look at him, he's crying. Can you believe that?" Like any viewer Monty rooted for the contestants. But he kept noticing little things. "I shouldn't have turned my back there," he said. "And I should have done more with that gal."

A man won some furniture. "He seems happy," Monty

said. Later, the man risked the furniture and wound up with a year's supply of popcorn. Monty said sadly, "Poor Joe looks heartbroken." A lady won a fur coat, screamed with joy, and kissed Monty. "Well, she's happy, anyway," Monty said. "It was a good show," Marilyn observed. Monty shrugged. Sharon asked, "Can I go on the beach now?"

Monty walked to the balcony and stood there, looking out over the ocean. "Twenty-three hundred shows," he said.

I'm not the star of the show. The contestants are. When I watch the show, I can't help watching myself to see if I'm the way I should be. But otherwise I watch the expressions on the people's faces. Their reactions make this show. They become performers on the show.

Norman Brokaw, the William Morris agent, called it a "happening." That's as good a description of it as any. Most critics rap the show, but they don't really represent the public. And they miss the point of the professionals, which is to please viewers and draw the largest possible audience to which a sponsor may sell his product. I don't know what is wrong with pleasing the audience. Isn't that what any entertainer tries to do? And I'm not sure why a Bob Hope standing up there telling his writers' jokes and acting in comic skits is performing on a higher plane than we are, wringing varied reactions from excited and very real people. The show should be judged for what it is, not what it isn't. It should be measured against its ambitions and its competition. It is the sheerest sort of snobbery to suggest that the millions who watch us are idiots.

I am proud of how I do the show and of the recognition I get. Signed to do a show with Jimmy Durante, I entered the studio when he was twenty steps up on stage. He came bounding down, this aging great, and threw his arms around me, saying, "I just love this guy. I just love this guy." What a thrill that was! And then I answered a knock at my dressing room door and found Jimmy Stewart standing there. He said, "I just wanted to let you know that my wife and I are great fans of yours and your show."

At Chasen's Restaurant one night someone said, "Jack Benny's been trying to get your attention." Startled, I looked up. There at a table fifteen feet away was Benny. He shouted at me, "My wife is crazy about you." I walked over and spoke to Jack, whom I'd never met, and he introduced me to Mary, and she said, "I adore you," and pulled me down and gave me a great big kiss.

I'd heard Red Skelton stopped whatever he was doing to watch my show. At a luncheon, his wife repeated this to me, then Red himself confirmed it, saying, "It's an exciting show and you do an exciting job." At a Friar's Club luncheon Phil Silvers asked the show business people there if they realized I did a daily half hour without a script. "He's fantastic," said Silvers. And at a dinner the great Metropolitan Opera singer Richard Tucker told me, "I'm thrilled to meet you. I watch your show all the time." Well, I am in awe of such people, and their plaudits mean more to me than all the raps of all the critics. As do the compliments paid me by all sorts of people wherever I go.

Let's Make a Deal is a tough show to do. But I am quick and I can talk. I think the real reason for my success is I sincerely like people. People like to be liked. I have a knack for relaxing them. Most people want recognition. When a celebrity treats them as if they were important, it matters to them. Few can be one of the beautiful people. But with a smile, a handshake, a hug, you can give them a dignity and an importance that they seldom get in everyday life, and I enjoy giving this to them.

I think it is the genuine excitement of the people who are on our show that makes it go. And I do not believe it stems strictly from the value of the prizes to be won. The reaction of wealthy people to the winning of a prize is the same as that of poor people. And the reaction is almost the same to small prizes as to large prizes. And even losers do not seem too disappointed. The "zonks" seem to amuse them. The prizes vary, but the fun is always the same.

I watch the contestants like a hawk when they win big. A little old Italian lady gave me a belt that bruised a rib. I said, "I always rated Rocky Marciano the greatest Italian boxer until now." One seventy-year-old grandmother from Nebraska hugged me, lifted me straight up, and threw me over her shoulder like a sack of wheat. I dangled there helplessly while the show stalled, but the audience loved it. I was scared to death. One big guy picked me up and threw me straight up in the air, and when I came down I tore a cartilage in my knee. Another fellow hooked me with a fishing pole. The women's kisses are sweet. Three men have kissed me, too. I couldn't get out of the way fast enough. One was an elderly man who was simply exuberant. Another was a European, where such is a custom. But the third was terribly suspect.

It has been a consistently entertaining and popular show. Morton Moss in the Los Angeles *Herald-Examiner* wrote, "Prizes aside, it lives off the vitality of its emcee." Well, I don't expect to win an Oscar for acting, but I do want to be appreciated as an emcee. There are fewer top men qualified to host game shows on television in this country than there are performers able to handle the roles in every other kind of show.

When I leave *Let's Make a Deal*, it will be a sad day. But I will leave it, sooner or later. Before long, I will have done 3000 shows. A person just cannot do the same show forever, especially one with a tough schedule. I get tired. I feel dead. But when the lights go

up, I come alive again. I don't look forward to doing it
the way I once did, yet when I get to it, it's still great.

I may go on with *Deal*. But ten or fifteen years is
a long time to be doing the same show. It flatters me
to say no one else could do it, but I prefer to feel it
eventually will carry on successfully without me.

Let's Make a Deal is unique in that it has been
staffed by the same people for the whole ten years of its
existence. They have been paid well, and we have provided them with pension and profit-sharing plans and
other benefits. Steve Hatos and I not only created and
sold the show, but have stayed with it as executive producer and emcee, respectively.

Steve Hatos is a smart, tough man. He has been an
almost perfect partner. We have complemented each
other perfectly. He was strongest where I was weakest,
and I was strongest where he was weakest. We have
had our disagreements, especially in the early years,
but there has been no behind-the-back stuff, and we
still work together wonderfully well. We have different
personalities and life styles, but we have enjoyed considerable success and made a lot of money together.
He is a proud man, and I know he resents it when interviews with me appear and don't mention him. I
have never, absolutely never, discussed our shows without crediting Steve, but writers usually leave him out.

Steve does not like the thought of my leaving *Let's
Make a Deal*. He does not want to disrupt a smooth
team performance, and I don't blame him. But I must
make my own life, too. Steve is content where he is.
I am not. I am a good emcee, but that is only one of
the things I can do well. There is much of me that does
not show. I am not putting down an emcee's role or the
show by saying I want to do other things. I have to protect myself by proving myself in other roles while I can.
I can command other opportunities only while I'm on top.

Look, it's a brutal business. It is run by ratings. We
brag about them when they are good and rap them

when they are bad, but we live and die by them. And it doesn't matter who you are or what you do. The ratings are based on a small sample, and a few people in Oklahoma can knock a star right out of the sky.

If I don't make my move now, when can I? I have compromised in the past. I remember going to Grant Tinker, at that time an executive at NBC (and the husband of Mary Tyler Moore), to ask his advice about a talk show. "Why leave a hit for something uncertain?" he asked me. "It doesn't matter whether it is a game show or a talk show, a hit is a hit and a miss is a miss, and if you have a hit, you stick with it. It doesn't matter whether it is daytime, nighttime, anytime; if you are winning, you go with it as long as it lasts." I didn't make a move. I wanted the other show in the worst way. But I didn't have the courage to give up a secure thing to take a chance.

I have been a guest on many shows—*The Dean Martin Show, That Girl, The Flip Wilson Show, The Odd Couple*, and others—and have done well. But for every show I have taken, I have had to turn down ten others because my *Let's Make a Deal* schedule would not permit it. I want time to do these things and more —a variety show, perhaps, and especially a talk show.

I am no fool. I know Vegas didn't work. I can't be kidded that it was better than it was. But there were facts in that failure that went beyond Monty Hall alone. I wasn't tough enough to see that everything was done the way I wanted it done. The same was true of the television special in 1972. It wasn't what I had planned or hoped for, but there were some good things in it—and it could have been all good if I'd been tough enough to insist on having things my way.

As always, there are discouraging defeats in life and in a fellow's career, but they don't have to defeat him. I'm not the kind of guy to give up in the face of disappointment.

13

As I BEGAN to rise in show business, as my brother began to rise in his legal practice, we began to be able to help our parents. First, we contributed to a fund that would allow them to feel secure. Then we backed my father in a move of his butcher shop to a better part of town. It went well for a while, then competition crowded them. We sold out and invested in a pair of drive-in restaurants for him to run in Toronto. Proudly, he said, "I've traded my butcher's apron for a brief case." However, we had bought a bad business, and in time we had to sell it.

By then our parents were in their late sixties and it was time they retired. So in 1968 we moved them into a condominium in Palm Springs. I turned a new car over to them. When they reached their new home, tears were in their eyes. They were like Mr. and Mrs. Rockefeller. They called it, "The Garden of Eden." Sadly, paradise paled. My mother became ill and returned to Toronto for surgery.

I flew there to bring her two pieces of news that I

thought would cheer her. The first was an invitation to be the guest of honor at a large charity banquet in Winnipeg. Because the cause was close to her heart, she had always told me that when I was invited to speak at this dinner, I would have "made" it. She already knew that I was going to appear there in October. Then I went on to describe the offer of my first special on ABC. Attempting to take her mind off her illness, I tried to involve her in the various formats I was considering. She sat, looking out the window, as I ran out of things to say about the special. The room grew silent. After the longest time, my mother began to speak. "I want it to be the best you have ever done." Quickly I broke in, "You mean the special." Without turning her head, still gazing out the window, she replied, "No, October . . . October. . . ."

In July 1970, my mother died at the age of sixty-nine. Her death was a blow to all of us. Tributes to Rose Halparin poured in from everywhere. She was beloved by many, but especially by her family. My wife has meant as much to me as a woman can mean to a man, but I must admit my mother was the most unforgettable person I've known, and even today I feel her loss daily.

My father was as though cast adrift. Eleven months later, he remarried. Five months after that, they were divorced. More than a year after that, he married a third time. But I think this one was not so much from desperation, and it may endure. His new wife is a lady he has known on and off since he was very young. He is a man who cannot bear to be alone, and perhaps she can be a companion to him and give to him and take from him and it will be good for both of them.

A few months after his divorce, he suffered a heart attack. I don't think he had been ill for forty years and he recovered remarkably. He tends to set too fast a pace. He has his cronies and his card games and his part-time volunteer work at the hospital. He has had hard times and he has managed to survive. I have resented his rough treatment of me in the past, but I have come to know him better in recent years and I respect him. He is a remarkably resilient man.

I am close to my brother, although we are parted by many miles. We slept in the same bed for many years. He grew up as Monty's brother, in my shadow. But he overcame this and became his own man, earning himself an outstanding reputation in Canada. We disagree on some things, but with respect. I am proud of my brother.

I think my feelings for my wife must have shown through throughout this book. Marriage is not an easy matter. But it has not been hard for us. We got married young and got through a lot of tough times together and stress seemed to strengthen us. I suspect we have had fewer disagreements and more real love between us than most couples. We suit each other, so we have been fortunate. We celebrated our silver wedding anniversary in September of 1972.

Our oldest child, Joanne, who, for professional purposes, has changed her name to Joanna, has graduated with honors in Theater Arts from Occidental College and has begun to seek a career on stage on her own. She is singularly attractive, a good actress and a good singer, has won awards and received some marvelous notices in various local productions. She has a shot at stardom. She doesn't like to be called Monty Hall's daughter, but I'd like the day to come when I am called Joanna Hall's father. I am proud of her and close to her.

I am equally proud of my son. Richard has overcome a bad back problem which has plagued him since youth. He wants to be a journalist and has shown a talent for it. He is very much a mod young man, long hair and all. He is very much his own man. We argue politics. Like many young men today, he is impatient with the state of things. He has stirred up some sparks in high school and at Yale, but a guidance counsellor once told me, "You don't have to worry about this young man."

Once, when we met at Sardi's on Broadway, he arrived looking like a hippie while I had on a conservative suit. I held out my hand, but he went right past me and embraced me and kissed me on the lips. I will never forget it. I will not worry about him. He will do all right.

Sharon came along late in 1964. She was a surprise, but a marvelous one. She took away the free life we thought we'd be entering by then and gave us the best life we could ever have had. She is another Joanne, only more so. She is the most natural little person I've ever known. She's a great mimic and a born actress. When she was five, she and the twins next door got together and worked up a sketch on Cinderella. After rehearsing it for hours, they came into the den where I was watching a football game on television. "Daddy," she asked, "the twins and I have an act for television. We'd like to put it on *Let's Make a Deal*. Can we?" "No!" I roared, "and leave me alone!" They left, and after a caucus they came back and confronted me again. "Daddy, are you sure we can't go on *Let's Make a Deal?*" "No!" I replied emphatically. "Okay, then," she answered, "we're going to take it to Art Linkletter." She has been a blessing.

I have been a scrounger. I always would pick up any work I could get. I worked around the clock if necessary. I always got by financially. But success changes you. After *Let's Make a Deal* was a big success, our company got *Chain Letter* on the air, too. I was emceeing the first and producing the second and it was just too much. The show had troubles. I went out to Malibu and when they started to call me with their troubles, I said, for the first time in my life, "I don't care." And when they offered us only a part-time renewal, I said, "Just cancel the show. I am not going to commit suicide for a few weeks. If not this show, there'll be another show. Life is too short and I want to enjoy it." It was a turning point for me.

I will go on with *Let's Make a Deal* as long as it is made attractive for me to do so. I love it, but I have been doing it a long time and I want to do other things that attract me as they come up. I am not afraid to fail. I am sure I will in time succeed. It is not a matter of money. It is a matter of pride. I am a performer. There is more to me than the public has yet seen.

I have made, and am making, a lot of money. I have made some investments, some good, some bad. I will continue to make major contributions to charity, but I will, if I can, cut down on my charitable works because I have reached the point where I want more time for myself and my wife and my youngest child and my two older children as they may need me. It is time my family came first.

We have lived in the same home in Beverly Hills for eleven years. It is a nice home and we are happy with it. We could afford something grander, but we don't feel the need for it. Then there's the condominium, provided for my father in Palm Springs, which we use sometimes. And we have gone in with friends on another one on Malibu Beach, which we use sparingly.

We don't enjoy the social swirl in Hollywood. It all gets gossipy. Once I appeared at a Cardinal McIntyre Communion Breakfast and was photographed with the four Lennon Sisters and the Cardinal. I happened to be standing next to Peggy Lennon. A TV-movie magazine cropped us out and ran the picture with a hint that we were a new twosome about town. Who needs that?

Marilyn and I like to go out to concerts and to the theater, and to good restaurants, but the fans keep looking at us and coming at me for autographs and it's difficult to relax, so we usually just stay home or go to someone else's home and relax with our best friends, some of whom are in the business and many of whom are not.

I still serve as toastmaster at banquets. In the summer of 1972 when I emceed the B'nai B'rith "Man of the Year" tribute to Gordon Stulberg, the president of 20th-Century Fox, I introduced him with a biblical parody I'd worked out myself. It received tremendous favorable recognition from both the audience and my peers. I enjoy that sort of challenge.

Some appearances are satisfying. Some are not. At a "Salute to Israel," a flag standard was knocked into my face, cut me, and nearly took out my eye. I said, "I'd give blood for Israel, but this is ridiculous." They laughed, I bled.

But there is always the challenge of coming up with the right speech for the right audience at the right time. So whether it's Jacksonville, Phoenix, Vancouver, Albany, Montreal, you tailor your speech to the audience; and your success is measured in applause and laughter. And don't kid yourself—applause and laughter still mean more to a performer than money. And there have been some great reactions to my work.

Perhaps the most unforgettable came in Israel. My wife and I like to travel, we are able to, and we have enjoyed many marvelous moments with many marvelous people. One that will never be forgotten was when we attended a dinner party at the home of the noted Israeli prosecutor, Gideon Hausner, who took us around and introduced us to a stunning list of celebrated guests. One, who turned out to be an Israeli delegate to the United Nations, asked, "Mr. Hall, from American television? What do you do on television?" And I was immediately embarrassed in front of all these highly educated accomplished persons to say that I was emcee of an audience participation game show. Hesitating, I said, "Well, I am what you would call in this country a *compère*," which was, roughly, the European name for master of ceremonies. "Ah," said this man, "a *compère*." And the others gathered around and nodded.

And then the man asked, "And what type of program do you moderate?" They all looked at me ex-
pectantly, I found myself wishing I could really say I
was Lawrence Spivak and my program was *Meet the
Press* and I brought on important persons to be interviewed by expert journalists. But I could not say that,
could I? Stammering, I said, "Well, I am not a moderator, exactly. I am more a master of ceremonies. And it
is an . . . audience participation show." And the man
said, "Audience participation? What does that mean?"
How could I explain it to him?

Struggling, I said, "Well, we have a show in which I
perform in the middle of an arena of people . . ." I
realized I was trying to make it sound as if I was
working the state senate floor. I said, "They get an
opportunity to win prizes and then they get further
opportunities to trade them in for unknown prizes,
which may be better or worse . . ."

And as I was struggling, the man said, "Wait, do
they dress in costumes?" Surprised, I said, "Yes. Yes,
they do." And he said, "Oh, my, why, when I am in
your country I always watch that show. When I am in
New York for United Nations sessions and I am in my
hotel room I always look to see if that show is on
because it is so diverting and you, whom I recognize
now, are marvelous and it always gives me much plea-
sure and much enjoyment. I am what you might call
a fan."